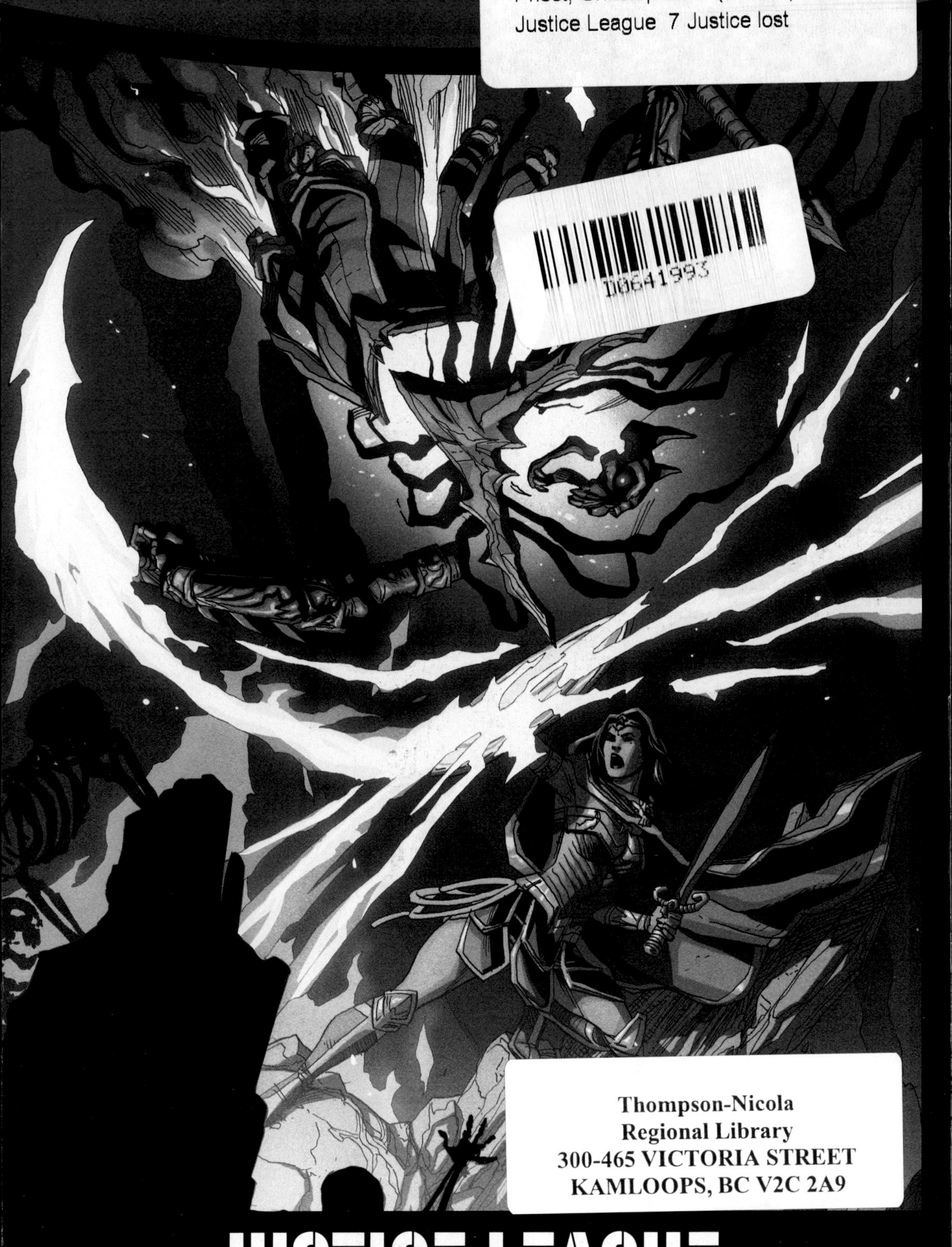

JUSTICE LEAGUE

VOL.7 JUSTICE LOST

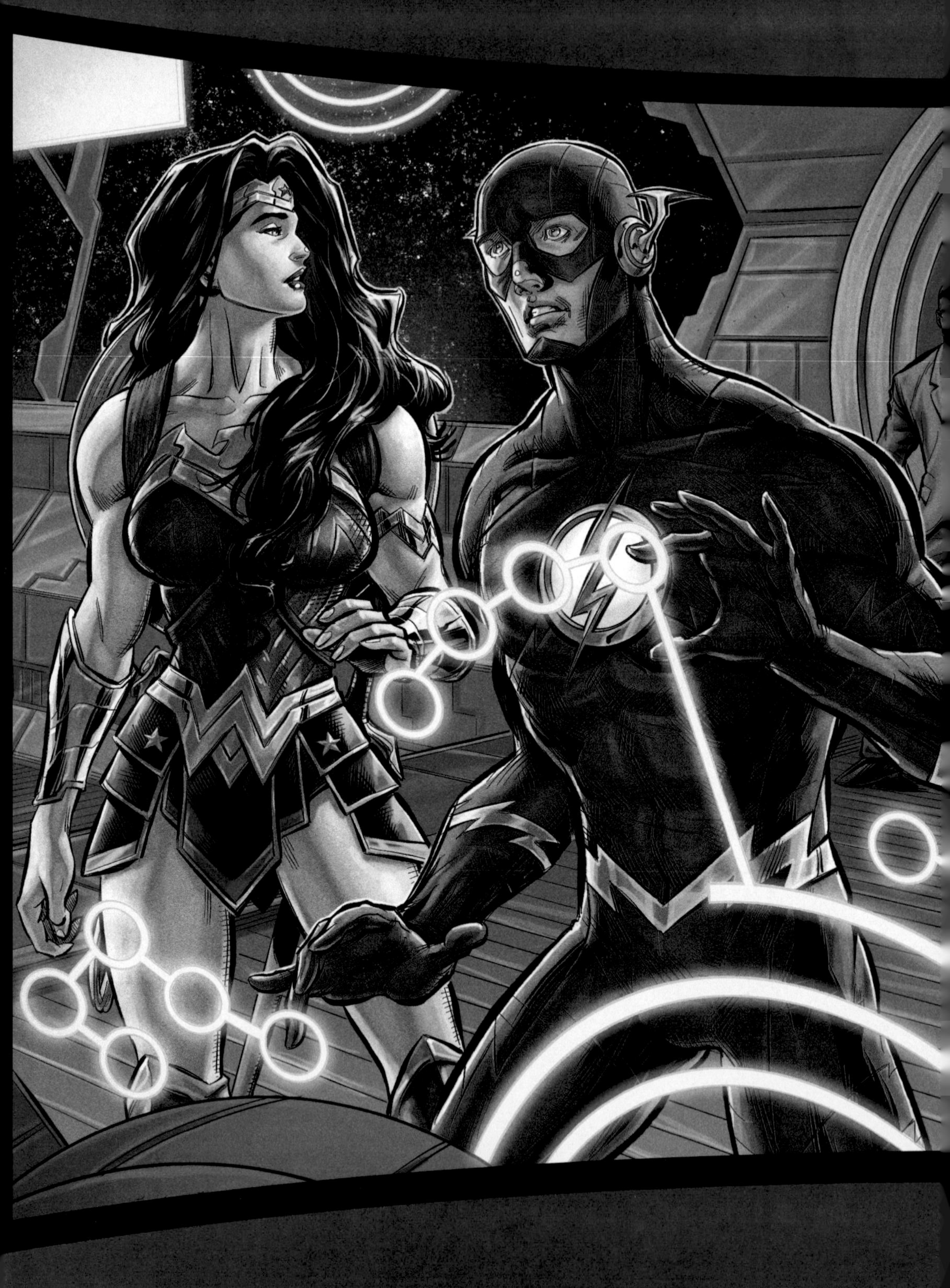

JUSTICE LEAGUE
VOL.7 JUSTICE LOST

CHRISTOPHER PRIEST
writer

PETE WOODS * IAN CHURCHILL * PHILIPPE BRIONES
artists

PETE WOODS * ALEX SOLLAZZO
CHRIS SOTOMAYOR * JEROMY COX
colorists

WILLIE SCHUBERT
letterer

DAVID YARDIN
collection cover artist

SUPERMAN created by **JERRY SIEGEL** and **JOE SHUSTER**
By special arrangement with the Jerry Siegel family

WONDER WOMAN created by **WILLIAM MOULTON MARSTON**

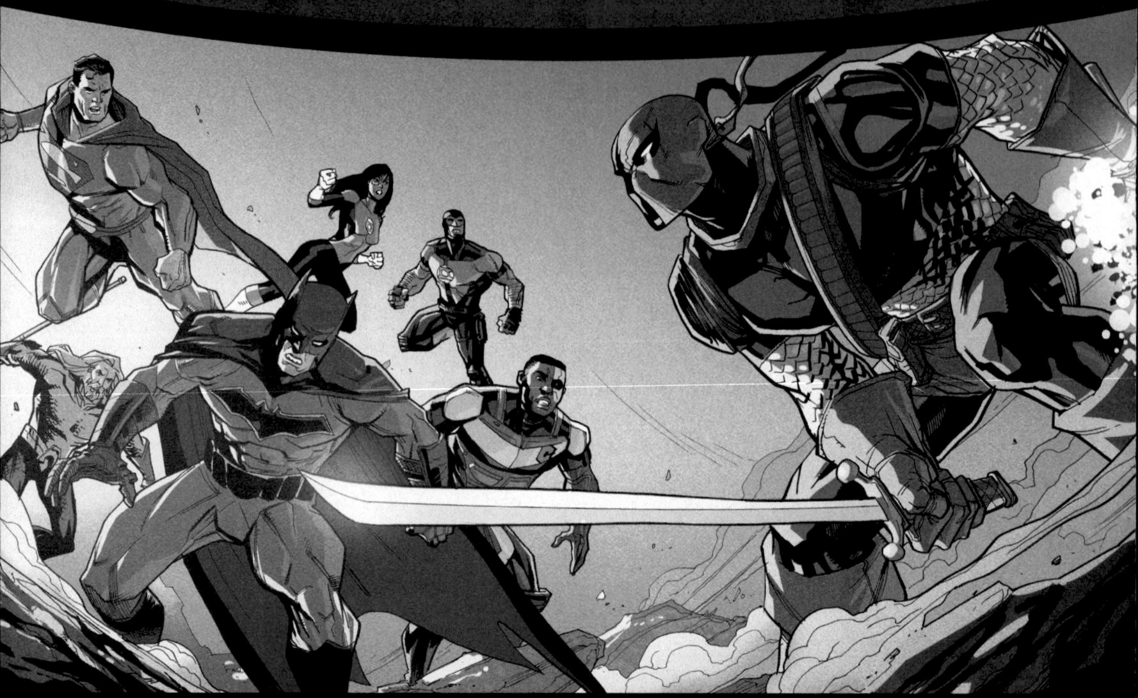

BRIAN CUNNINGHAM REBECCA TAYLOR Editors - Original Series
JEB WOODARD Group Editor - Collected Editions * **ROBIN WILDMAN** Editor - Collected Edition
STEVE COOK Design Director - Books * **MEGEN BELLERSEN** Publication Design

BOB HARRAS Senior VP - Editor-in-Chief, DC Comics
PAT McCALLUM Executive Editor, DC Comics

DAN DiDIO Publisher * **JIM LEE** Publisher & Chief Creative Officer
AMIT DESAI Executive VP - Business & Marketing Strategy, Direct to Consumer & Global Franchise Management
BOBBIE CHASE VP & Executive Editor, Young Reader & Talent Development * **MARK CHIARELLO** Senior VP - Art, Design & Collected Editions
JOHN CUNNINGHAM Senior VP - Sales & Trade Marketing * **BRIAR DARDEN** VP - Business Affairs
ANNE DePIES Senior VP - Business Strategy, Finance & Administration * **DON FALLETTI** VP - Manufacturing Operations
LAWRENCE GANEM VP - Editorial Administration & Talent Relations * **ALISON GILL** Senior VP - Manufacturing & Operations
JASON GREENBERG VP - Business Strategy & Finance * **HANK KANALZ** Senior VP - Editorial Strategy & Administration * **JAY KOGAN** Senior VP - Legal Affairs
NICK J. NAPOLITANO VP - Manufacturing Administration * **LISETTE OSTERLOH** VP - Digital Marketing & Events * **EDDIE SCANNELL** VP - Consumer Marketing
COURTNEY SIMMONS Senior VP - Publicity & Communications * **JIM (SKI) SOKOLOWSKI** VP - Comic Book Specialty Sales & Trade Marketing
NANCY SPEARS VP - Mass, Book, Digital Sales & Trade Marketing * **MICHELE R. WELLS** VP - Content Strategy

JUSTICE LEAGUE VOL. 7: JUSTICE LOST

DC Comics, 2900 West Alameda Ave., Burbank, CA 91505
Printed by LSC Communications, Owensville, MO, USA. 8/10/18. First Printing.
ISBN: 978-1-4012-8425-1

Library of Congress Cataloging-in-Publication Data is available.

PEFC Certified
Printed on paper from sustainably managed forests, controlled sources
PEFC
PEFC/29-31-337
www.pefc.org

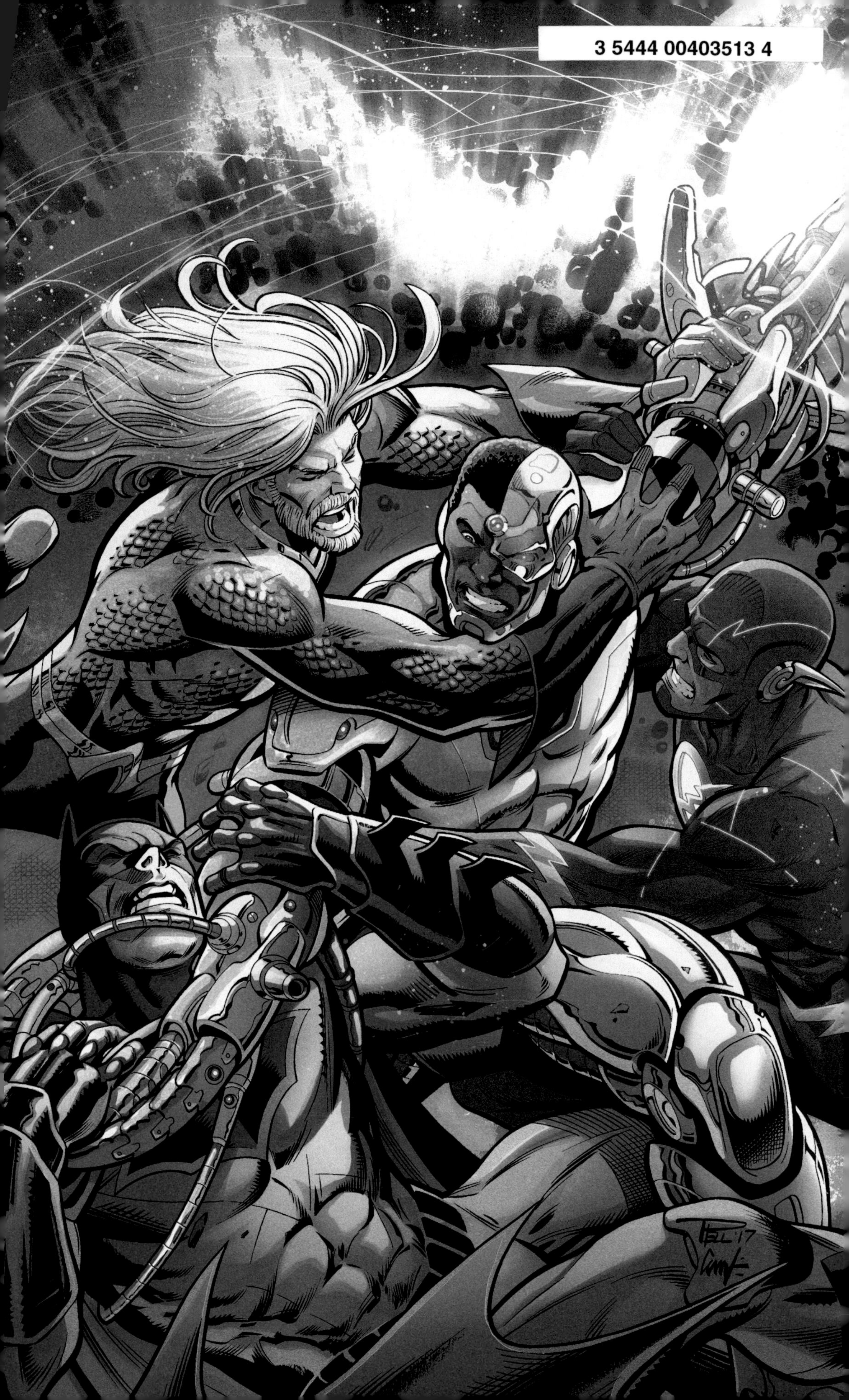

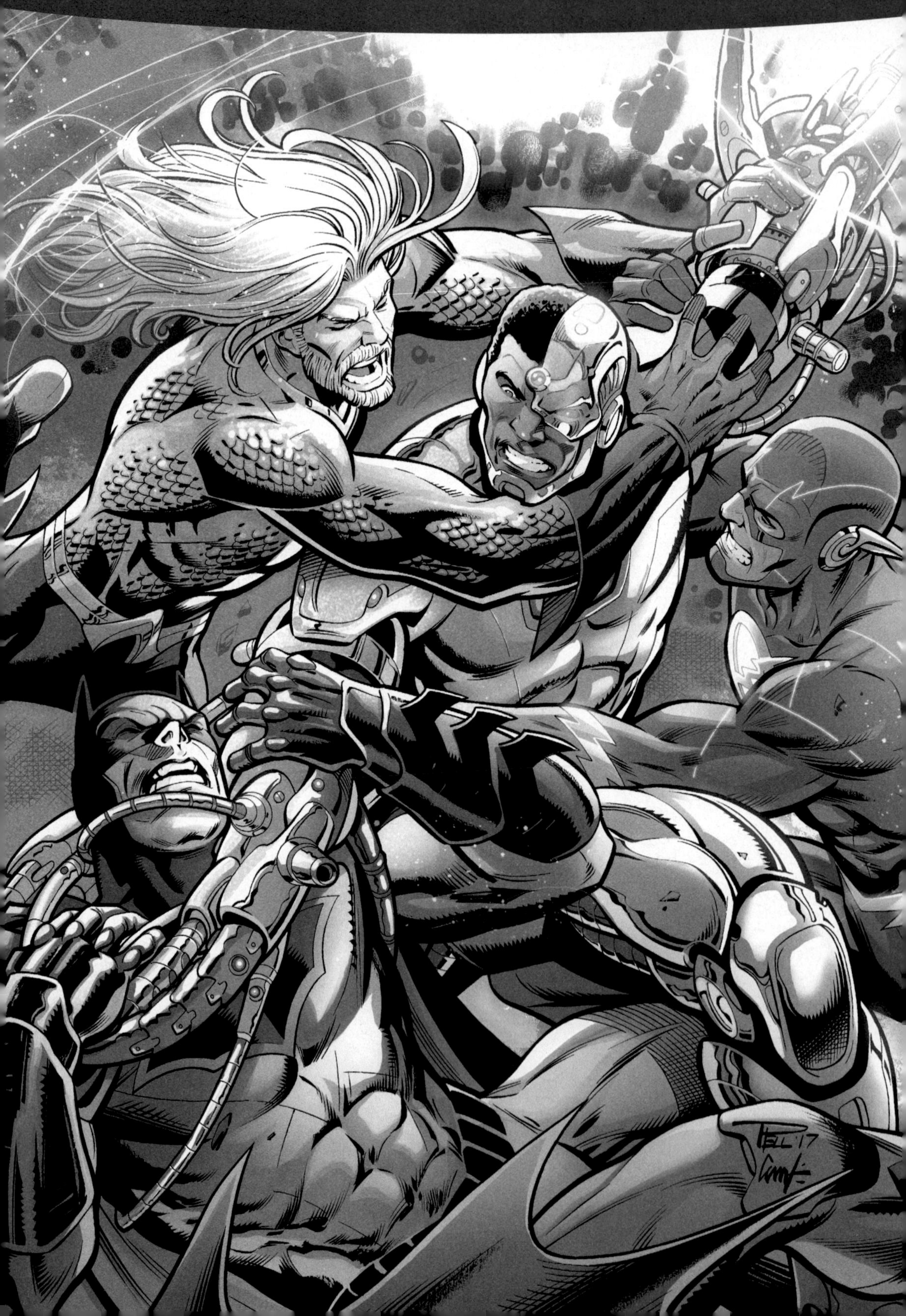

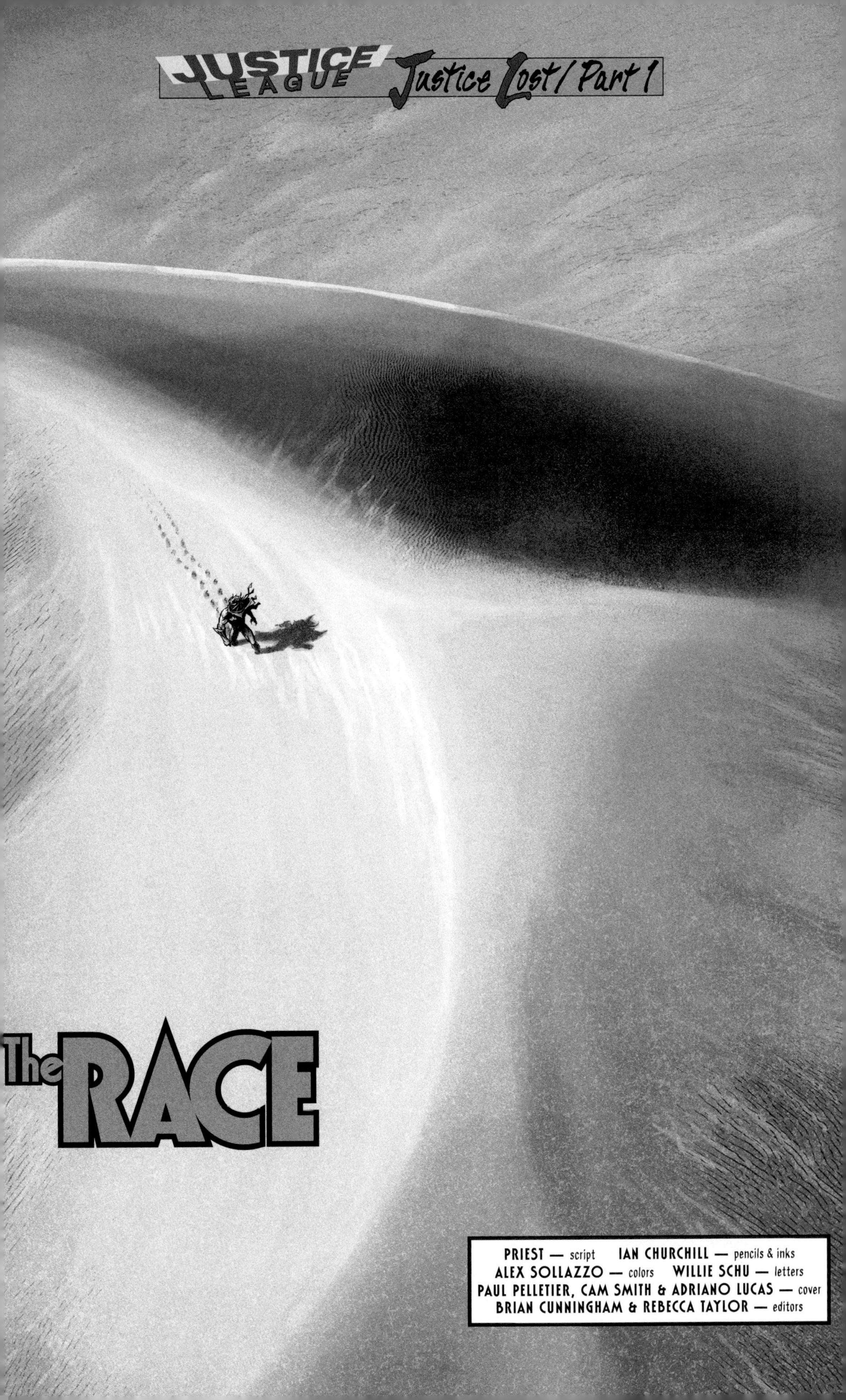
JUSTICE LEAGUE Justice Lost / Part 1
The RACE
PRIEST — script IAN CHURCHILL — pencils & inks
ALEX SOLLAZZO — colors WILLIE SCHU — letters
PAUL PELLETIER, CAM SMITH & ADRIANO LUCAS — cover
BRIAN CUNNINGHAM & REBECCA TAYLOR — editors

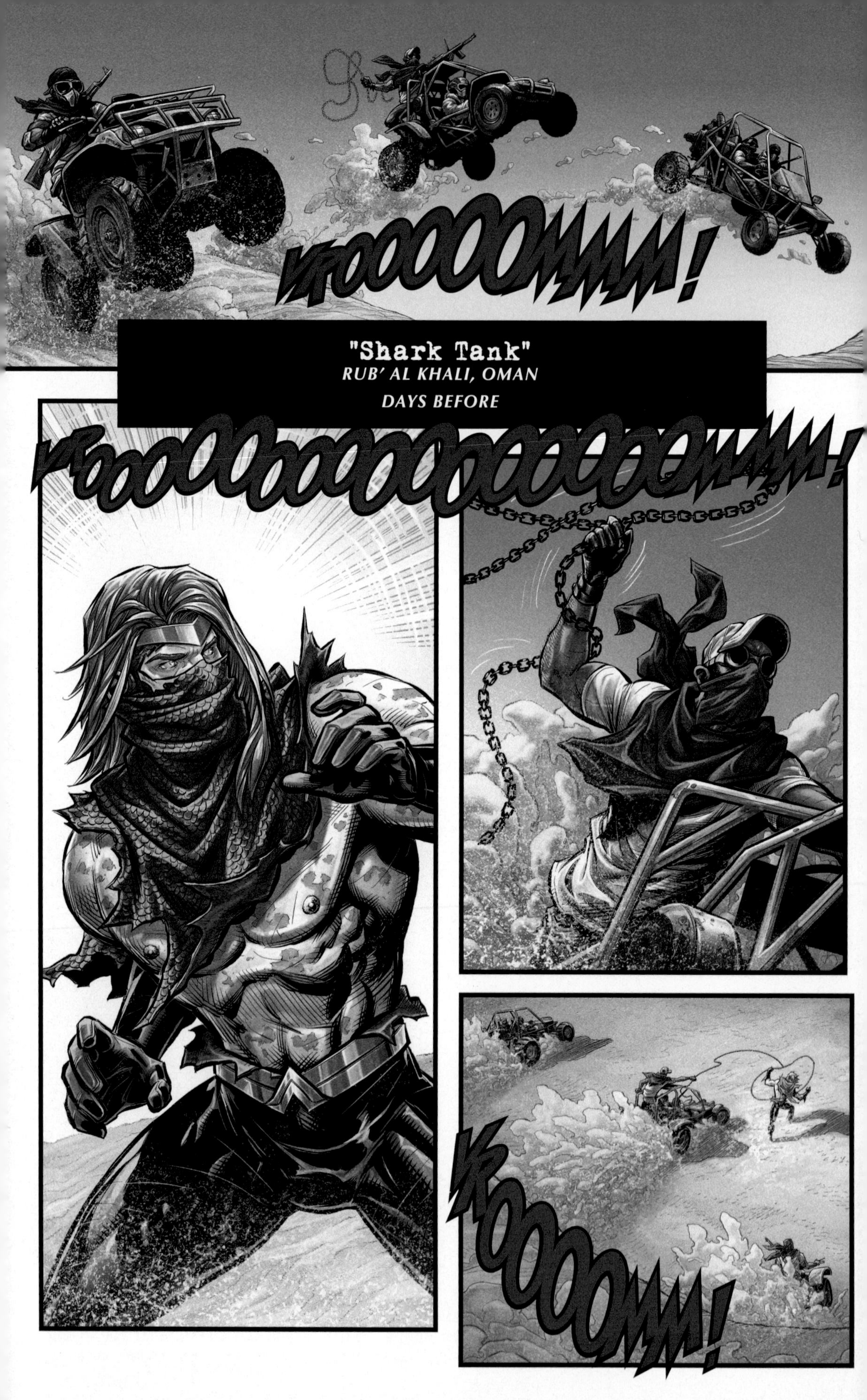
VROOOOOOMMMM!
"Shark Tank"
RUB' AL KHALI, OMAN
DAYS BEFORE
VROOOOOOOOOOOOOOOOMMM!
VROOOOOMMM!

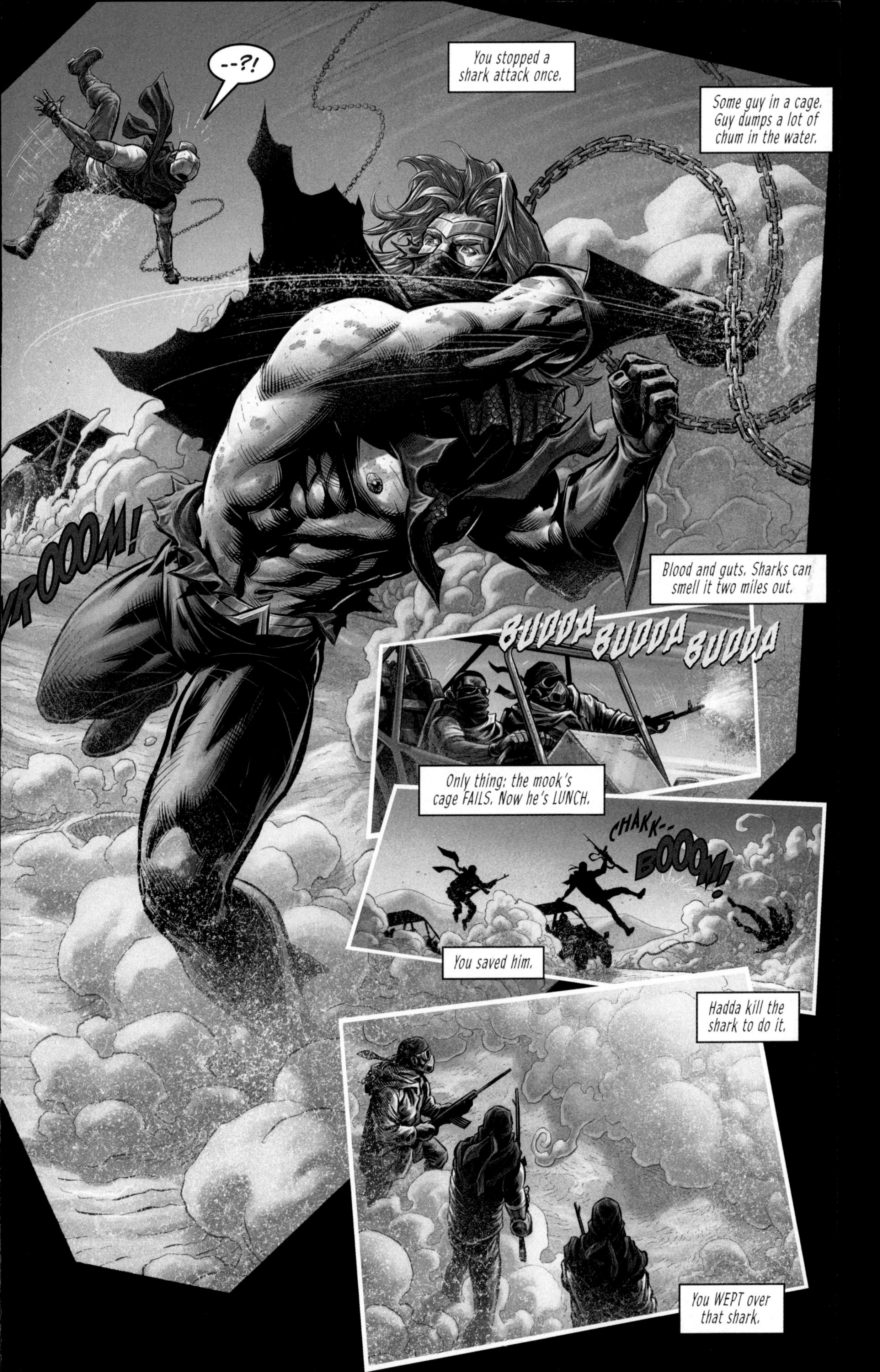
--?!
You stopped a shark attack once.
Some guy in a cage. Guy dumps a lot of chum in the water.
VROOOOM!
Blood and guts. Sharks can smell it two miles out.
BUDDA BUDDA BUDDA
Only thing: the mook's cage FAILS. Now he's LUNCH.
CHAKK--
BOOOM!
You saved him.
Hadda kill the shark to do it.
You WEPT over that shark.

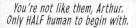

You're not like them, Arthur. Only HALF human to begin with.

Dense muscle tissue and night vision to survive miles below where even the most advanced submarines can't operate.

Got yourself dethroned by your own people for caring too much about "peace with the surface" and not putting Atlantis first.

I don't get why you even BOTHER with a lace-curtain sorority like the Justice League.

Defenders of the Earth, they build their clubhouse 22,000 miles ABOVE it.

Above US.

Which, I suppose, makes more sense than the joint you people built on the MOON.

The MOON. Seriously.

I'm here to help with that.

You people need to do better.

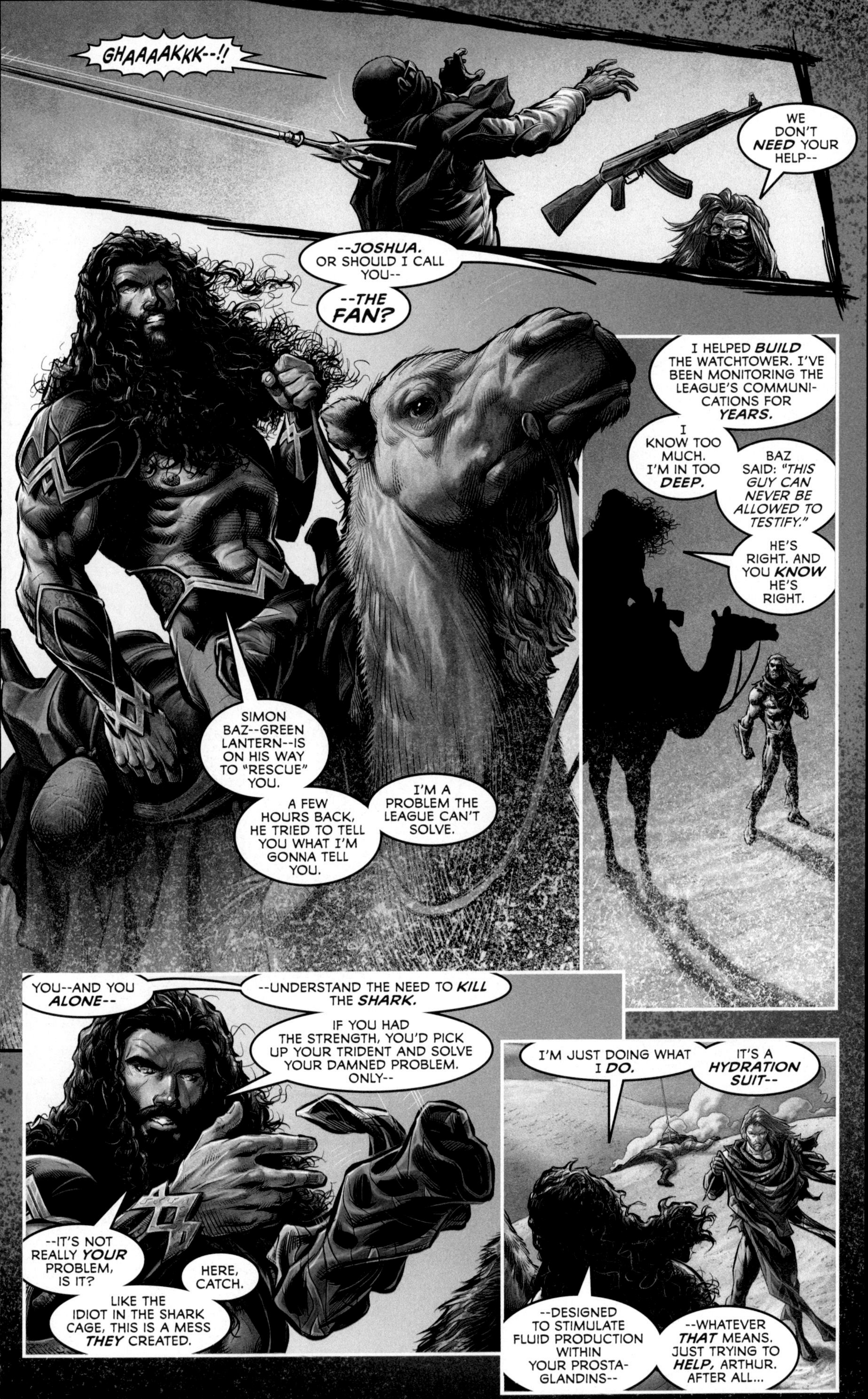
GHAAAAKKK--!!
WE DON'T NEED YOUR HELP--
--JOSHUA. OR SHOULD I CALL YOU--
--THE FAN?
I HELPED BUILD THE WATCHTOWER. I'VE BEEN MONITORING THE LEAGUE'S COMMUNICATIONS FOR YEARS.
I KNOW TOO MUCH. I'M IN TOO DEEP.
BAZ SAID: "THIS GUY CAN NEVER BE ALLOWED TO TESTIFY."
HE'S RIGHT. AND YOU KNOW HE'S RIGHT.
SIMON BAZ--GREEN LANTERN--IS ON HIS WAY TO "RESCUE" YOU.
A FEW HOURS BACK, HE TRIED TO TELL YOU WHAT I'M GONNA TELL YOU.
I'M A PROBLEM THE LEAGUE CAN'T SOLVE.
YOU--AND YOU ALONE--
--UNDERSTAND THE NEED TO KILL THE SHARK.
IF YOU HAD THE STRENGTH, YOU'D PICK UP YOUR TRIDENT AND SOLVE YOUR DAMNED PROBLEM. ONLY--
--IT'S NOT REALLY YOUR PROBLEM, IS IT?
HERE, CATCH.
LIKE THE IDIOT IN THE SHARK CAGE, THIS IS A MESS THEY CREATED.
I'M JUST DOING WHAT I DO.
IT'S A HYDRATION SUIT--
--DESIGNED TO STIMULATE FLUID PRODUCTION WITHIN YOUR PROSTA-GLANDINS--
--WHATEVER THAT MEANS. JUST TRYING TO HELP, ARTHUR. AFTER ALL...

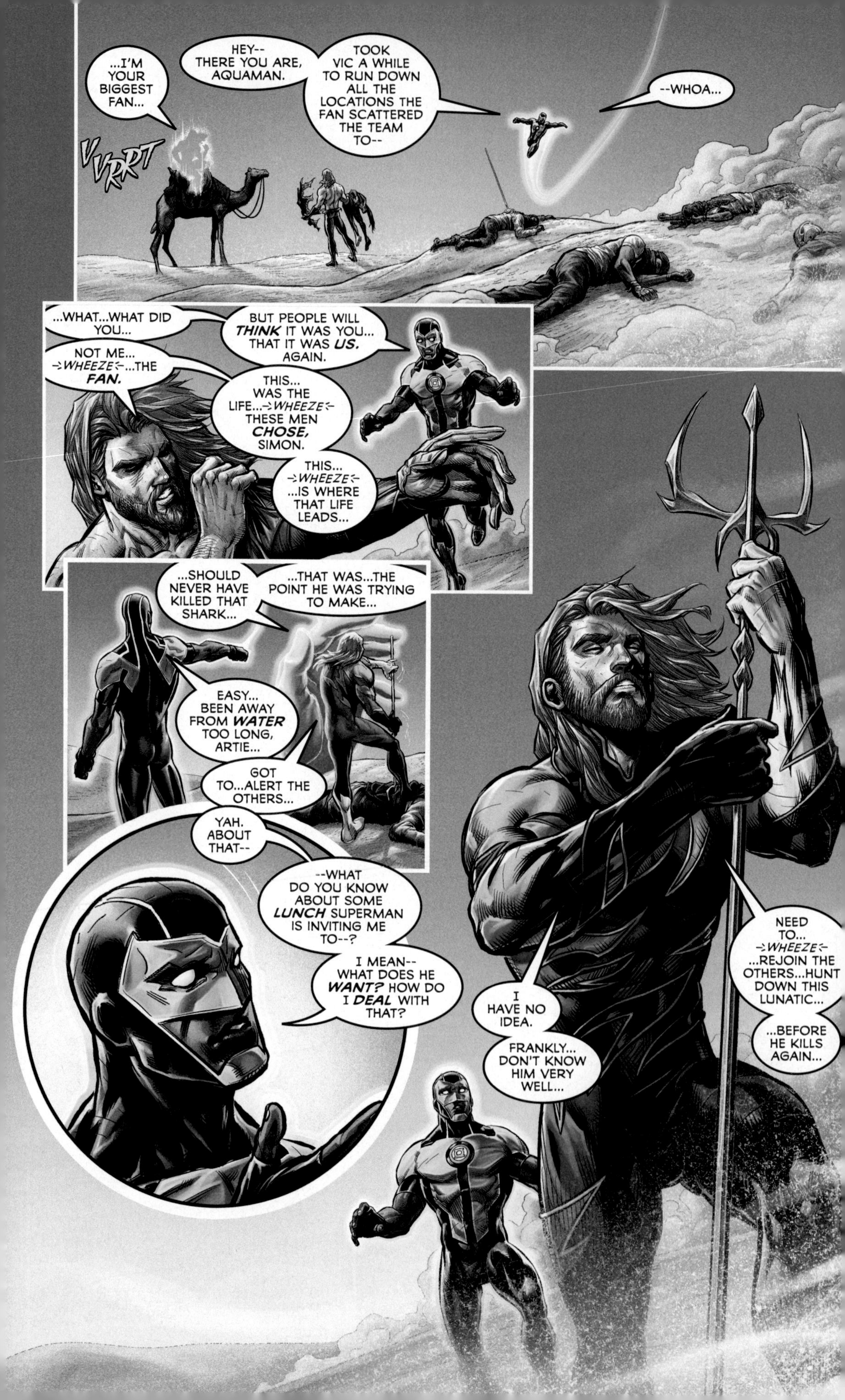

...I'M YOUR BIGGEST FAN...
V VRRT
HEY-- THERE YOU ARE, AQUAMAN.
TOOK VIC A WHILE TO RUN DOWN ALL THE LOCATIONS THE FAN SCATTERED THE TEAM TO--
--WHOA...
...WHAT...WHAT DID YOU...
BUT PEOPLE WILL THINK IT WAS YOU... THAT IT WAS US. AGAIN.
NOT ME... →WHEEZE←...THE FAN.
THIS... WAS THE LIFE...→WHEEZE← THESE MEN CHOSE, SIMON.
THIS... →WHEEZE← ...IS WHERE THAT LIFE LEADS...
...SHOULD NEVER HAVE KILLED THAT SHARK...
...THAT WAS...THE POINT HE WAS TRYING TO MAKE...
EASY... BEEN AWAY FROM WATER TOO LONG, ARTIE...
GOT TO...ALERT THE OTHERS...
YAH. ABOUT THAT--
--WHAT DO YOU KNOW ABOUT SOME LUNCH SUPERMAN IS INVITING ME TO--?
I MEAN-- WHAT DOES HE WANT? HOW DO I DEAL WITH THAT?
I HAVE NO IDEA.
FRANKLY... DON'T KNOW HIM VERY WELL...
NEED TO... →WHEEZE← ...REJOIN THE OTHERS...HUNT DOWN THIS LUNATIC...
...BEFORE HE KILLS AGAIN...

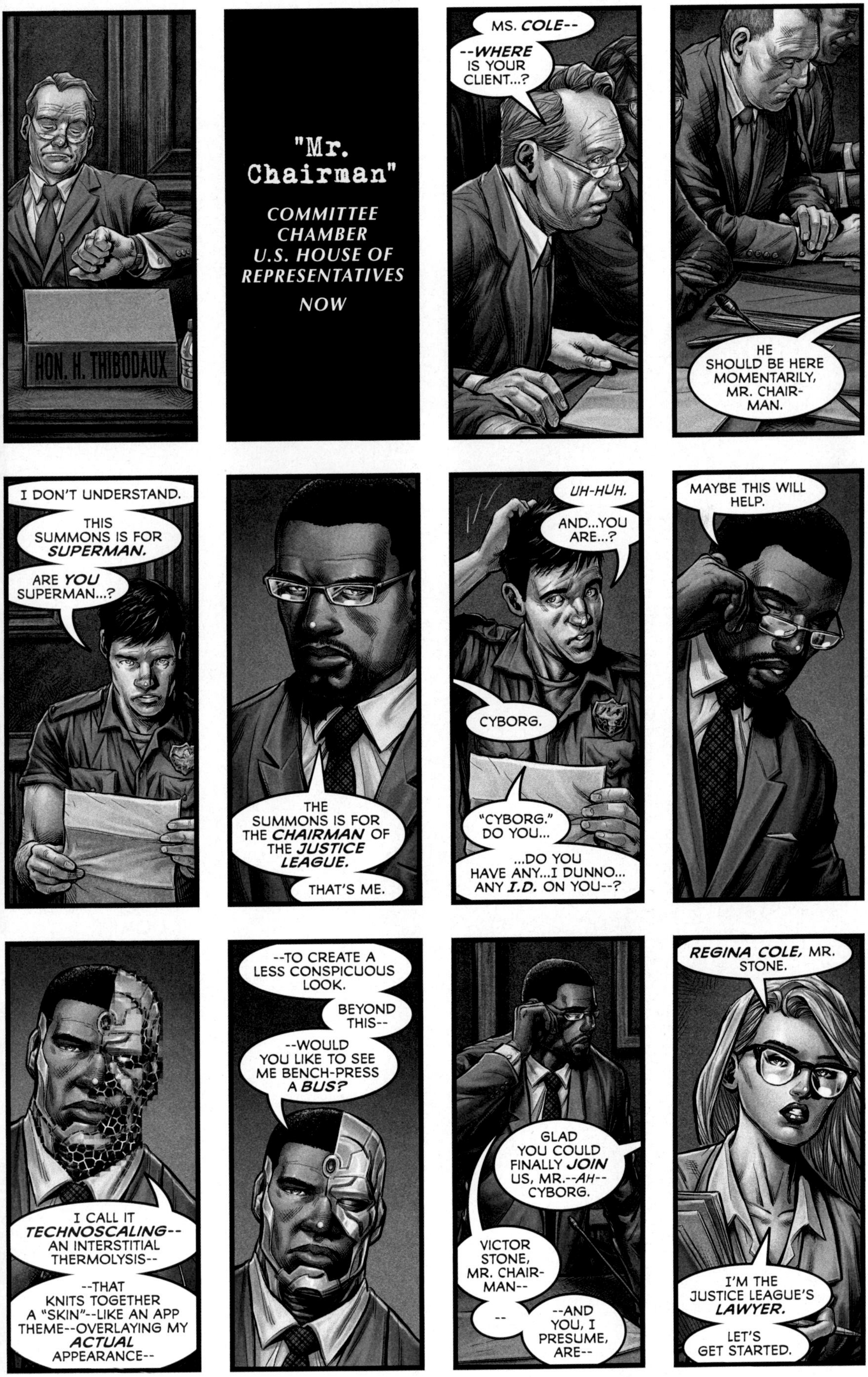
HON. H. THIBODAUX
"Mr. Chairman"
COMMITTEE CHAMBER U.S. HOUSE OF REPRESENTATIVES
NOW
MS. COLE--
--WHERE IS YOUR CLIENT...?
HE SHOULD BE HERE MOMENTARILY, MR. CHAIR-MAN.
I DON'T UNDERSTAND.
THIS SUMMONS IS FOR SUPERMAN.
ARE YOU SUPERMAN...?
THE SUMMONS IS FOR THE CHAIRMAN OF THE JUSTICE LEAGUE.
THAT'S ME.
UH-HUH.
AND...YOU ARE...?
CYBORG.
"CYBORG." DO YOU...
...DO YOU HAVE ANY...I DUNNO... ANY I.D. ON YOU--?
MAYBE THIS WILL HELP.
I CALL IT TECHNOSCALING-- AN INTERSTITIAL THERMOLYSIS--
--THAT KNITS TOGETHER A "SKIN"--LIKE AN APP THEME--OVERLAYING MY ACTUAL APPEARANCE--
--TO CREATE A LESS CONSPICUOUS LOOK.
BEYOND THIS--
--WOULD YOU LIKE TO SEE ME BENCH-PRESS A BUS?
GLAD YOU COULD FINALLY JOIN US, MR.--AH-- CYBORG.
VICTOR STONE, MR. CHAIR-MAN--
--
--AND YOU, I PRESUME, ARE--
REGINA COLE, MR. STONE.
I'M THE JUSTICE LEAGUE'S LAWYER.
LET'S GET STARTED.

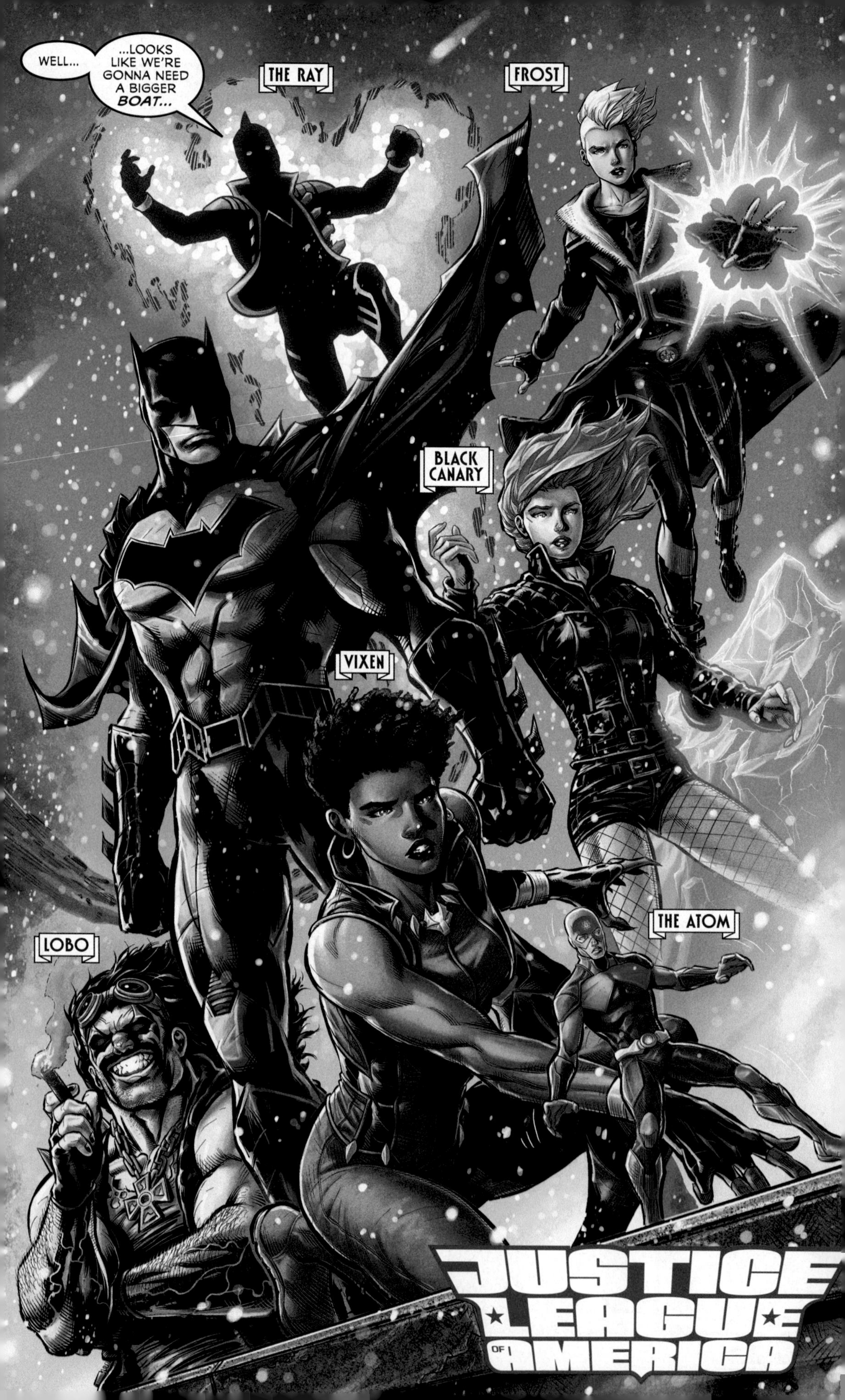
WELL...
...LOOKS LIKE WE'RE GONNA NEED A BIGGER *BOAT*...
THE RAY
FROST
BLACK CANARY
VIXEN
THE ATOM
LOBO
JUSTICE LEAGUE OF AMERICA

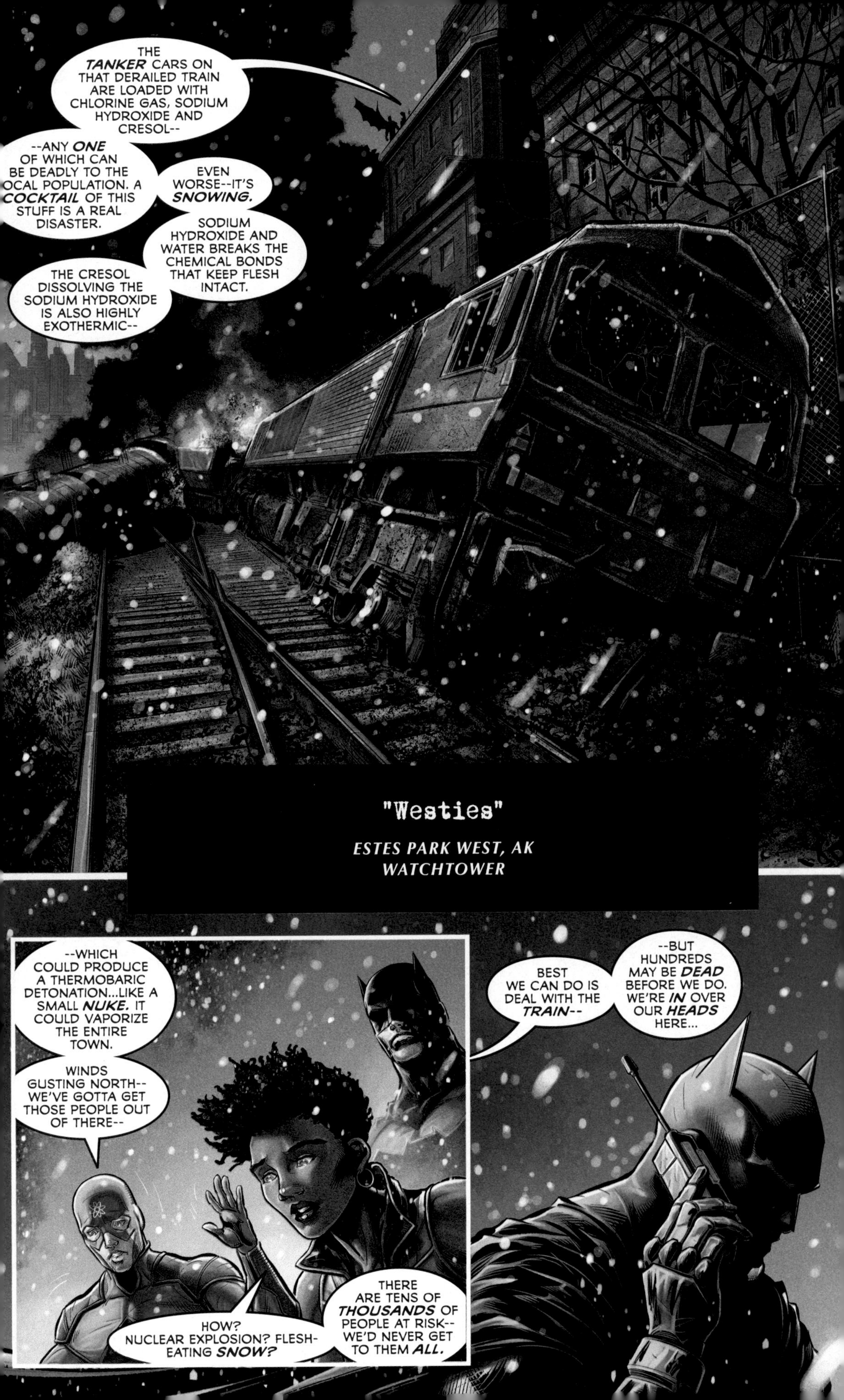
THE TANKER CARS ON THAT DERAILED TRAIN ARE LOADED WITH CHLORINE GAS, SODIUM HYDROXIDE AND CRESOL--
--ANY ONE OF WHICH CAN BE DEADLY TO THE OCAL POPULATION. A COCKTAIL OF THIS STUFF IS A REAL DISASTER.
EVEN WORSE--IT'S SNOWING.
SODIUM HYDROXIDE AND WATER BREAKS THE CHEMICAL BONDS THAT KEEP FLESH INTACT.
THE CRESOL DISSOLVING THE SODIUM HYDROXIDE IS ALSO HIGHLY EXOTHERMIC--
"Westies"
ESTES PARK WEST, AK
WATCHTOWER
--WHICH COULD PRODUCE A THERMOBARIC DETONATION...LIKE A SMALL NUKE. IT COULD VAPORIZE THE ENTIRE TOWN.
WINDS GUSTING NORTH-- WE'VE GOTTA GET THOSE PEOPLE OUT OF THERE--
HOW? NUCLEAR EXPLOSION? FLESH-EATING SNOW?
THERE ARE TENS OF THOUSANDS OF PEOPLE AT RISK-- WE'D NEVER GET TO THEM ALL.
BEST WE CAN DO IS DEAL WITH THE TRAIN--
--BUT HUNDREDS MAY BE DEAD BEFORE WE DO. WE'RE IN OVER OUR HEADS HERE...

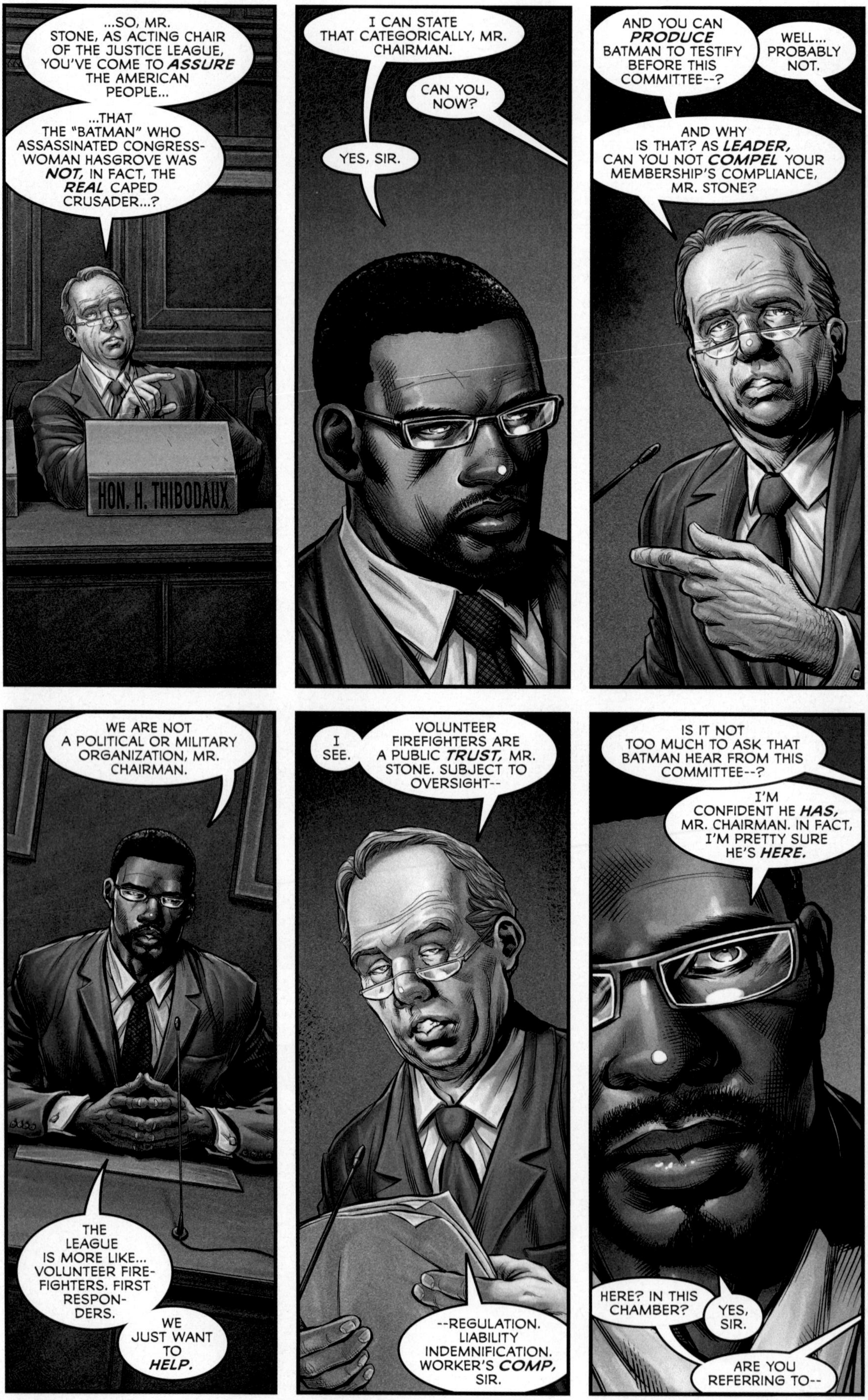
...SO, MR. STONE, AS ACTING CHAIR OF THE JUSTICE LEAGUE, YOU'VE COME TO ASSURE THE AMERICAN PEOPLE...
...THAT THE "BATMAN" WHO ASSASSINATED CONGRESS-WOMAN HASGROVE WAS NOT, IN FACT, THE REAL CAPED CRUSADER...?
HON. H. THIBODAUX
I CAN STATE THAT CATEGORICALLY, MR. CHAIRMAN.
CAN YOU, NOW?
YES, SIR.
AND YOU CAN PRODUCE BATMAN TO TESTIFY BEFORE THIS COMMITTEE--?
WELL... PROBABLY NOT.
AND WHY IS THAT? AS LEADER, CAN YOU NOT COMPEL YOUR MEMBERSHIP'S COMPLIANCE, MR. STONE?
WE ARE NOT A POLITICAL OR MILITARY ORGANIZATION, MR. CHAIRMAN.
THE LEAGUE IS MORE LIKE... VOLUNTEER FIRE-FIGHTERS. FIRST RESPON-DERS.
WE JUST WANT TO HELP.
I SEE.
VOLUNTEER FIREFIGHTERS ARE A PUBLIC TRUST, MR. STONE. SUBJECT TO OVERSIGHT--
--REGULATION. LIABILITY INDEMNIFICATION. WORKER'S COMP, SIR.
IS IT NOT TOO MUCH TO ASK THAT BATMAN HEAR FROM THIS COMMITTEE--?
I'M CONFIDENT HE HAS, MR. CHAIRMAN. IN FACT, I'M PRETTY SURE HE'S HERE.
HERE? IN THIS CHAMBER?
YES, SIR.
ARE YOU REFERRING TO--

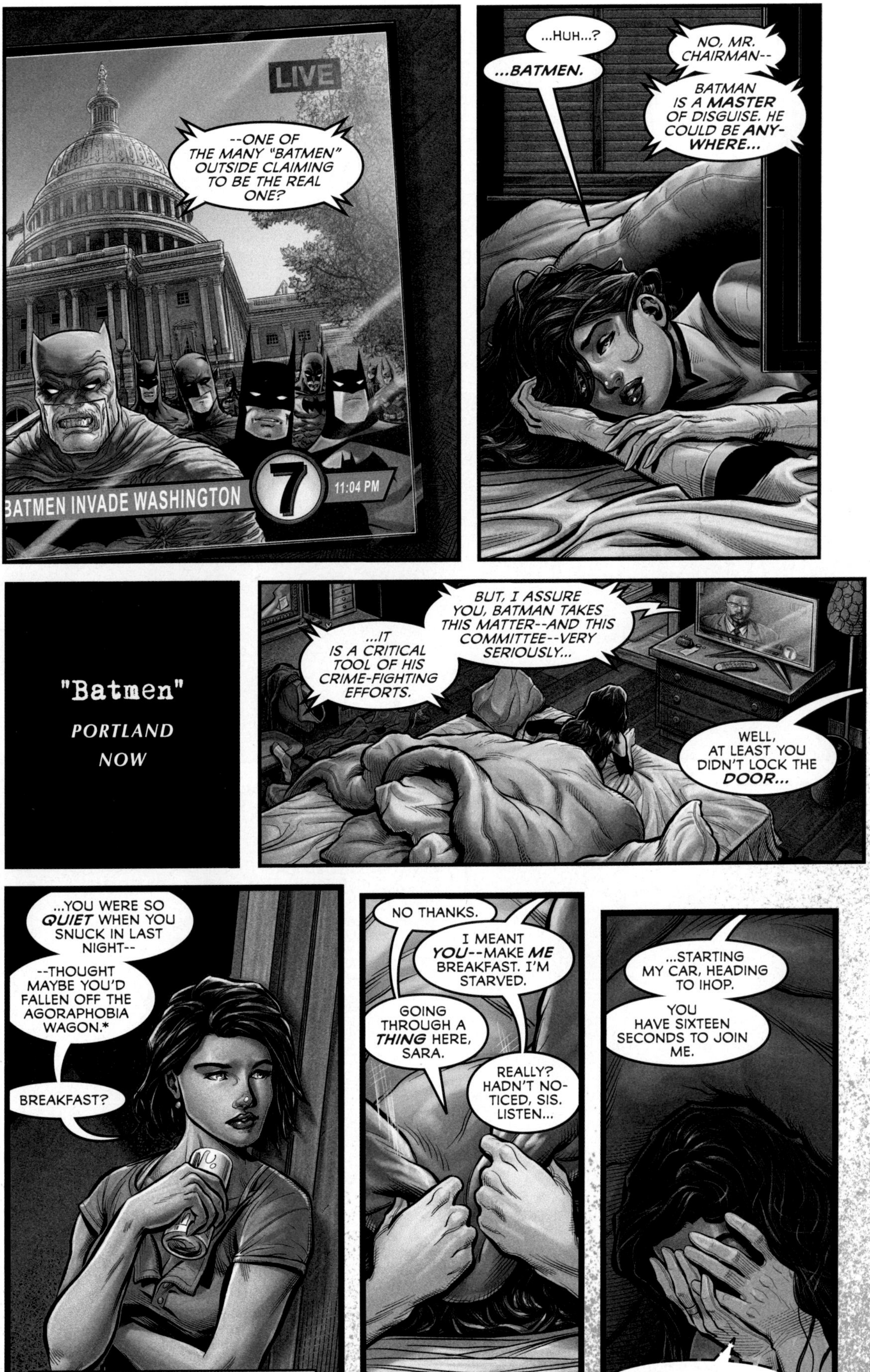
LIVE
--ONE OF THE MANY "BATMEN" OUTSIDE CLAIMING TO BE THE REAL ONE?
BATMEN INVADE WASHINGTON
7
11:04 PM
...HUH...?
...BATMEN.
NO, MR. CHAIRMAN--
BATMAN IS A MASTER OF DISGUISE. HE COULD BE ANY-WHERE...
"Batmen"
PORTLAND
NOW
BUT, I ASSURE YOU, BATMAN TAKES THIS MATTER--AND THIS COMMITTEE--VERY SERIOUSLY...
...IT IS A CRITICAL TOOL OF HIS CRIME-FIGHTING EFFORTS.
WELL, AT LEAST YOU DIDN'T LOCK THE DOOR...
...YOU WERE SO QUIET WHEN YOU SNUCK IN LAST NIGHT--
--THOUGHT MAYBE YOU'D FALLEN OFF THE AGORAPHOBIA WAGON.*
BREAKFAST?
*JESSICA CRUZ SUFFERS FROM AN IRRATIONAL FEAR OF CROWDED SPACES OR ENCLOSED PUBLIC PLACES. --BRIAN
NO THANKS.
I MEANT YOU--MAKE ME BREAKFAST. I'M STARVED.
GOING THROUGH A THING HERE, SARA.
REALLY? HADN'T NO-TICED, SIS. LISTEN...
...STARTING MY CAR, HEADING TO IHOP.
YOU HAVE SIXTEEN SECONDS TO JOIN ME.
WHAT HAVE I DONE? WHAT HAVE I DONE?!

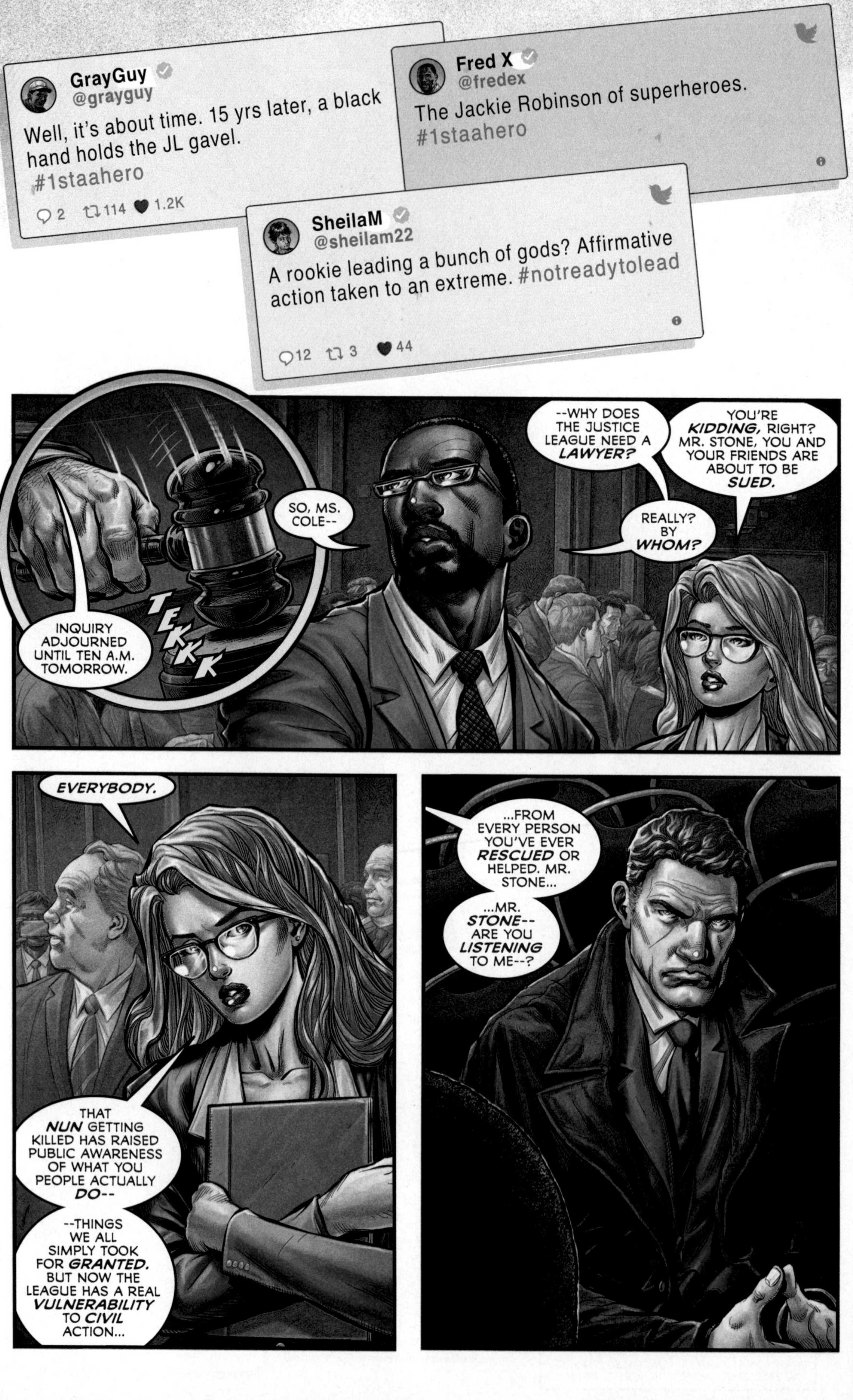

GrayGuy
@grayguy
Well, it's about time. 15 yrs later, a black hand holds the JL gavel. #1staahero
2 114 1.2K
Fred X
@fredex
The Jackie Robinson of superheroes. #1staahero
SheilaM
@sheilam22
A rookie leading a bunch of gods? Affirmative action taken to an extreme. #notreadytolead
12 3 44
INQUIRY ADJOURNED UNTIL TEN A.M. TOMORROW.
TEKKK
SO, MS. COLE--
--WHY DOES THE JUSTICE LEAGUE NEED A LAWYER?
YOU'RE KIDDING, RIGHT? MR. STONE, YOU AND YOUR FRIENDS ARE ABOUT TO BE SUED.
REALLY? BY WHOM?
EVERYBODY.
THAT NUN GETTING KILLED HAS RAISED PUBLIC AWARENESS OF WHAT YOU PEOPLE ACTUALLY DO--
--THINGS WE ALL SIMPLY TOOK FOR GRANTED. BUT NOW THE LEAGUE HAS A REAL VULNERABILITY TO CIVIL ACTION...
...FROM EVERY PERSON YOU'VE EVER RESCUED OR HELPED. MR. STONE...
...MR. STONE-- ARE YOU LISTENING TO ME--?

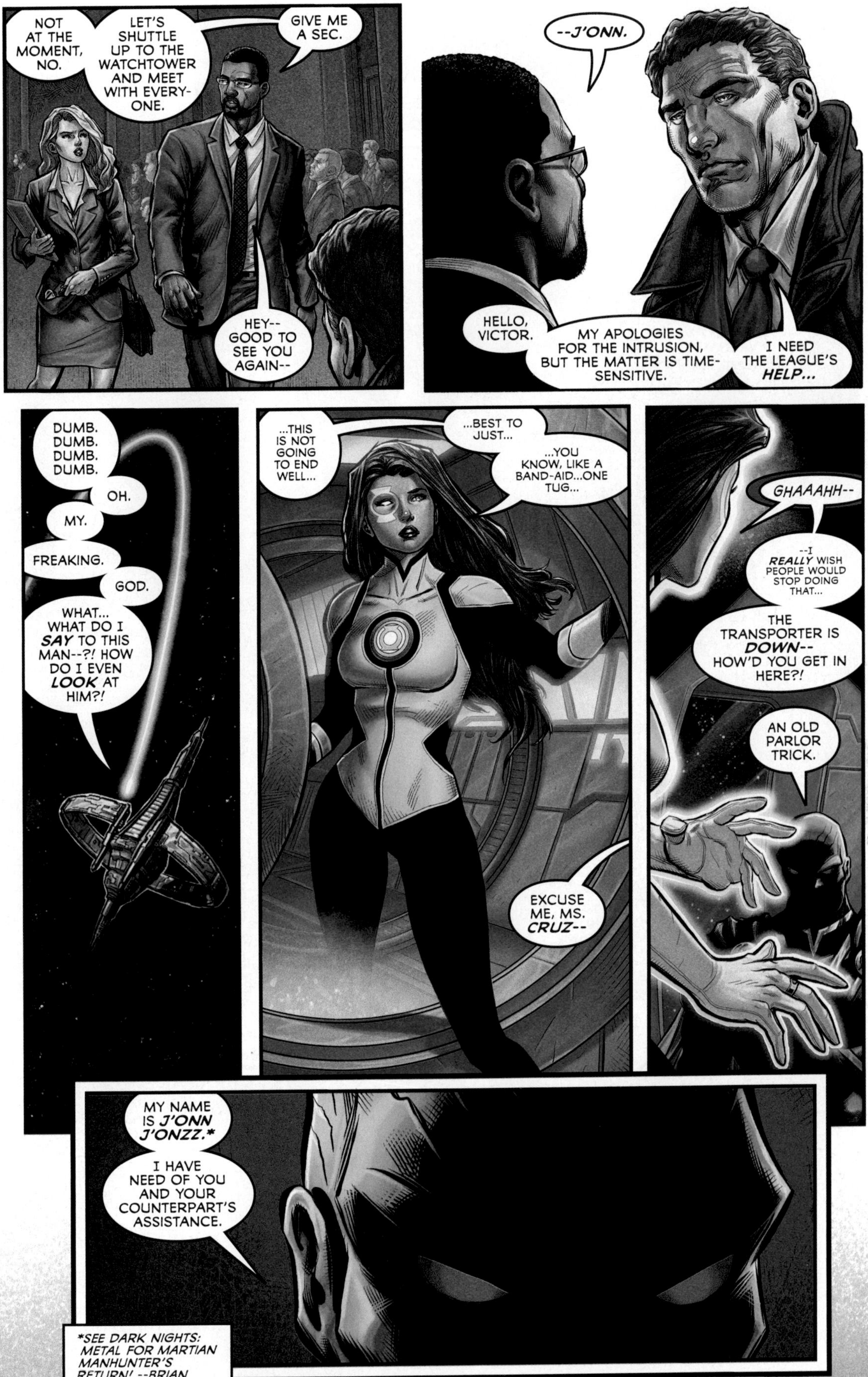
NOT AT THE MOMENT, NO.
LET'S SHUTTLE UP TO THE WATCHTOWER AND MEET WITH EVERY-ONE.
GIVE ME A SEC.
HEY-- GOOD TO SEE YOU AGAIN--
--J'ONN.
HELLO, VICTOR.
MY APOLOGIES FOR THE INTRUSION, BUT THE MATTER IS TIME-SENSITIVE.
I NEED THE LEAGUE'S HELP...
DUMB. DUMB. DUMB. DUMB.
OH.
MY.
FREAKING.
GOD.
WHAT... WHAT DO I SAY TO THIS MAN--?! HOW DO I EVEN LOOK AT HIM?!
...THIS IS NOT GOING TO END WELL...
...BEST TO JUST...
...YOU KNOW, LIKE A BAND-AID...ONE TUG...
EXCUSE ME, MS. CRUZ--
GHAAAHH--
--I REALLY WISH PEOPLE WOULD STOP DOING THAT...
THE TRANSPORTER IS DOWN-- HOW'D YOU GET IN HERE?!
AN OLD PARLOR TRICK.
MY NAME IS J'ONN J'ONZZ.*
I HAVE NEED OF YOU AND YOUR COUNTERPART'S ASSISTANCE.
*SEE DARK NIGHTS: METAL FOR MARTIAN MANHUNTER'S RETURN! --BRIAN

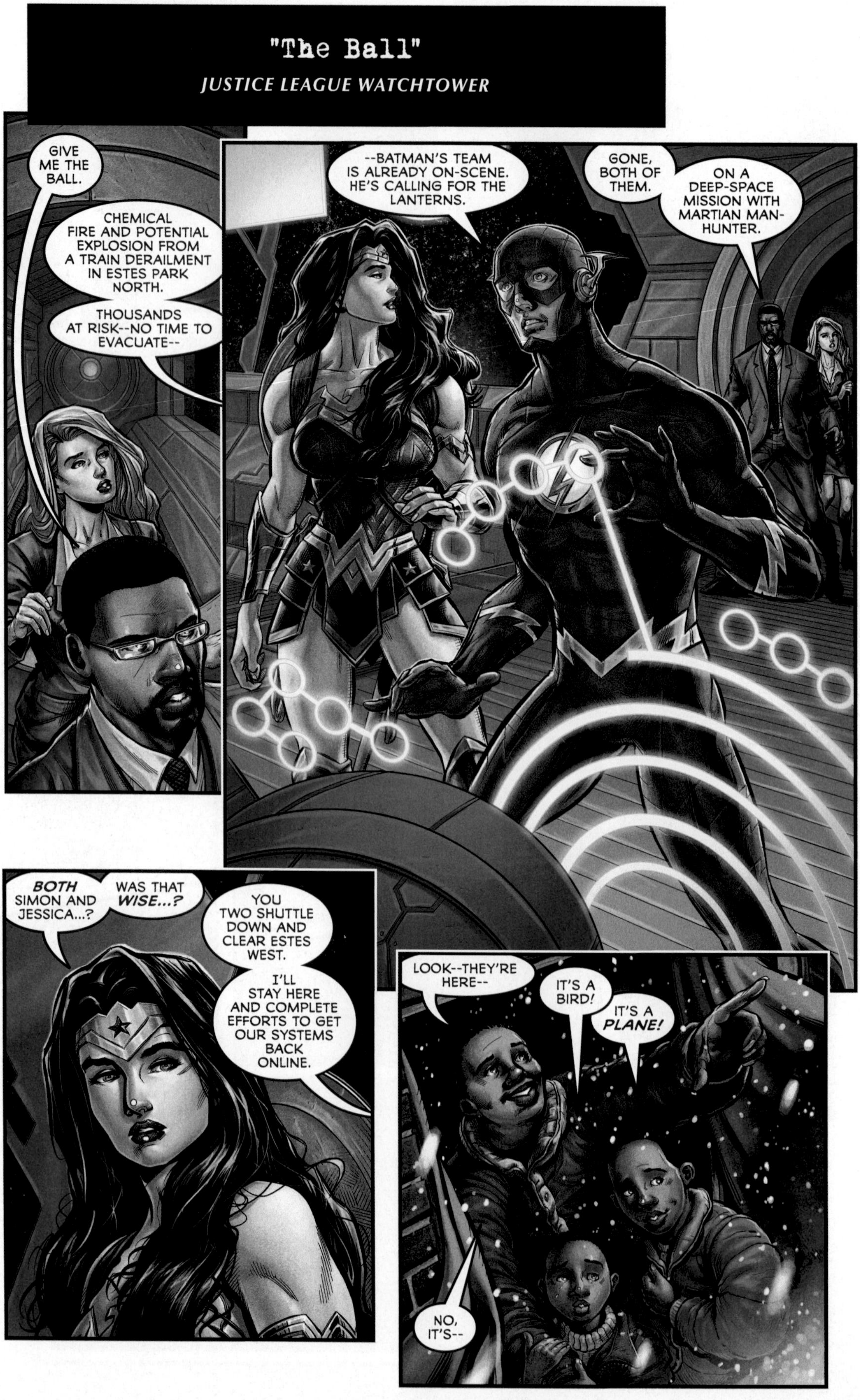
"The Ball"
JUSTICE LEAGUE WATCHTOWER
GIVE ME THE BALL.
CHEMICAL FIRE AND POTENTIAL EXPLOSION FROM A TRAIN DERAILMENT IN ESTES PARK NORTH.
THOUSANDS AT RISK--NO TIME TO EVACUATE--
--BATMAN'S TEAM IS ALREADY ON-SCENE. HE'S CALLING FOR THE LANTERNS.
GONE, BOTH OF THEM.
ON A DEEP-SPACE MISSION WITH MARTIAN MAN-HUNTER.
BOTH SIMON AND JESSICA...?
WAS THAT *WISE...?*
YOU TWO SHUTTLE DOWN AND CLEAR ESTES WEST.
I'LL STAY HERE AND COMPLETE EFFORTS TO GET OUR SYSTEMS BACK ONLINE.
LOOK--THEY'RE HERE--
IT'S A BIRD!
IT'S A *PLANE!*
NO, IT'S--

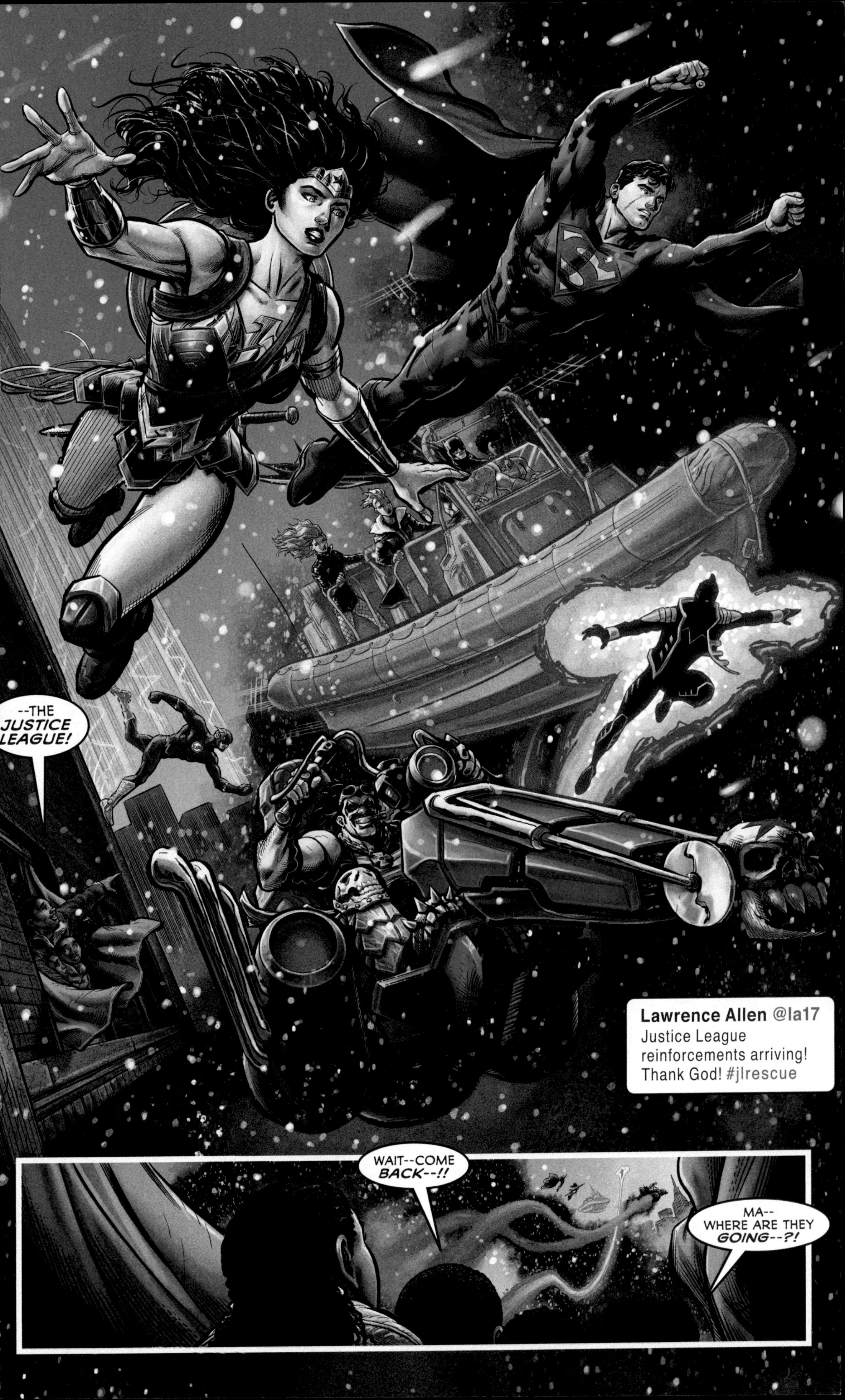
--THE JUSTICE LEAGUE!
Lawrence Allen @la17
Justice League reinforcements arriving! Thank God! #jlrescue
WAIT--COME BACK--!!
MA-- WHERE ARE THEY GOING--?!

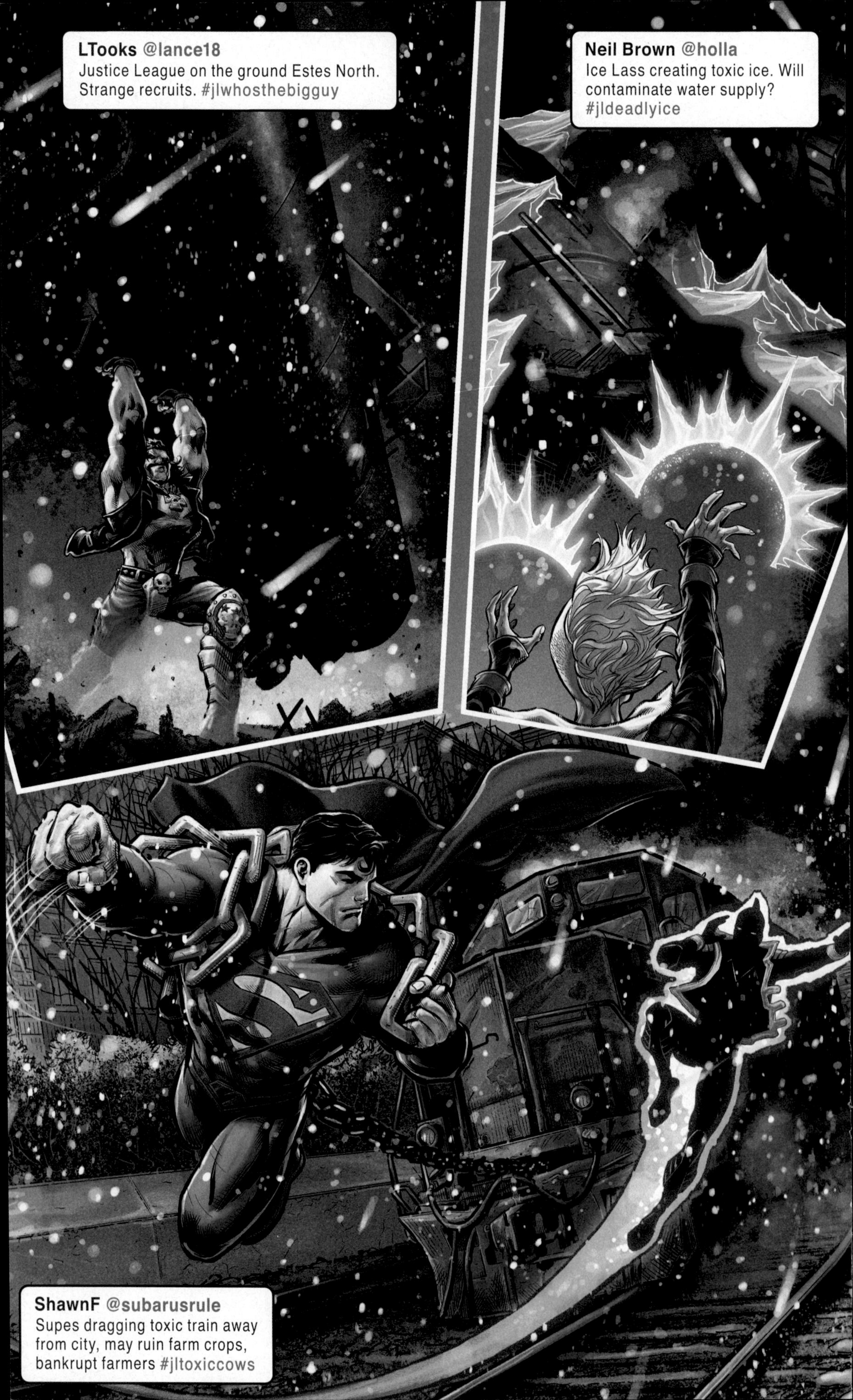
LTooks @lance18
Justice League on the ground Estes North. Strange recruits. #jlwhosthebigguy
Neil Brown @holla
Ice Lass creating toxic ice. Will contaminate water supply? #jldeadlyice
ShawnF @subarusrule
Supes dragging toxic train away from city, may ruin farm crops, bankrupt farmers #jltoxiccows

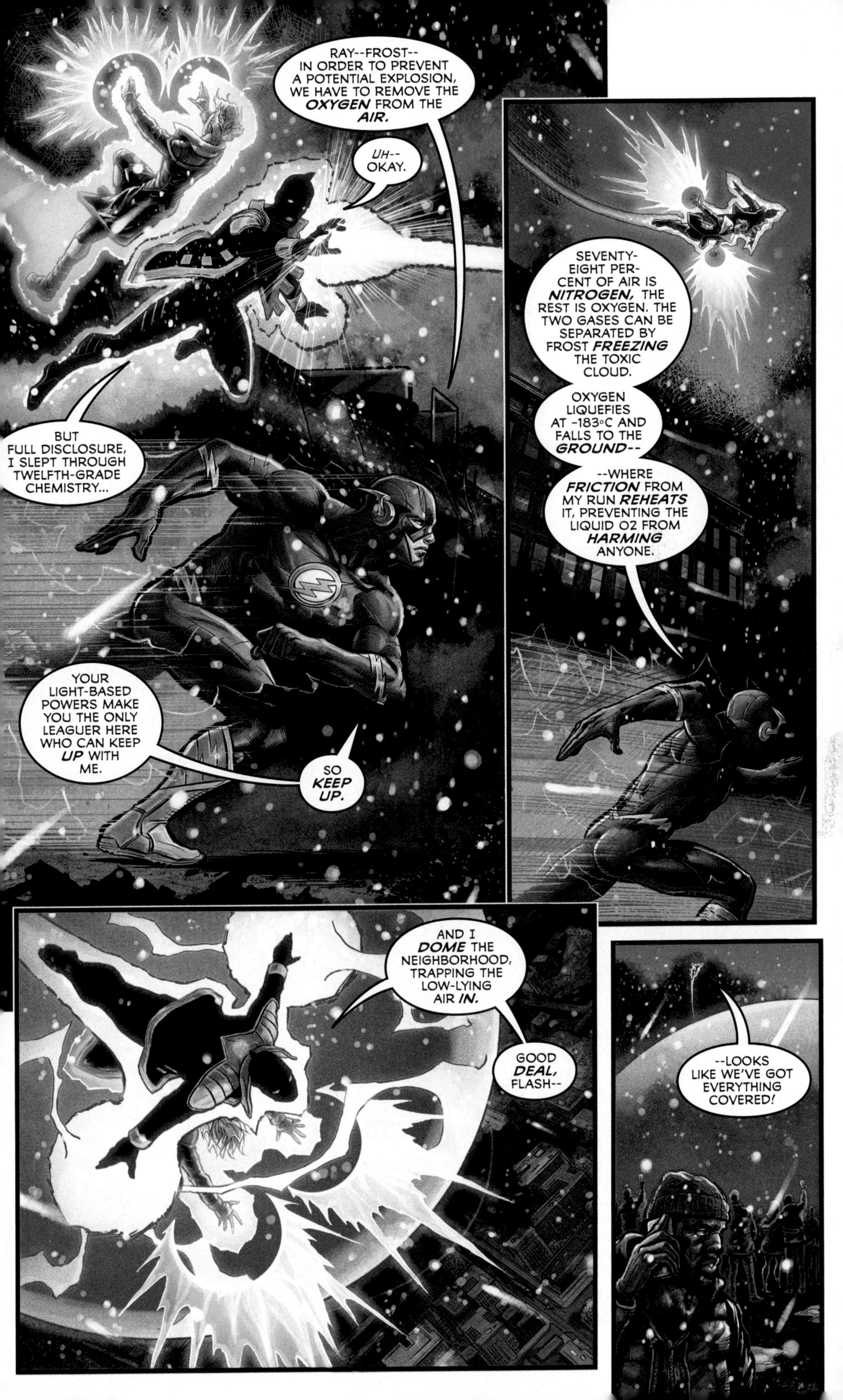
RAY--FROST--
IN ORDER TO PREVENT A POTENTIAL EXPLOSION, WE HAVE TO REMOVE THE OXYGEN FROM THE AIR.
UH-- OKAY.
BUT FULL DISCLOSURE, I SLEPT THROUGH TWELFTH-GRADE CHEMISTRY...
YOUR LIGHT-BASED POWERS MAKE YOU THE ONLY LEAGUER HERE WHO CAN KEEP UP WITH ME.
SO KEEP UP.
SEVENTY-EIGHT PERCENT OF AIR IS NITROGEN, THE REST IS OXYGEN. THE TWO GASES CAN BE SEPARATED BY FROST FREEZING THE TOXIC CLOUD.
OXYGEN LIQUEFIES AT -183°C AND FALLS TO THE GROUND--
--WHERE FRICTION FROM MY RUN REHEATS IT, PREVENTING THE LIQUID O2 FROM HARMING ANYONE.
AND I DOME THE NEIGHBORHOOD, TRAPPING THE LOW-LYING AIR IN.
GOOD DEAL, FLASH--
--LOOKS LIKE WE'VE GOT EVERYTHING COVERED!

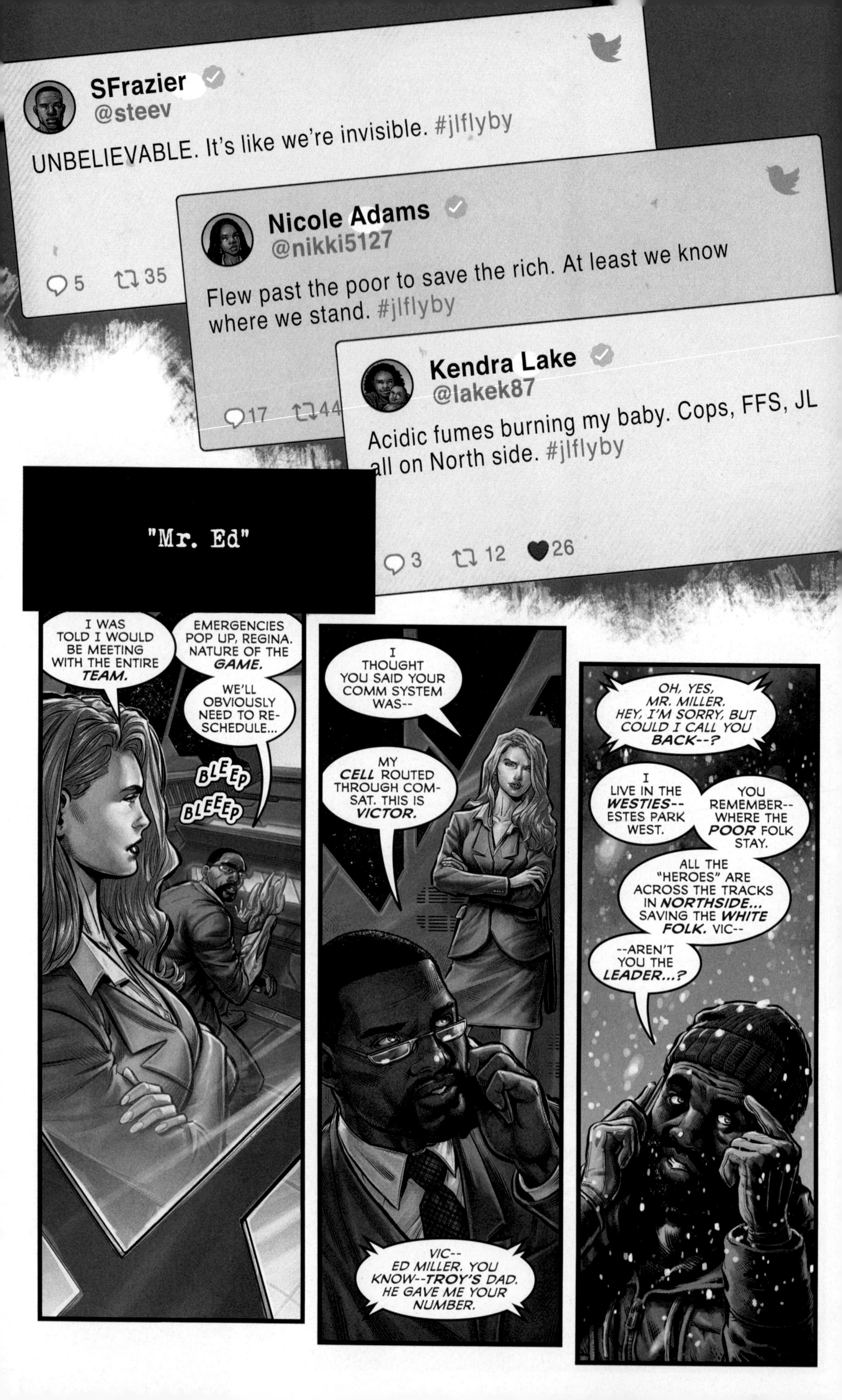
SFrazier
@steev
UNBELIEVABLE. It's like we're invisible. #jlflyby
5 35
Nicole Adams
@nikki5127
Flew past the poor to save the rich. At least we know where we stand. #jlflyby
17 44
Kendra Lake
@lakek87
Acidic fumes burning my baby. Cops, FFS, JL all on North side. #jlflyby
3 12 26
"Mr. Ed"
I WAS TOLD I WOULD BE MEETING WITH THE ENTIRE TEAM.
EMERGENCIES POP UP, REGINA. NATURE OF THE GAME.
WE'LL OBVIOUSLY NEED TO RE-SCHEDULE...
BLEEP
BLEEEP
I THOUGHT YOU SAID YOUR COMM SYSTEM WAS--
MY CELL ROUTED THROUGH COM-SAT. THIS IS VICTOR.
VIC-- ED MILLER. YOU KNOW--TROY'S DAD. HE GAVE ME YOUR NUMBER.
OH, YES, MR. MILLER. HEY, I'M SORRY, BUT COULD I CALL YOU BACK--?
I LIVE IN THE WESTIES-- ESTES PARK WEST.
YOU REMEMBER-- WHERE THE POOR FOLK STAY.
ALL THE "HEROES" ARE ACROSS THE TRACKS IN NORTHSIDE... SAVING THE WHITE FOLK. VIC--
--AREN'T YOU THE LEADER...?

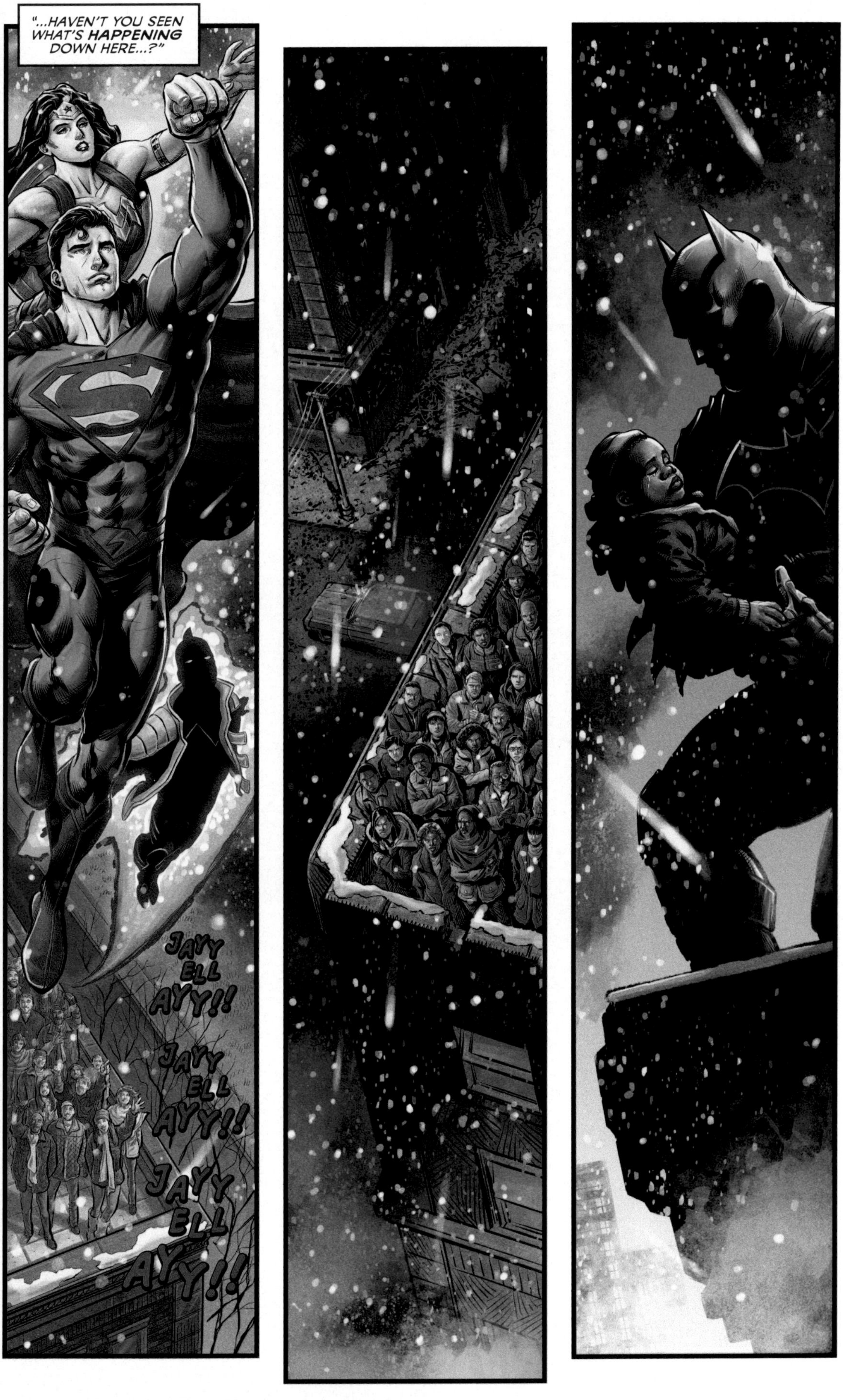
"...HAVEN'T YOU SEEN WHAT'S **HAPPENING** DOWN HERE...?"
JAYY ELL AYY!!
JAYY ELL AYY!!
JAYY ELL AYY!!

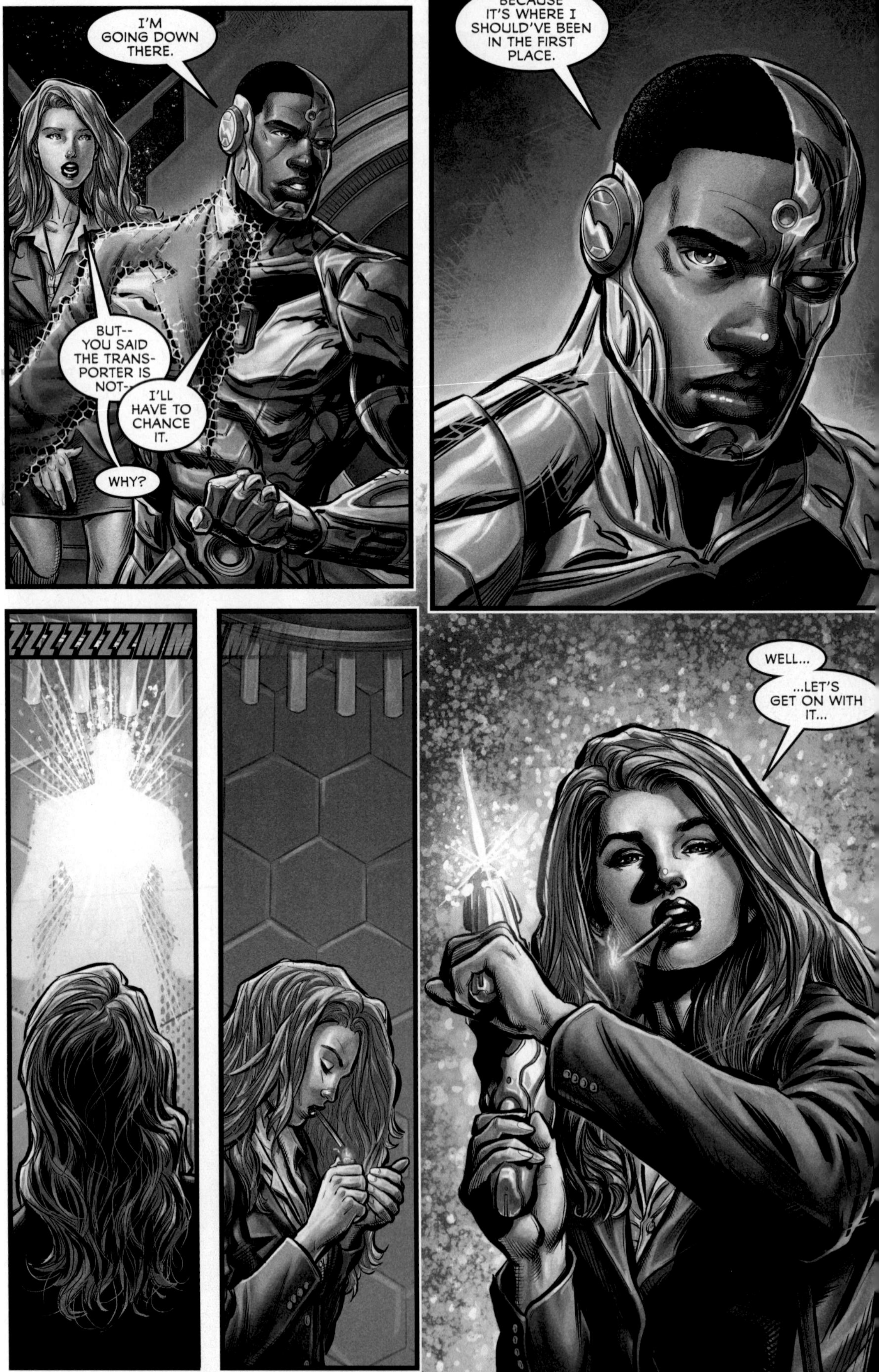
I'M GOING DOWN THERE.
BUT-- YOU SAID THE TRANS-PORTER IS NOT--
I'LL HAVE TO CHANCE IT.
WHY?
BECAUSE IT'S WHERE I SHOULD'VE BEEN IN THE FIRST PLACE.
ZZZZZZZMMM
WELL...
...LET'S GET ON WITH IT...

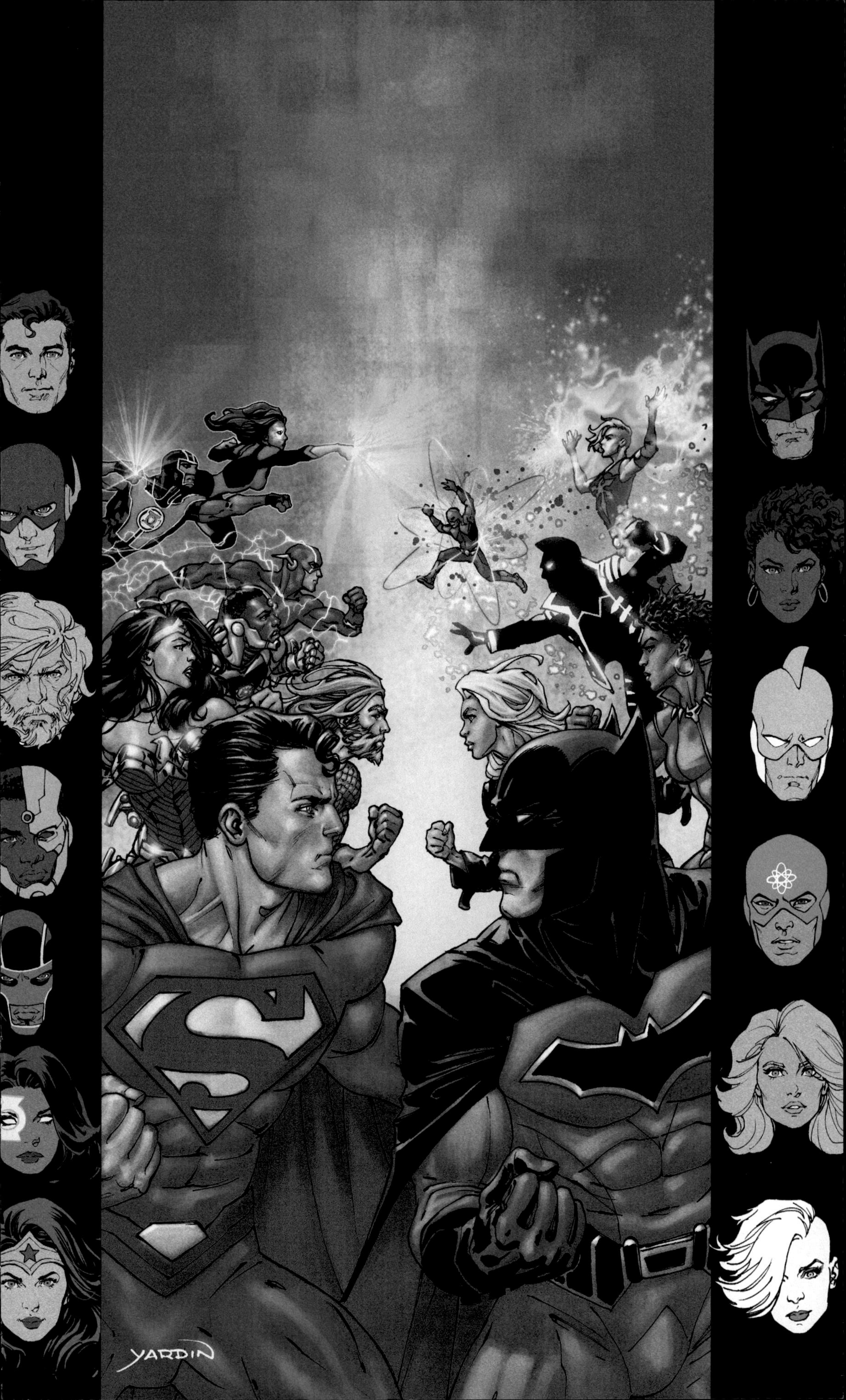
YARDIN

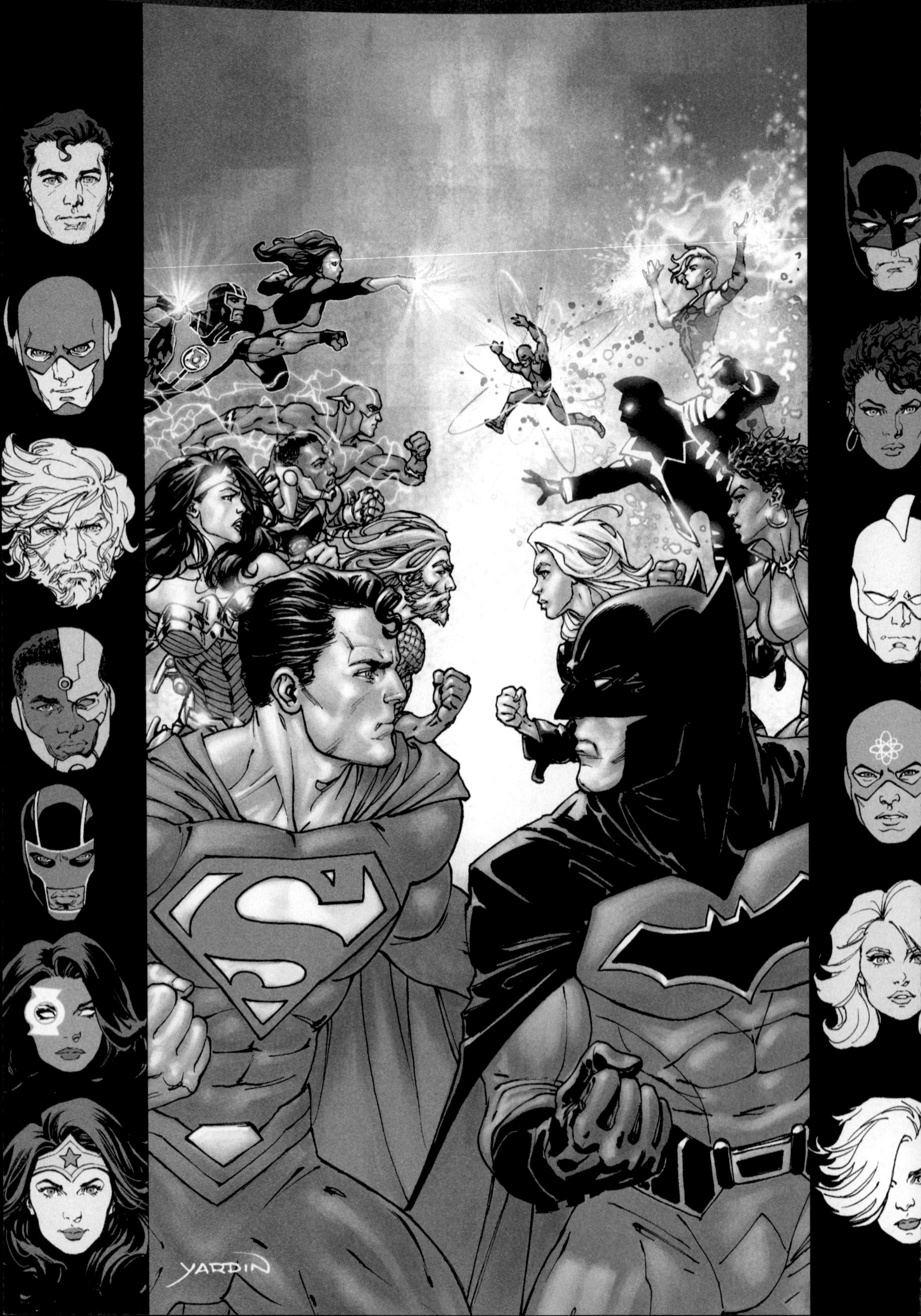
YARDIN

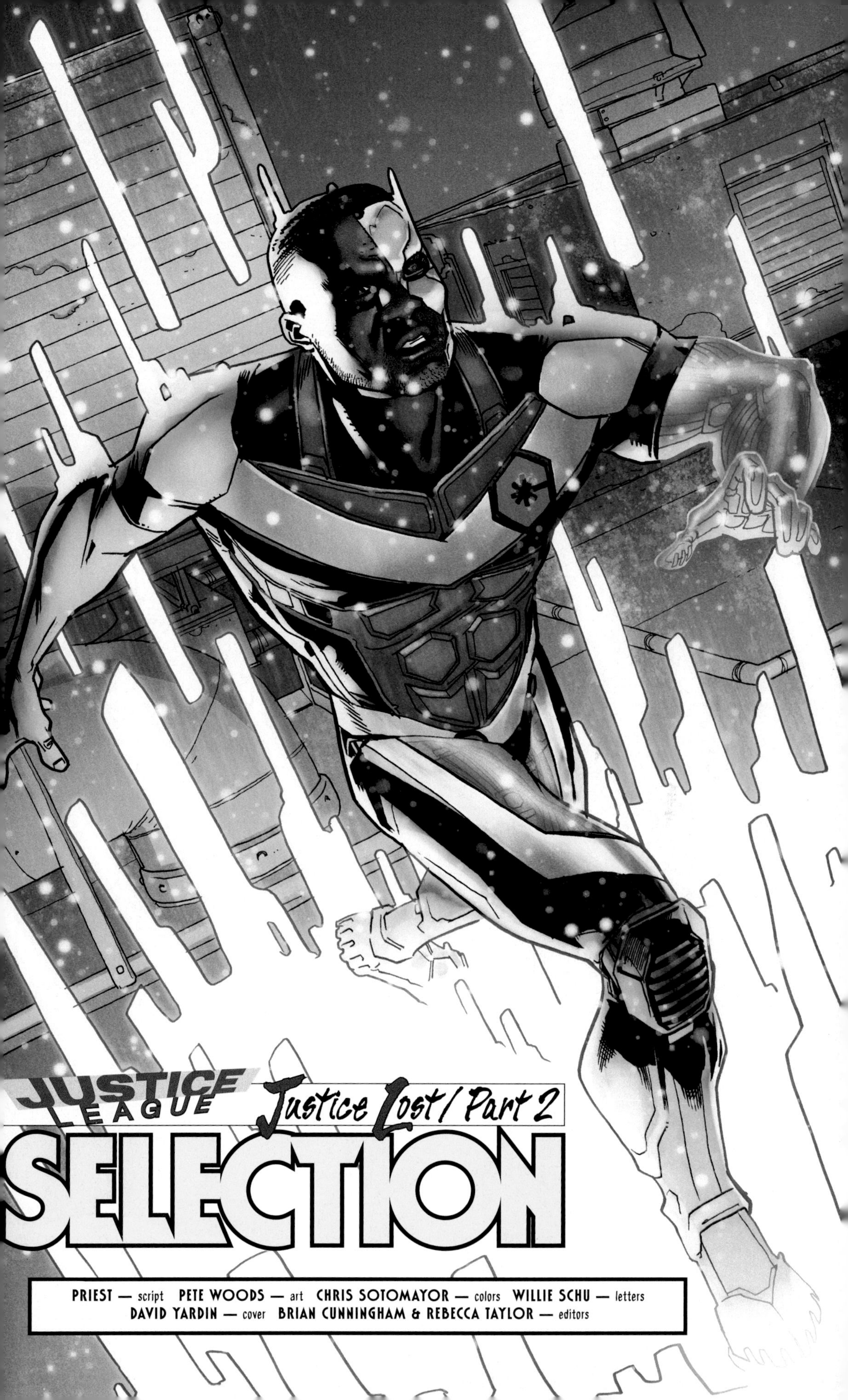

JUSTICE LEAGUE
Justice Lost / Part 2
SELECTION
PRIEST — script PETE WOODS — art CHRIS SOTOMAYOR — colors WILLIE SCHU — letters
DAVID YARDIN — cover BRIAN CUNNINGHAM & REBECCA TAYLOR — editors

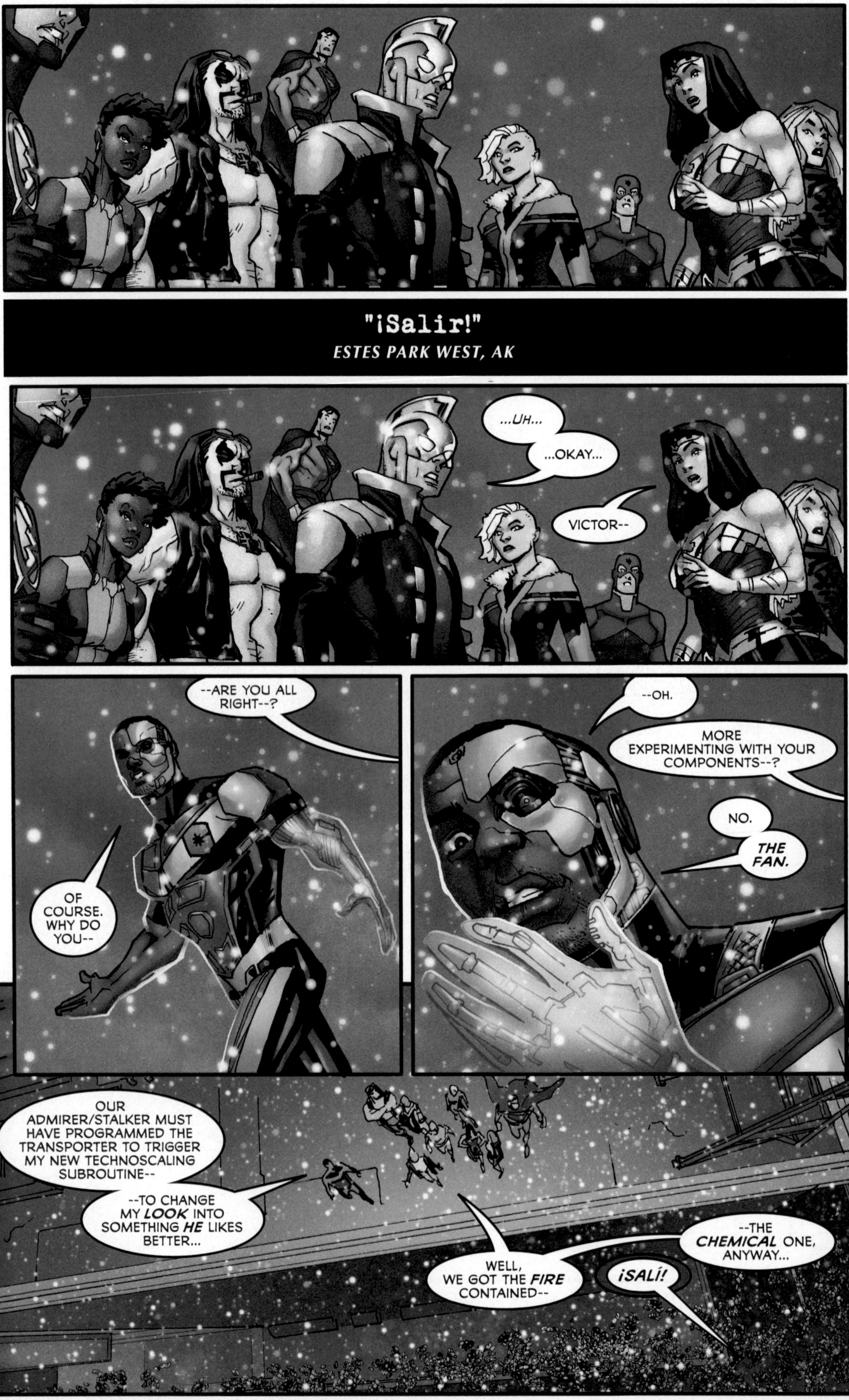
"¡Salir!"
ESTES PARK WEST, AK
...UH...
...OKAY...
VICTOR--
--ARE YOU ALL RIGHT--?
OF COURSE. WHY DO YOU--
--OH.
MORE EXPERIMENTING WITH YOUR COMPONENTS--?
NO. THE FAN.
OUR ADMIRER/STALKER MUST HAVE PROGRAMMED THE TRANSPORTER TO TRIGGER MY NEW TECHNOSCALING SUBROUTINE--
--TO CHANGE MY LOOK INTO SOMETHING HE LIKES BETTER...
WELL, WE GOT THE FIRE CONTAINED--
--THE CHEMICAL ONE, ANYWAY...
¡SALÍ!

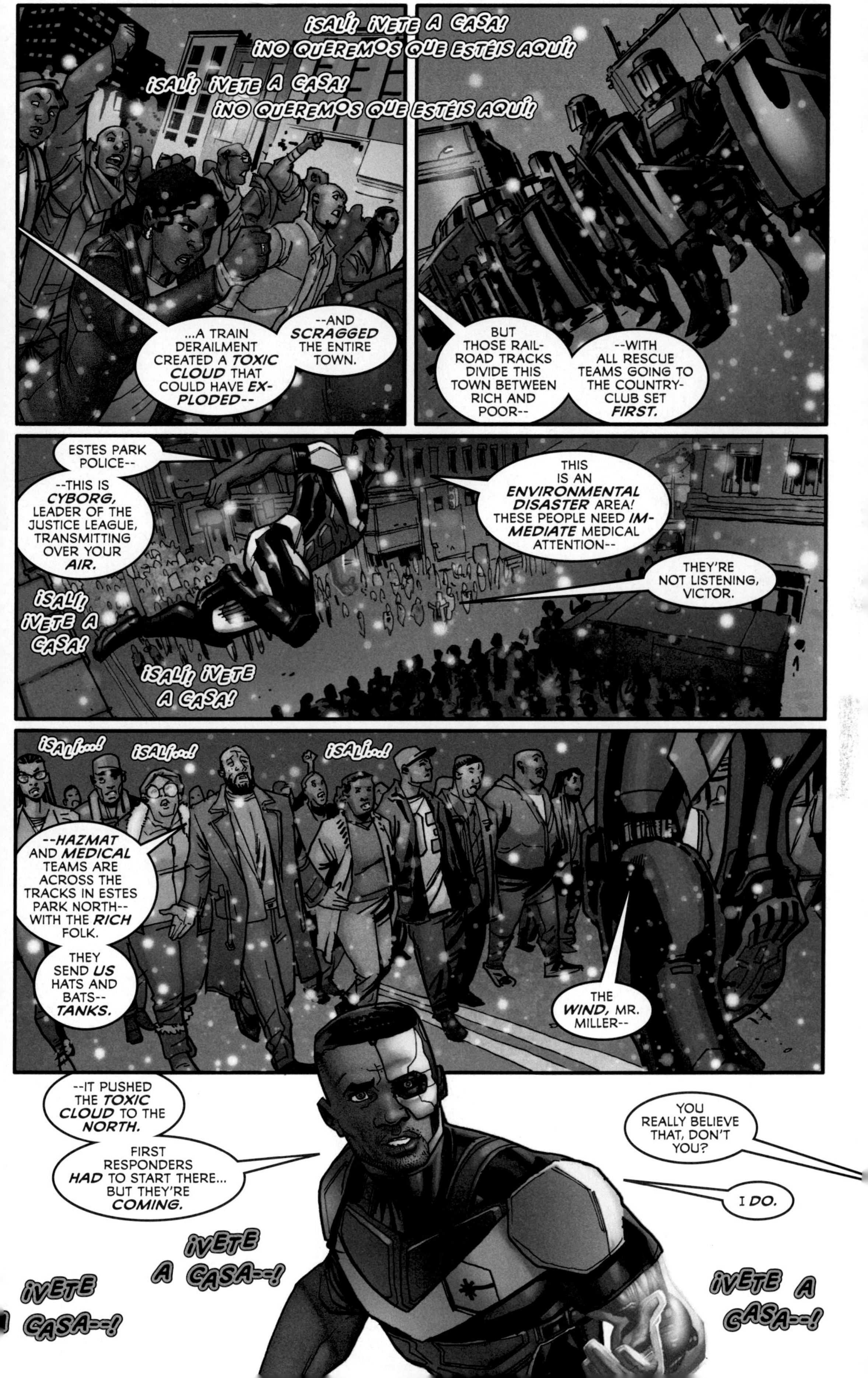
¡SALÍ! ¡VETE A CASA!
¡NO QUEREMOS QUE ESTÉIS AQUÍ!
¡SALÍ! ¡VETE A CASA!
¡NO QUEREMOS QUE ESTÉIS AQUÍ!
...A TRAIN DERAILMENT CREATED A TOXIC CLOUD THAT COULD HAVE EXPLODED--
--AND SCRAGGED THE ENTIRE TOWN.
BUT THOSE RAILROAD TRACKS DIVIDE THIS TOWN BETWEEN RICH AND POOR--
--WITH ALL RESCUE TEAMS GOING TO THE COUNTRY-CLUB SET FIRST.
ESTES PARK POLICE--
--THIS IS CYBORG, LEADER OF THE JUSTICE LEAGUE, TRANSMITTING OVER YOUR AIR.
THIS IS AN ENVIRONMENTAL DISASTER AREA! THESE PEOPLE NEED IMMEDIATE MEDICAL ATTENTION--
THEY'RE NOT LISTENING, VICTOR.
¡SALÍ! ¡VETE A CASA!
¡SALÍ! ¡VETE A CASA!
¡SALÍ...!
¡SALÍ...!
¡SALÍ...!
--HAZMAT AND MEDICAL TEAMS ARE ACROSS THE TRACKS IN ESTES PARK NORTH--WITH THE RICH FOLK.
THEY SEND US HATS AND BATS--TANKS.
THE WIND, MR. MILLER--
--IT PUSHED THE TOXIC CLOUD TO THE NORTH.
FIRST RESPONDERS HAD TO START THERE... BUT THEY'RE COMING.
YOU REALLY BELIEVE THAT, DON'T YOU?
I DO.
¡VETE A CASA--!
¡VETE A CASA--!
¡VETE A CASA--!

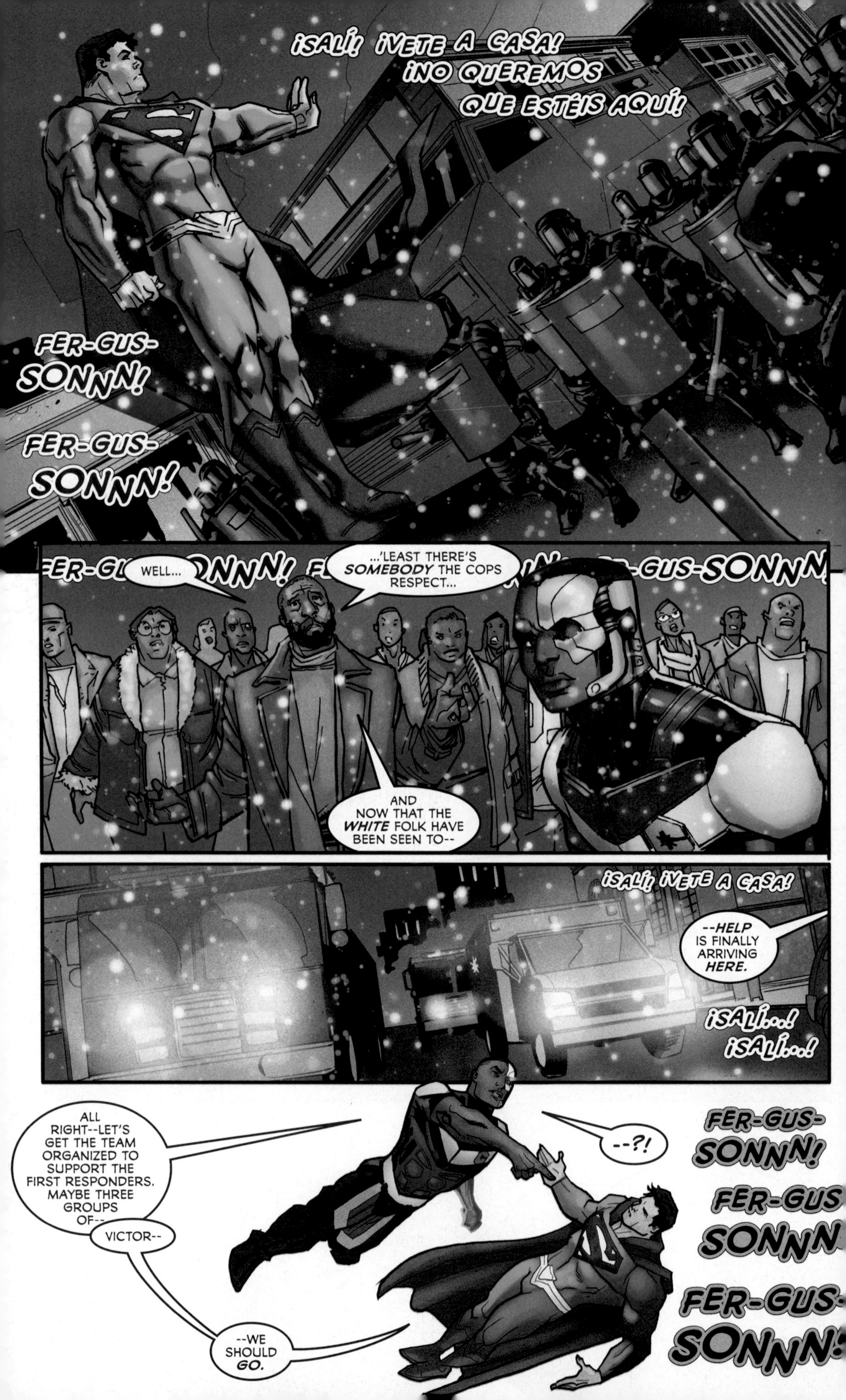

¡SALÍ! ¡VETE A CASA! ¡NO QUEREMOS QUE ESTÉIS AQUÍ!
FER-GUS-SONNN!
FER-GUS-SONNN!
WELL...
...'LEAST THERE'S SOMEBODY THE COPS RESPECT...
AND NOW THAT THE WHITE FOLK HAVE BEEN SEEN TO--
¡SALÍ! ¡VETE A CASA!
--HELP IS FINALLY ARRIVING HERE.
¡SALÍ...! ¡SALÍ...!
ALL RIGHT--LET'S GET THE TEAM ORGANIZED TO SUPPORT THE FIRST RESPONDERS. MAYBE THREE GROUPS OF--
VICTOR--
--WE SHOULD GO.
--?!
FER-GUS-SONNN!

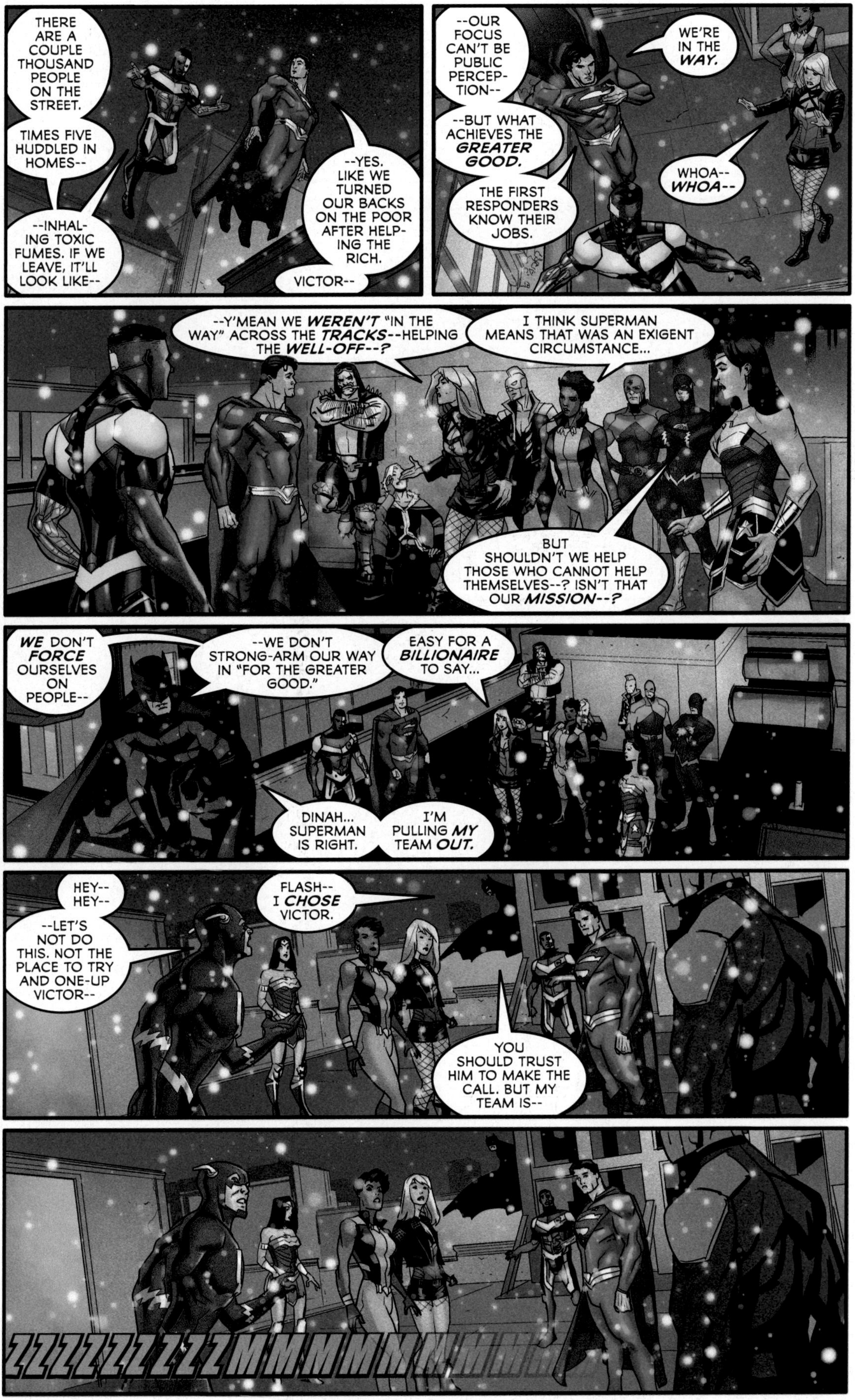
THERE ARE A COUPLE THOUSAND PEOPLE ON THE STREET.
TIMES FIVE HUDDLED IN HOMES--
--INHALING TOXIC FUMES. IF WE LEAVE, IT'LL LOOK LIKE--
--YES. LIKE WE TURNED OUR BACKS ON THE POOR AFTER HELPING THE RICH.
VICTOR--
--OUR FOCUS CAN'T BE PUBLIC PERCEPTION--
--BUT WHAT ACHIEVES THE GREATER GOOD.
THE FIRST RESPONDERS KNOW THEIR JOBS.
WE'RE IN THE WAY.
WHOA-- WHOA--
--Y'MEAN WE WEREN'T "IN THE WAY" ACROSS THE TRACKS--HELPING THE WELL-OFF--?
I THINK SUPERMAN MEANS THAT WAS AN EXIGENT CIRCUMSTANCE...
BUT SHOULDN'T WE HELP THOSE WHO CANNOT HELP THEMSELVES--? ISN'T THAT OUR MISSION--?
WE DON'T FORCE OURSELVES ON PEOPLE--
--WE DON'T STRONG-ARM OUR WAY IN "FOR THE GREATER GOOD."
EASY FOR A BILLIONAIRE TO SAY...
DINAH... SUPERMAN IS RIGHT.
I'M PULLING MY TEAM OUT.
HEY-- HEY--
--LET'S NOT DO THIS. NOT THE PLACE TO TRY AND ONE-UP VICTOR--
FLASH-- I CHOSE VICTOR.
YOU SHOULD TRUST HIM TO MAKE THE CALL. BUT MY TEAM IS--
ZZZZZZZZZZZMMMMMMMMMMMMM

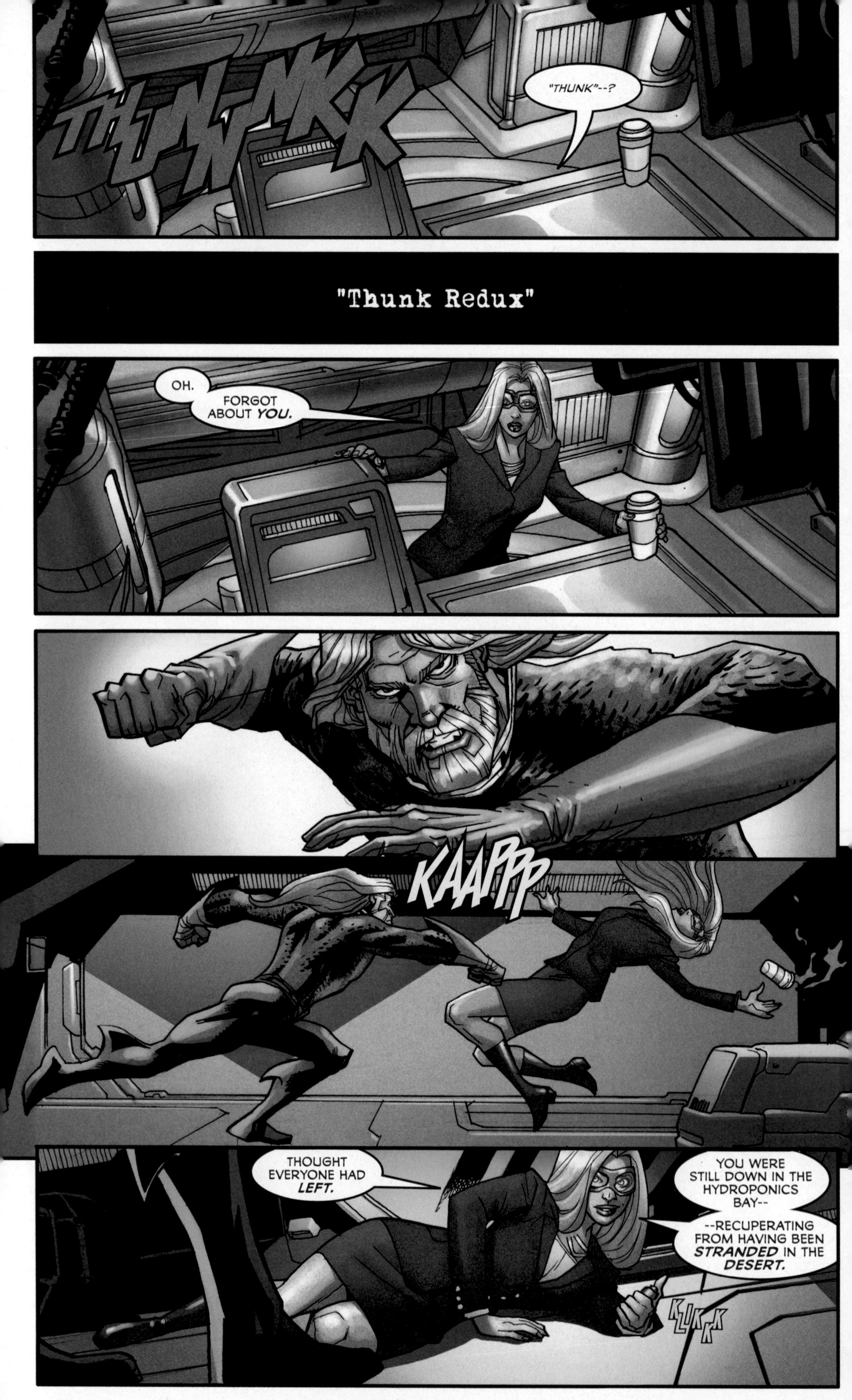
THUNNKK
"THUNK"--?
"Thunk Redux"
OH.
FORGOT ABOUT YOU.
KAAPPP
THOUGHT EVERYONE HAD LEFT.
YOU WERE STILL DOWN IN THE HYDROPONICS BAY--
--RECUPERATING FROM HAVING BEEN STRANDED IN THE DESERT.
KLIKKK

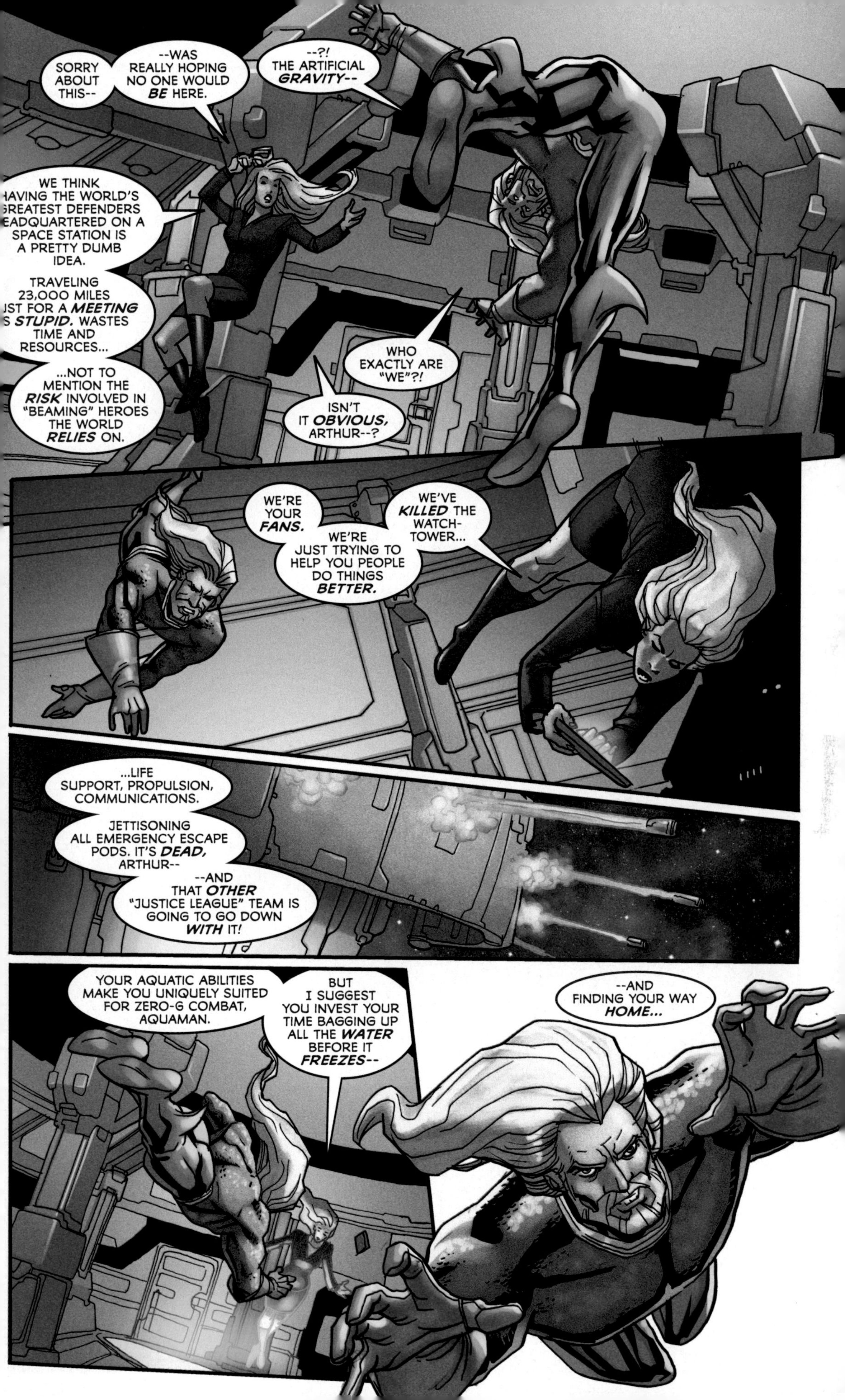
SORRY ABOUT THIS--
--WAS REALLY HOPING NO ONE WOULD BE HERE.
--?! THE ARTIFICIAL GRAVITY--
WE THINK HAVING THE WORLD'S GREATEST DEFENDERS HEADQUARTERED ON A SPACE STATION IS A PRETTY DUMB IDEA.
TRAVELING 23,000 MILES JUST FOR A MEETING IS STUPID. WASTES TIME AND RESOURCES...
...NOT TO MENTION THE RISK INVOLVED IN "BEAMING" HEROES THE WORLD RELIES ON.
WHO EXACTLY ARE "WE"?!
ISN'T IT OBVIOUS, ARTHUR--?
WE'RE YOUR FANS.
WE'RE JUST TRYING TO HELP YOU PEOPLE DO THINGS BETTER.
WE'VE KILLED THE WATCH-TOWER...
...LIFE SUPPORT, PROPULSION, COMMUNICATIONS.
JETTISONING ALL EMERGENCY ESCAPE PODS. IT'S DEAD, ARTHUR--
--AND THAT OTHER "JUSTICE LEAGUE" TEAM IS GOING TO GO DOWN WITH IT!
YOUR AQUATIC ABILITIES MAKE YOU UNIQUELY SUITED FOR ZERO-G COMBAT, AQUAMAN.
BUT I SUGGEST YOU INVEST YOUR TIME BAGGING UP ALL THE WATER BEFORE IT FREEZES--
--AND FINDING YOUR WAY HOME...

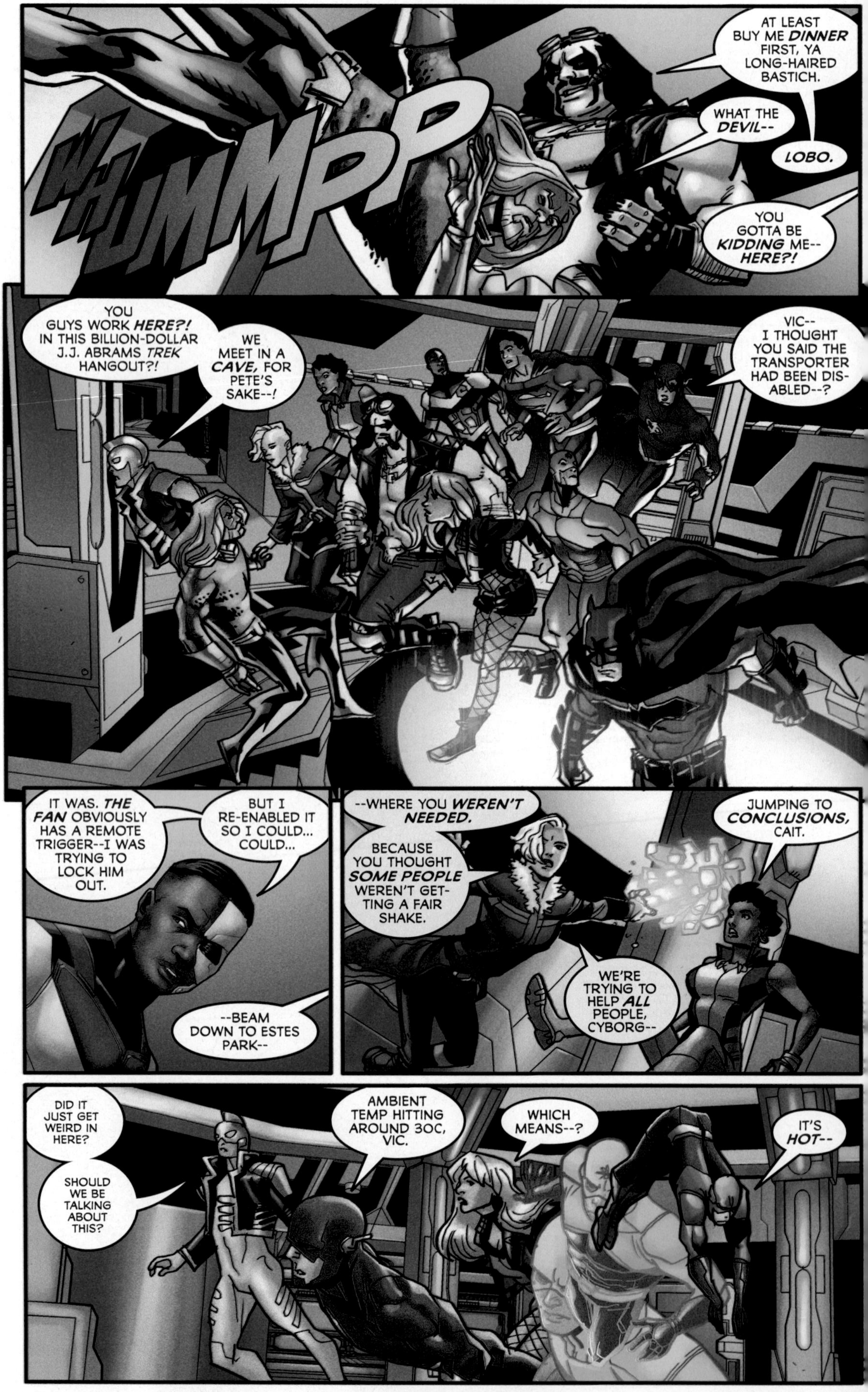
WHUMMPP
AT LEAST BUY ME *DINNER* FIRST, YA LONG-HAIRED BASTICH.
WHAT THE *DEVIL*--
LOBO.
YOU GOTTA BE *KIDDING* ME-- *HERE?!*
YOU GUYS WORK *HERE?!* IN THIS BILLION-DOLLAR J.J. ABRAMS *TREK* HANGOUT?!
WE MEET IN A *CAVE,* FOR PETE'S SAKE--!
VIC-- I THOUGHT YOU SAID THE TRANSPORTER HAD BEEN DIS-ABLED--?
IT WAS. *THE FAN* OBVIOUSLY HAS A REMOTE TRIGGER--I WAS TRYING TO LOCK HIM OUT.
BUT I RE-ENABLED IT SO I COULD... COULD...
--BEAM DOWN TO ESTES PARK--
--WHERE YOU *WEREN'T NEEDED.*
BECAUSE YOU THOUGHT *SOME PEOPLE* WEREN'T GET-TING A FAIR SHAKE.
JUMPING TO *CONCLUSIONS,* CAIT.
WE'RE TRYING TO HELP *ALL* PEOPLE, CYBORG--
DID IT JUST GET WEIRD IN HERE?
SHOULD WE BE TALKING ABOUT THIS?
AMBIENT TEMP HITTING AROUND 30C, VIC.
WHICH MEANS--?
IT'S *HOT--*

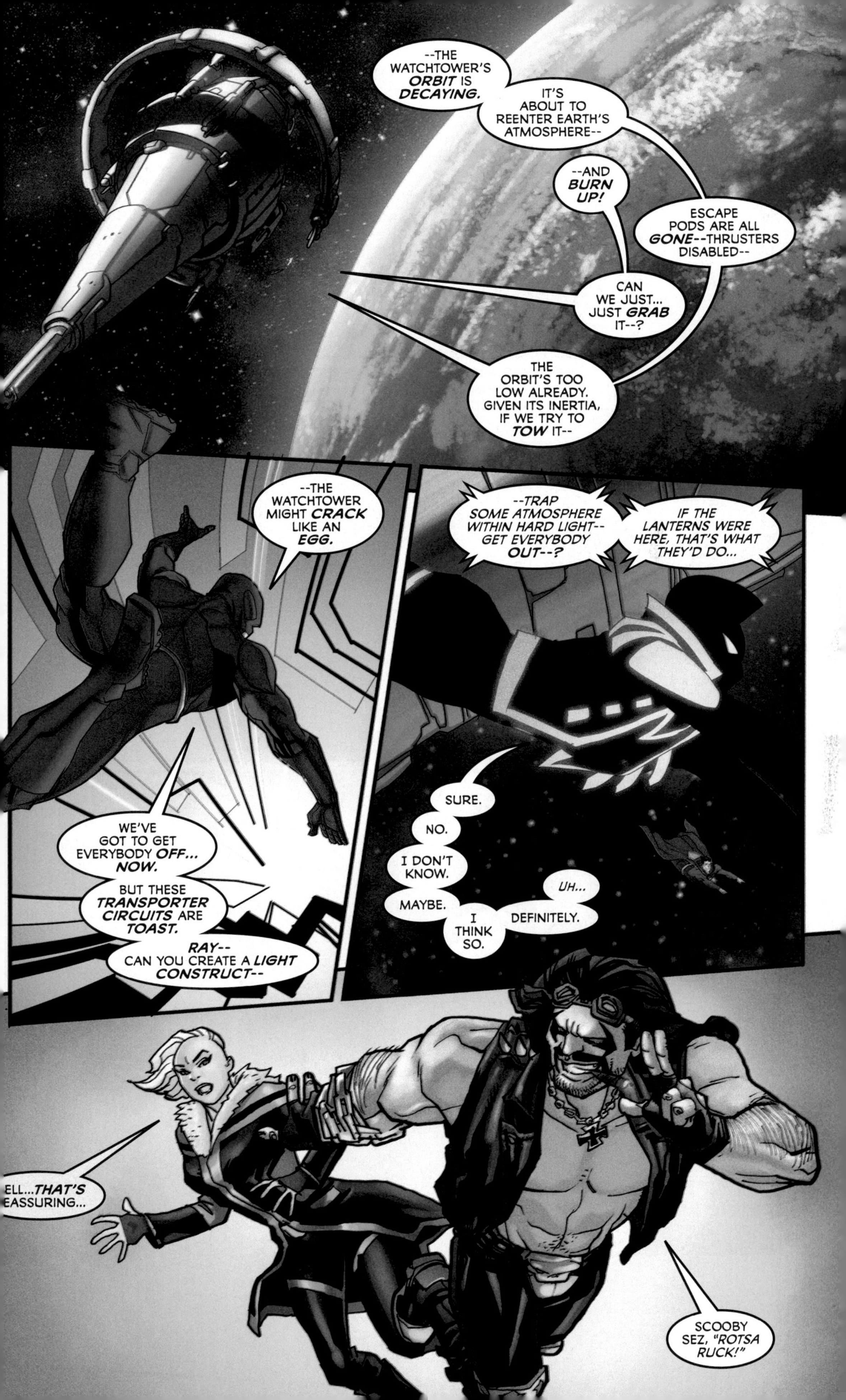
--THE WATCHTOWER'S ORBIT IS DECAYING.
IT'S ABOUT TO REENTER EARTH'S ATMOSPHERE--
--AND BURN UP!
ESCAPE PODS ARE ALL GONE--THRUSTERS DISABLED--
CAN WE JUST... JUST GRAB IT--?
THE ORBIT'S TOO LOW ALREADY. GIVEN ITS INERTIA, IF WE TRY TO TOW IT--
--THE WATCHTOWER MIGHT CRACK LIKE AN EGG.
WE'VE GOT TO GET EVERYBODY OFF... NOW.
BUT THESE TRANSPORTER CIRCUITS ARE TOAST.
RAY-- CAN YOU CREATE A LIGHT CONSTRUCT--
--TRAP SOME ATMOSPHERE WITHIN HARD LIGHT-- GET EVERYBODY OUT--?
IF THE LANTERNS WERE HERE, THAT'S WHAT THEY'D DO...
SURE.
NO.
I DON'T KNOW.
MAYBE.
I THINK SO.
UH...
DEFINITELY.
ELL...THAT'S EASSURING...
SCOOBY SEZ, "ROTSA RUCK!"

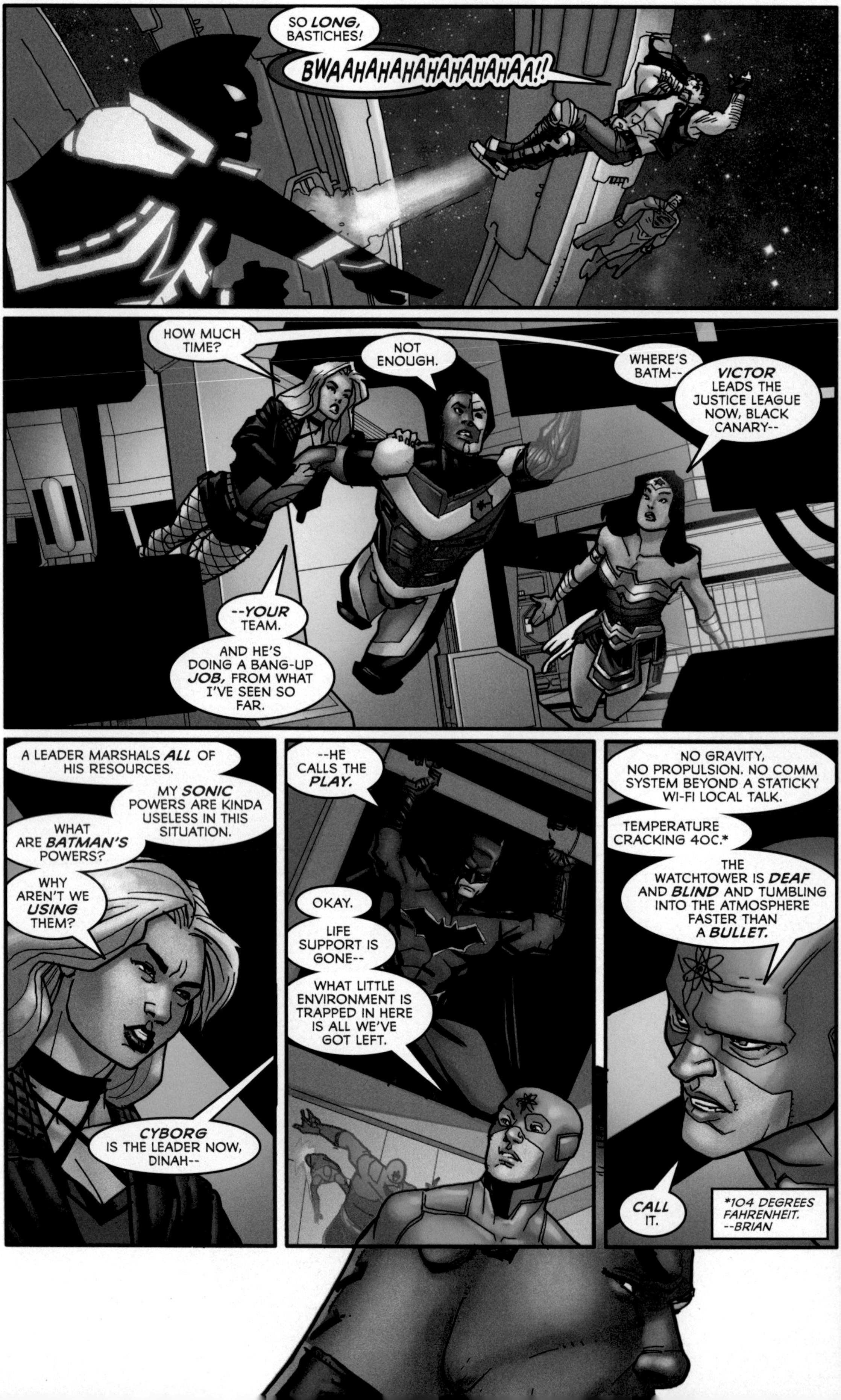
SO LONG, BASTICHES!
BWAAHAHAHAHAHAHAHAHAA!!
HOW MUCH TIME?
NOT ENOUGH.
WHERE'S BATM--
VICTOR LEADS THE JUSTICE LEAGUE NOW, BLACK CANARY--
--YOUR TEAM.
AND HE'S DOING A BANG-UP JOB, FROM WHAT I'VE SEEN SO FAR.
A LEADER MARSHALS ALL OF HIS RESOURCES.
MY SONIC POWERS ARE KINDA USELESS IN THIS SITUATION.
WHAT ARE BATMAN'S POWERS?
WHY AREN'T WE USING THEM?
CYBORG IS THE LEADER NOW, DINAH--
--HE CALLS THE PLAY.
OKAY.
LIFE SUPPORT IS GONE--
WHAT LITTLE ENVIRONMENT IS TRAPPED IN HERE IS ALL WE'VE GOT LEFT.
NO GRAVITY, NO PROPULSION. NO COMM SYSTEM BEYOND A STATICKY WI-FI LOCAL TALK.
TEMPERATURE CRACKING 40C.*
THE WATCHTOWER IS DEAF AND BLIND AND TUMBLING INTO THE ATMOSPHERE FASTER THAN A BULLET.
CALL IT.
*104 DEGREES FAHRENHEIT. --BRIAN

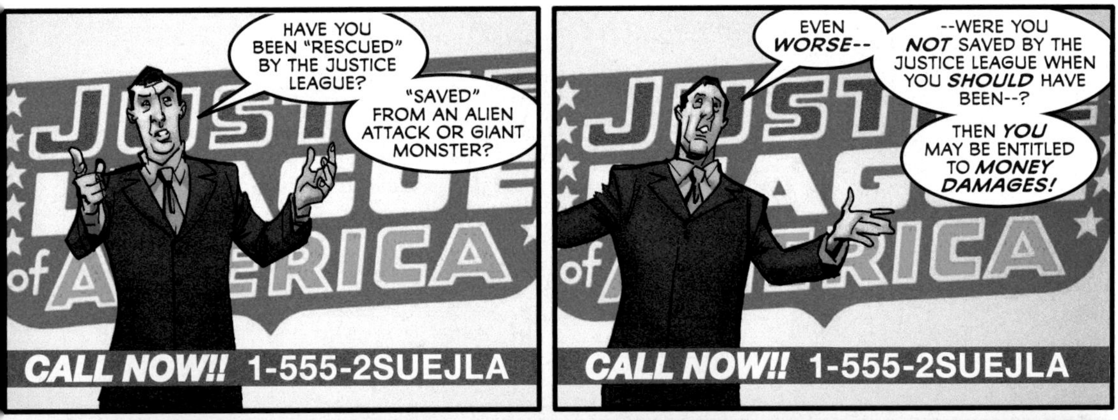
HAVE YOU BEEN "RESCUED" BY THE JUSTICE LEAGUE?
"SAVED" FROM AN ALIEN ATTACK OR GIANT MONSTER?
JUSTICE LEAGUE of AMERICA
CALL NOW!! 1-555-2SUEJLA
EVEN WORSE--
--WERE YOU NOT SAVED BY THE JUSTICE LEAGUE WHEN YOU SHOULD HAVE BEEN--?
THEN YOU MAY BE ENTITLED TO MONEY DAMAGES!
CALL NOW!! 1-555-2SUEJLA

"Ninety-Five Cents"

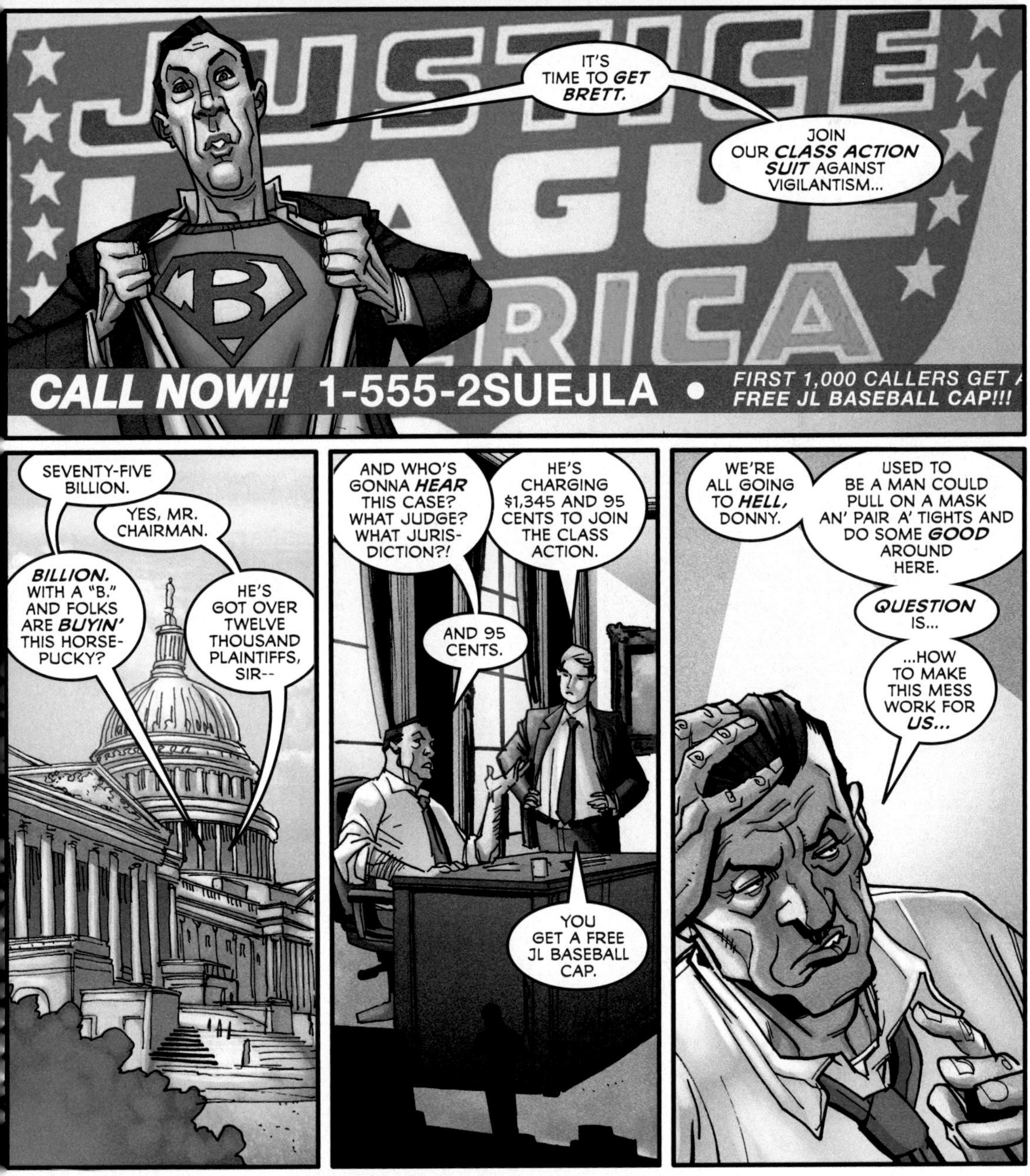
IT'S TIME TO GET BRETT.
JOIN OUR CLASS ACTION SUIT AGAINST VIGILANTISM...
CALL NOW!! 1-555-2SUEJLA • FIRST 1,000 CALLERS GET A FREE JL BASEBALL CAP!!!
SEVENTY-FIVE BILLION.
YES, MR. CHAIRMAN.
BILLION. WITH A "B." AND FOLKS ARE BUYIN' THIS HORSE-PUCKY?
HE'S GOT OVER TWELVE THOUSAND PLAINTIFFS, SIR--
AND WHO'S GONNA HEAR THIS CASE? WHAT JUDGE? WHAT JURIS-DICTION?!
HE'S CHARGING $1,345 AND 95 CENTS TO JOIN THE CLASS ACTION.
AND 95 CENTS.
YOU GET A FREE JL BASEBALL CAP.
WE'RE ALL GOING TO HELL, DONNY.
USED TO BE A MAN COULD PULL ON A MASK AN' PAIR A' TIGHTS AND DO SOME GOOD AROUND HERE.
QUESTION IS...
...HOW TO MAKE THIS MESS WORK FOR US...

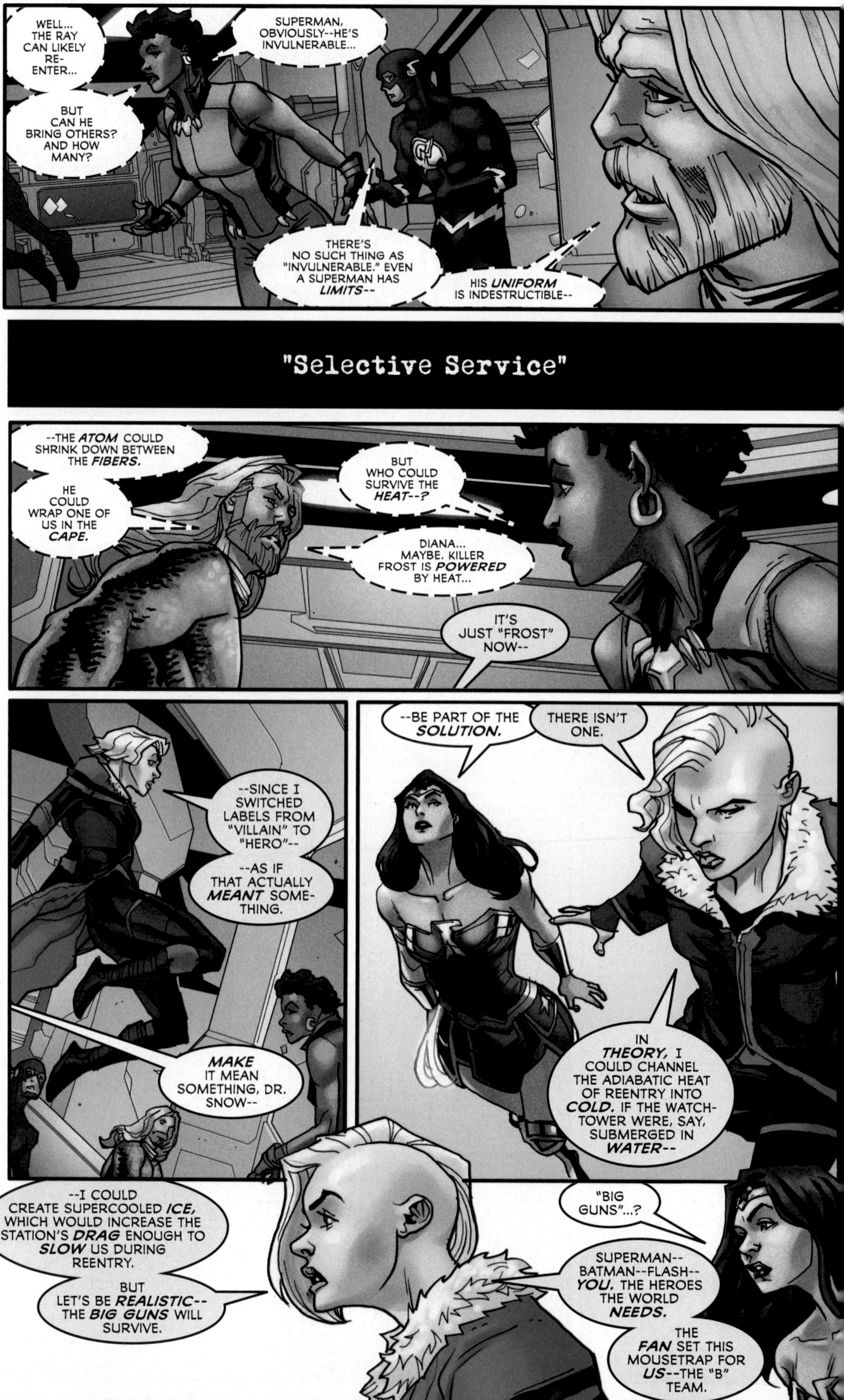
WELL... THE RAY CAN LIKELY RE-ENTER...
BUT CAN HE BRING OTHERS? AND HOW MANY?
SUPERMAN, OBVIOUSLY--HE'S INVULNERABLE...
THERE'S NO SUCH THING AS "INVULNERABLE." EVEN A SUPERMAN HAS LIMITS--
HIS UNIFORM IS INDESTRUCTIBLE--
"Selective Service"
--THE ATOM COULD SHRINK DOWN BETWEEN THE FIBERS.
HE COULD WRAP ONE OF US IN THE CAPE.
BUT WHO COULD SURVIVE THE HEAT--?
DIANA... MAYBE. KILLER FROST IS POWERED BY HEAT...
IT'S JUST "FROST" NOW--
--SINCE I SWITCHED LABELS FROM "VILLAIN" TO "HERO"--
--AS IF THAT ACTUALLY MEANT SOME-THING.
MAKE IT MEAN SOMETHING, DR. SNOW--
--BE PART OF THE SOLUTION.
THERE ISN'T ONE.
IN THEORY, I COULD CHANNEL THE ADIABATIC HEAT OF REENTRY INTO COLD. IF THE WATCH-TOWER WERE, SAY, SUBMERGED IN WATER--
--I COULD CREATE SUPERCOOLED ICE, WHICH WOULD INCREASE THE STATION'S DRAG ENOUGH TO SLOW US DURING REENTRY.
BUT LET'S BE REALISTIC-- THE BIG GUNS WILL SURVIVE.
"BIG GUNS"...?
SUPERMAN-- BATMAN--FLASH-- YOU. THE HEROES THE WORLD NEEDS.
THE FAN SET THIS MOUSETRAP FOR US--THE "B" TEAM.

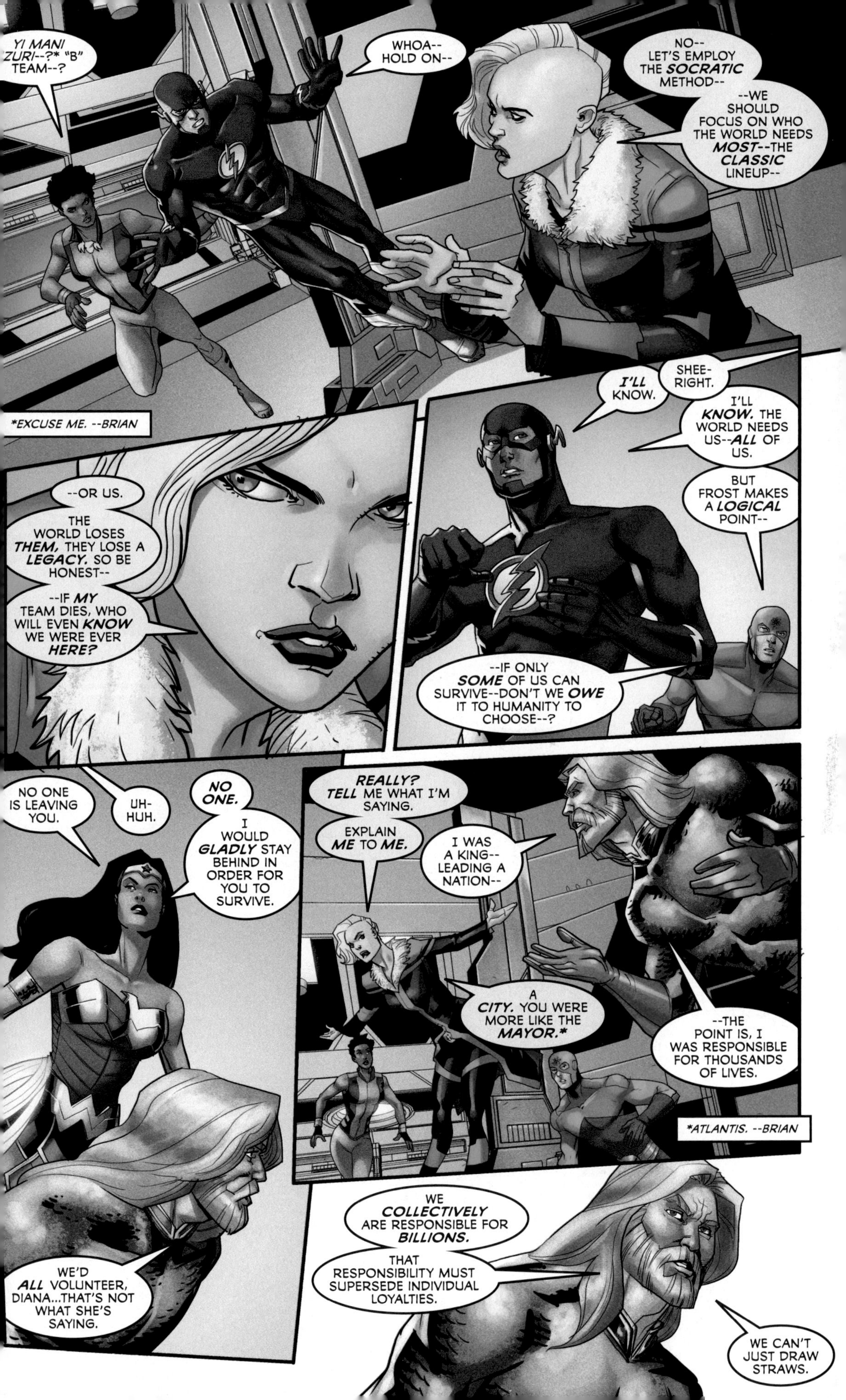
YI MANI ZURI--?* "B" TEAM--?
WHOA-- HOLD ON--
NO-- LET'S EMPLOY THE SOCRATIC METHOD--
--WE SHOULD FOCUS ON WHO THE WORLD NEEDS MOST--THE CLASSIC LINEUP--
*EXCUSE ME. --BRIAN
--OR US.
THE WORLD LOSES THEM, THEY LOSE A LEGACY. SO BE HONEST--
--IF MY TEAM DIES, WHO WILL EVEN KNOW WE WERE EVER HERE?
I'LL KNOW.
SHEE-RIGHT.
I'LL KNOW. THE WORLD NEEDS US--ALL OF US.
BUT FROST MAKES A LOGICAL POINT--
--IF ONLY SOME OF US CAN SURVIVE--DON'T WE OWE IT TO HUMANITY TO CHOOSE--?
NO ONE IS LEAVING YOU.
UH-HUH.
NO ONE.
I WOULD GLADLY STAY BEHIND IN ORDER FOR YOU TO SURVIVE.
WE'D ALL VOLUNTEER, DIANA...THAT'S NOT WHAT SHE'S SAYING.
REALLY? TELL ME WHAT I'M SAYING.
EXPLAIN ME TO ME.
I WAS A KING-- LEADING A NATION--
A CITY. YOU WERE MORE LIKE THE MAYOR.*
--THE POINT IS, I WAS RESPONSIBLE FOR THOUSANDS OF LIVES.
*ATLANTIS. --BRIAN
WE COLLECTIVELY ARE RESPONSIBLE FOR BILLIONS.
THAT RESPONSIBILITY MUST SUPERSEDE INDIVIDUAL LOYALTIES.
WE CAN'T JUST DRAW STRAWS.

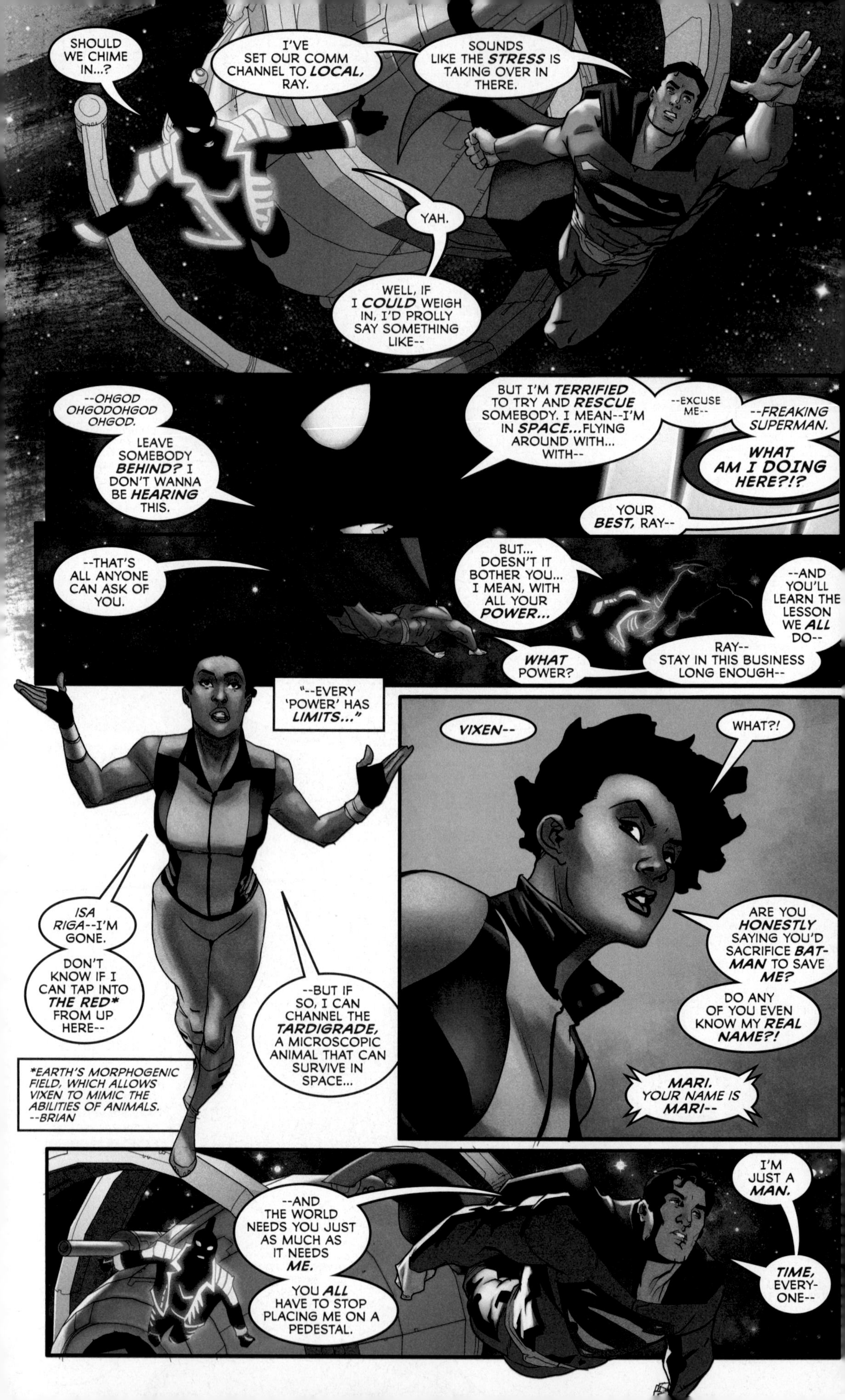
SHOULD WE CHIME IN...?
I'VE SET OUR COMM CHANNEL TO LOCAL, RAY.
SOUNDS LIKE THE STRESS IS TAKING OVER IN THERE.
YAH.
WELL, IF I COULD WEIGH IN, I'D PROLLY SAY SOMETHING LIKE--
--OHGOD OHGODOHGOD OHGOD.
LEAVE SOMEBODY BEHIND? I DON'T WANNA BE HEARING THIS.
BUT I'M TERRIFIED TO TRY AND RESCUE SOMEBODY. I MEAN--I'M IN SPACE...FLYING AROUND WITH... WITH--
--EXCUSE ME--
--FREAKING SUPERMAN.
WHAT AM I DOING HERE?!?
YOUR BEST, RAY--
--THAT'S ALL ANYONE CAN ASK OF YOU.
BUT... DOESN'T IT BOTHER YOU... I MEAN, WITH ALL YOUR POWER...
WHAT POWER?
RAY-- STAY IN THIS BUSINESS LONG ENOUGH--
--AND YOU'LL LEARN THE LESSON WE ALL DO--
"--EVERY 'POWER' HAS LIMITS..."
ISA RIGA--I'M GONE.
DON'T KNOW IF I CAN TAP INTO THE RED* FROM UP HERE--
--BUT IF SO, I CAN CHANNEL THE TARDIGRADE, A MICROSCOPIC ANIMAL THAT CAN SURVIVE IN SPACE...
*EARTH'S MORPHOGENIC FIELD, WHICH ALLOWS VIXEN TO MIMIC THE ABILITIES OF ANIMALS. --BRIAN
VIXEN--
WHAT?!
ARE YOU HONESTLY SAYING YOU'D SACRIFICE BATMAN TO SAVE ME?
DO ANY OF YOU EVEN KNOW MY REAL NAME?!
MARI. YOUR NAME IS MARI--
I'M JUST A MAN.
--AND THE WORLD NEEDS YOU JUST AS MUCH AS IT NEEDS ME.
YOU ALL HAVE TO STOP PLACING ME ON A PEDESTAL.
TIME, EVERYONE--

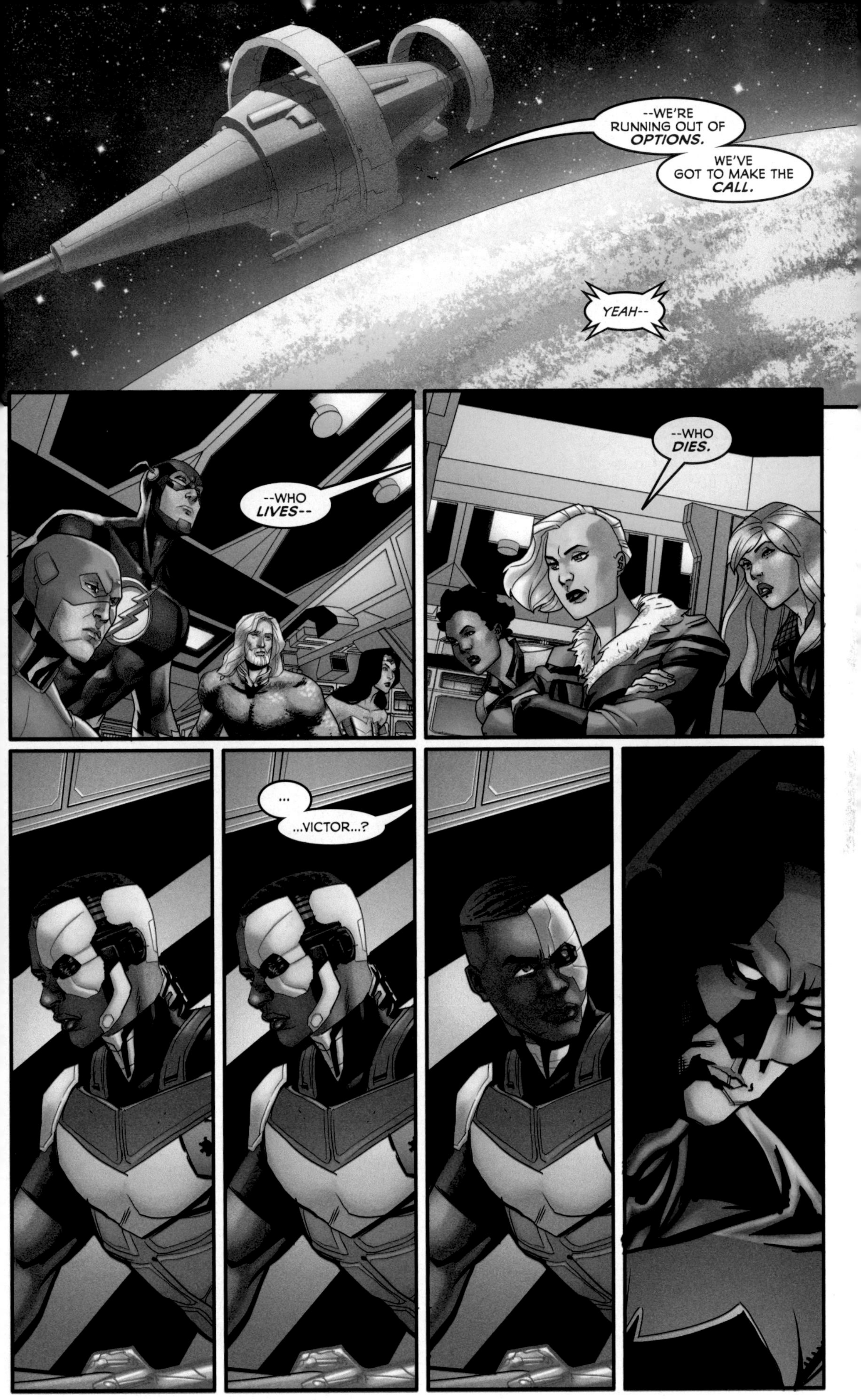
--WE'RE RUNNING OUT OF OPTIONS.
WE'VE GOT TO MAKE THE CALL.
YEAH--
--WHO LIVES--
--WHO DIES.
...
...VICTOR...?

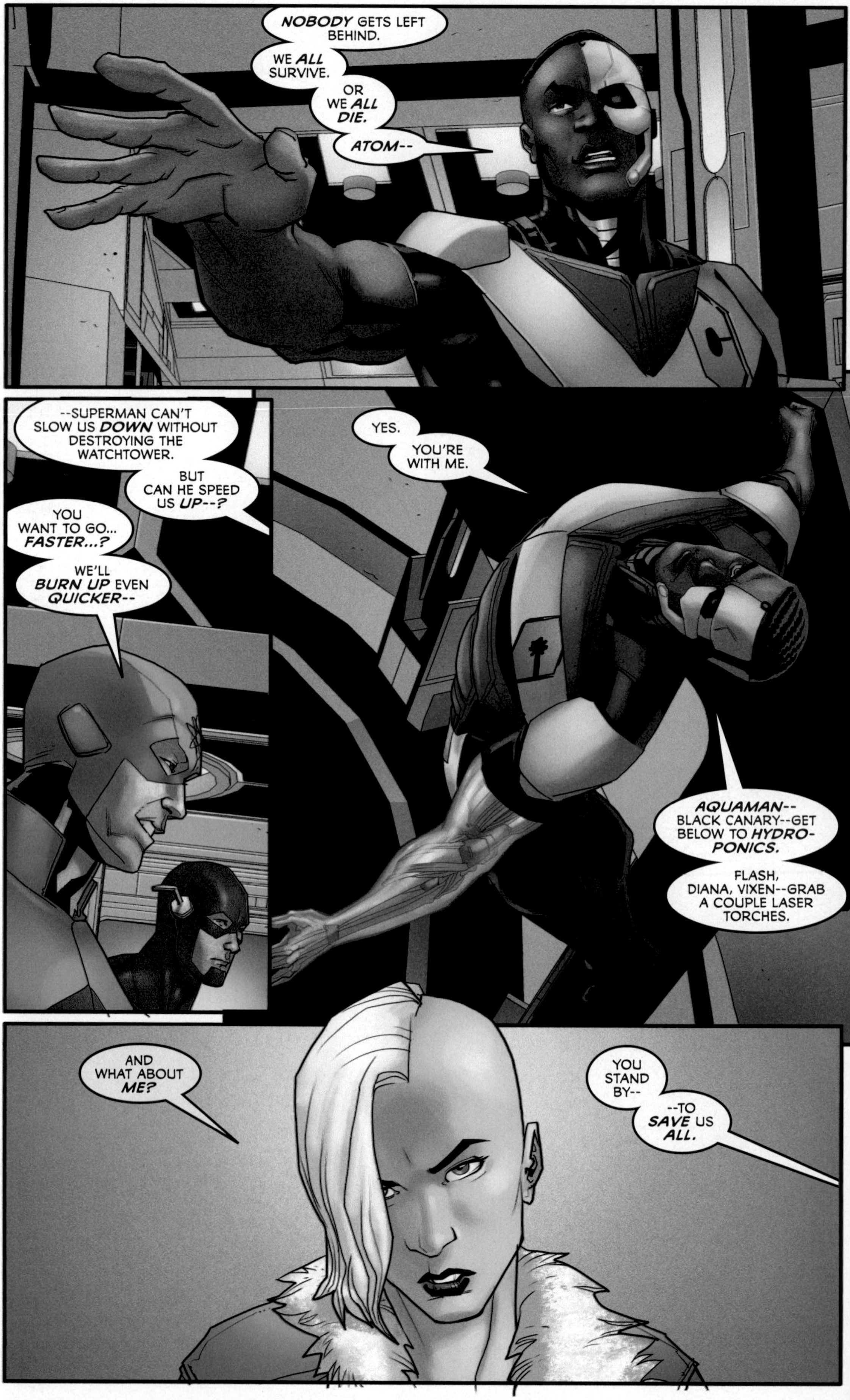
NOBODY GETS LEFT BEHIND.
WE ALL SURVIVE.
OR WE ALL DIE.
ATOM--
--SUPERMAN CAN'T SLOW US DOWN WITHOUT DESTROYING THE WATCHTOWER.
BUT CAN HE SPEED US UP--?
YOU WANT TO GO... FASTER...?
WE'LL BURN UP EVEN QUICKER--
YES.
YOU'RE WITH ME.
AQUAMAN--BLACK CANARY--GET BELOW TO HYDROPONICS.
FLASH, DIANA, VIXEN--GRAB A COUPLE LASER TORCHES.
AND WHAT ABOUT ME?
YOU STAND BY--
--TO SAVE US ALL.

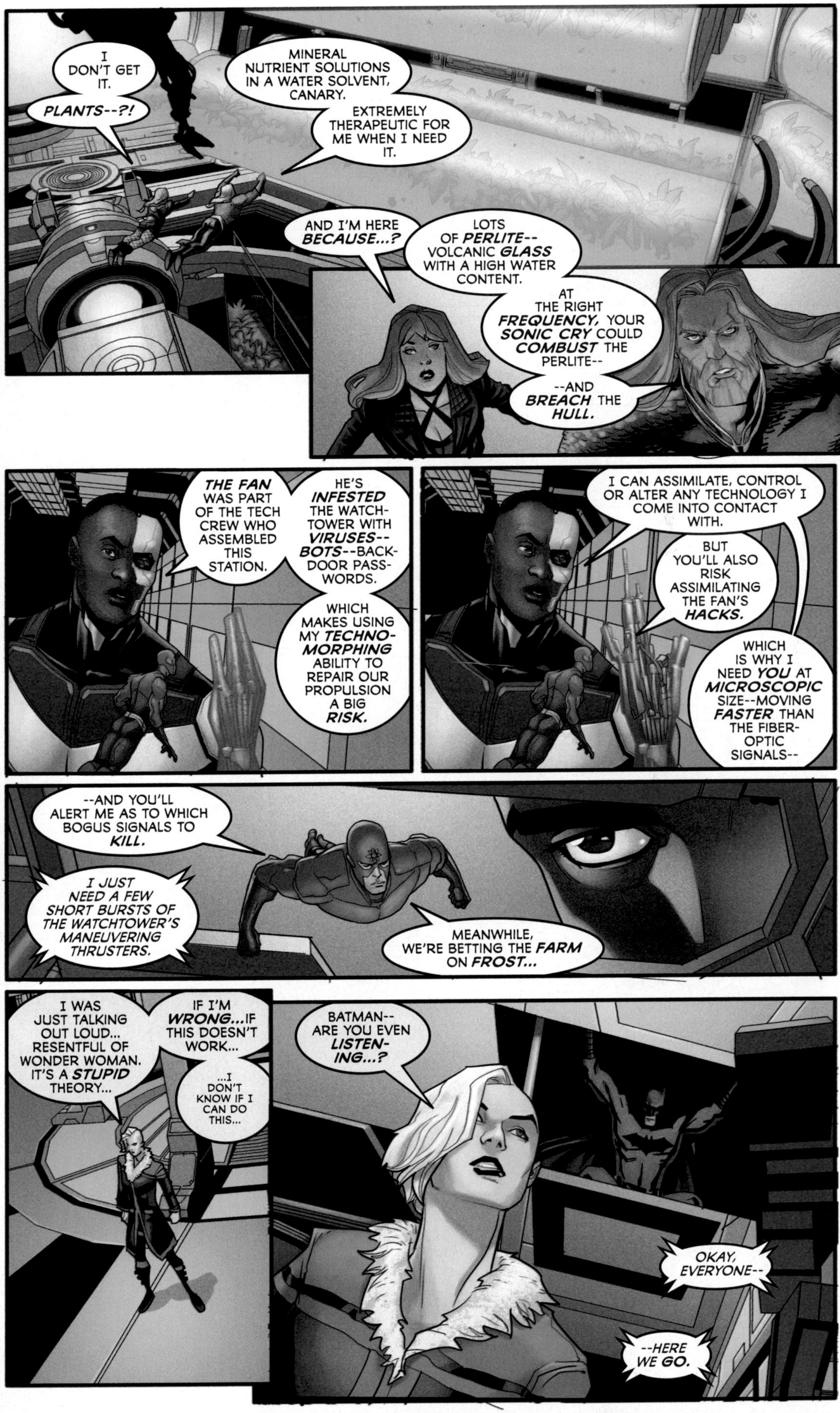

I DON'T GET IT.
PLANTS--?!
MINERAL NUTRIENT SOLUTIONS IN A WATER SOLVENT, CANARY.
EXTREMELY THERAPEUTIC FOR ME WHEN I NEED IT.
AND I'M HERE BECAUSE...?
LOTS OF PERLITE--VOLCANIC GLASS WITH A HIGH WATER CONTENT.
AT THE RIGHT FREQUENCY, YOUR SONIC CRY COULD COMBUST THE PERLITE--
--AND BREACH THE HULL.
THE FAN WAS PART OF THE TECH CREW WHO ASSEMBLED THIS STATION.
HE'S INFESTED THE WATCH-TOWER WITH VIRUSES--BOTS--BACK-DOOR PASS-WORDS.
WHICH MAKES USING MY TECHNO-MORPHING ABILITY TO REPAIR OUR PROPULSION A BIG RISK.
I CAN ASSIMILATE, CONTROL OR ALTER ANY TECHNOLOGY I COME INTO CONTACT WITH.
BUT YOU'LL ALSO RISK ASSIMILATING THE FAN'S HACKS.
WHICH IS WHY I NEED YOU AT MICROSCOPIC SIZE--MOVING FASTER THAN THE FIBER-OPTIC SIGNALS--
--AND YOU'LL ALERT ME AS TO WHICH BOGUS SIGNALS TO KILL.
I JUST NEED A FEW SHORT BURSTS OF THE WATCHTOWER'S MANEUVERING THRUSTERS.
MEANWHILE, WE'RE BETTING THE FARM ON FROST...
I WAS JUST TALKING OUT LOUD... RESENTFUL OF WONDER WOMAN. IT'S A STUPID THEORY...
IF I'M WRONG...IF THIS DOESN'T WORK...
...I DON'T KNOW IF I CAN DO THIS...
BATMAN--ARE YOU EVEN LISTEN-ING...?
OKAY, EVERYONE--
--HERE WE GO.

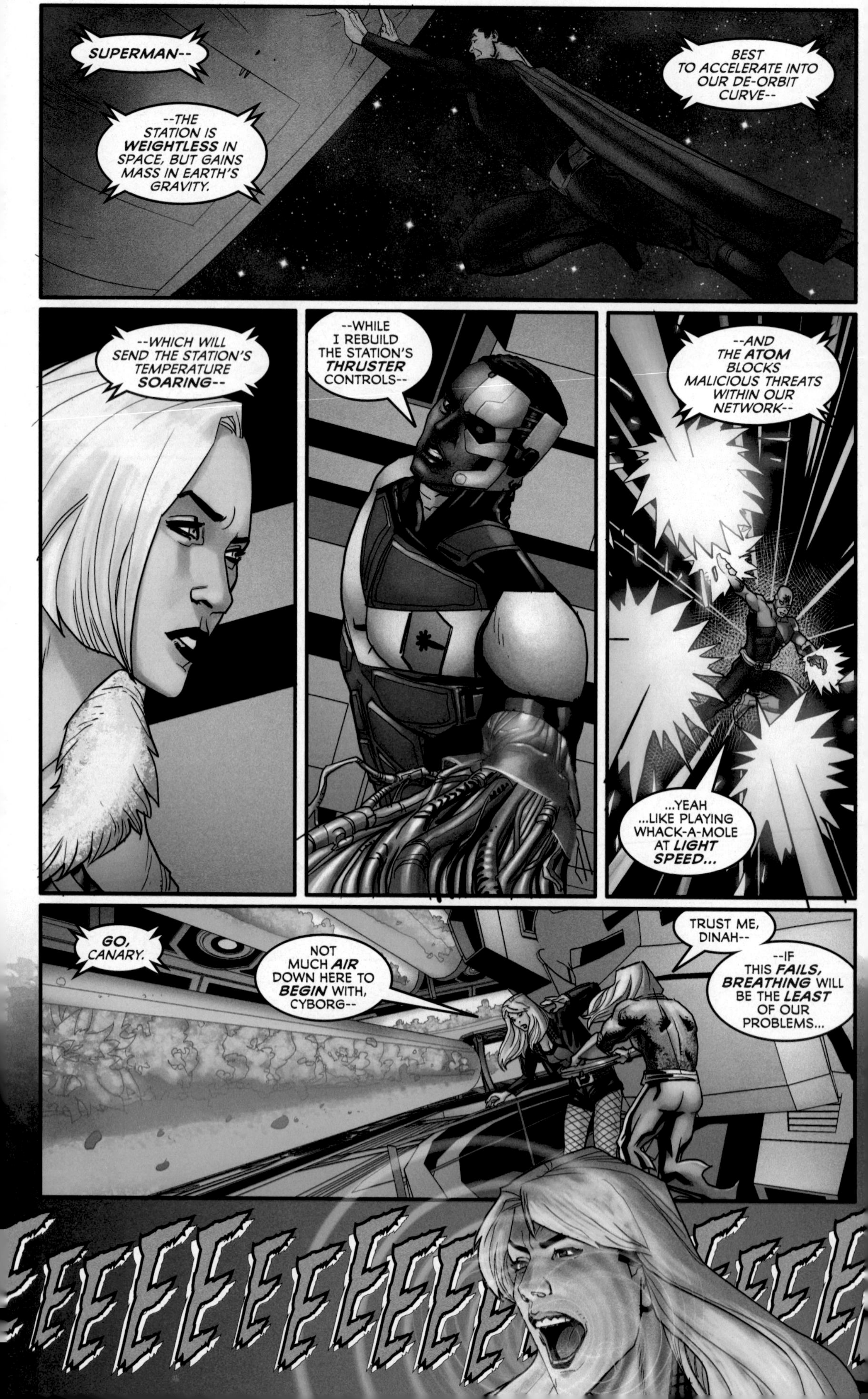
SUPERMAN--
--THE STATION IS WEIGHTLESS IN SPACE, BUT GAINS MASS IN EARTH'S GRAVITY.
BEST TO ACCELERATE INTO OUR DE-ORBIT CURVE--
--WHICH WILL SEND THE STATION'S TEMPERATURE SOARING--
--WHILE I REBUILD THE STATION'S THRUSTER CONTROLS--
--AND THE ATOM BLOCKS MALICIOUS THREATS WITHIN OUR NETWORK--
...YEAH ...LIKE PLAYING WHACK-A-MOLE AT LIGHT SPEED...
GO, CANARY.
NOT MUCH AIR DOWN HERE TO BEGIN WITH, CYBORG--
TRUST ME, DINAH--
--IF THIS FAILS, BREATHING WILL BE THE LEAST OF OUR PROBLEMS...
EEEEEEEEEEEEEEEEEEE

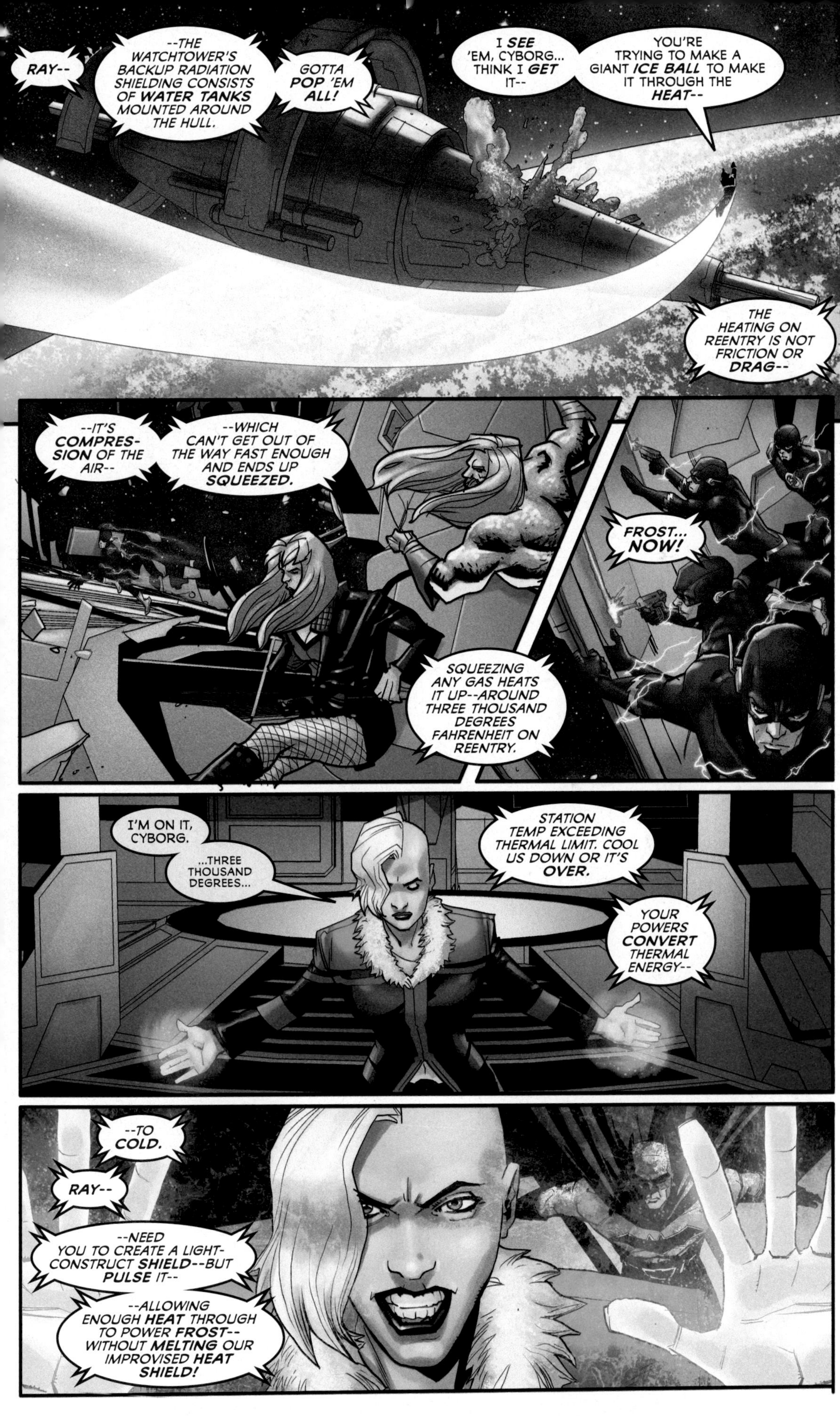
RAY--
--THE WATCHTOWER'S BACKUP RADIATION SHIELDING CONSISTS OF WATER TANKS MOUNTED AROUND THE HULL.
GOTTA POP 'EM ALL!
I SEE 'EM, CYBORG... THINK I GET IT--
YOU'RE TRYING TO MAKE A GIANT ICE BALL TO MAKE IT THROUGH THE HEAT--
THE HEATING ON REENTRY IS NOT FRICTION OR DRAG--
--IT'S COMPRESSION OF THE AIR--
--WHICH CAN'T GET OUT OF THE WAY FAST ENOUGH AND ENDS UP SQUEEZED.
FROST... NOW!
SQUEEZING ANY GAS HEATS IT UP--AROUND THREE THOUSAND DEGREES FAHRENHEIT ON REENTRY.
I'M ON IT, CYBORG.
...THREE THOUSAND DEGREES...
STATION TEMP EXCEEDING THERMAL LIMIT. COOL US DOWN OR IT'S OVER.
YOUR POWERS CONVERT THERMAL ENERGY--
--TO COLD.
RAY--
--NEED YOU TO CREATE A LIGHT-CONSTRUCT SHIELD--BUT PULSE IT--
--ALLOWING ENOUGH HEAT THROUGH TO POWER FROST--WITHOUT MELTING OUR IMPROVISED HEAT SHIELD!

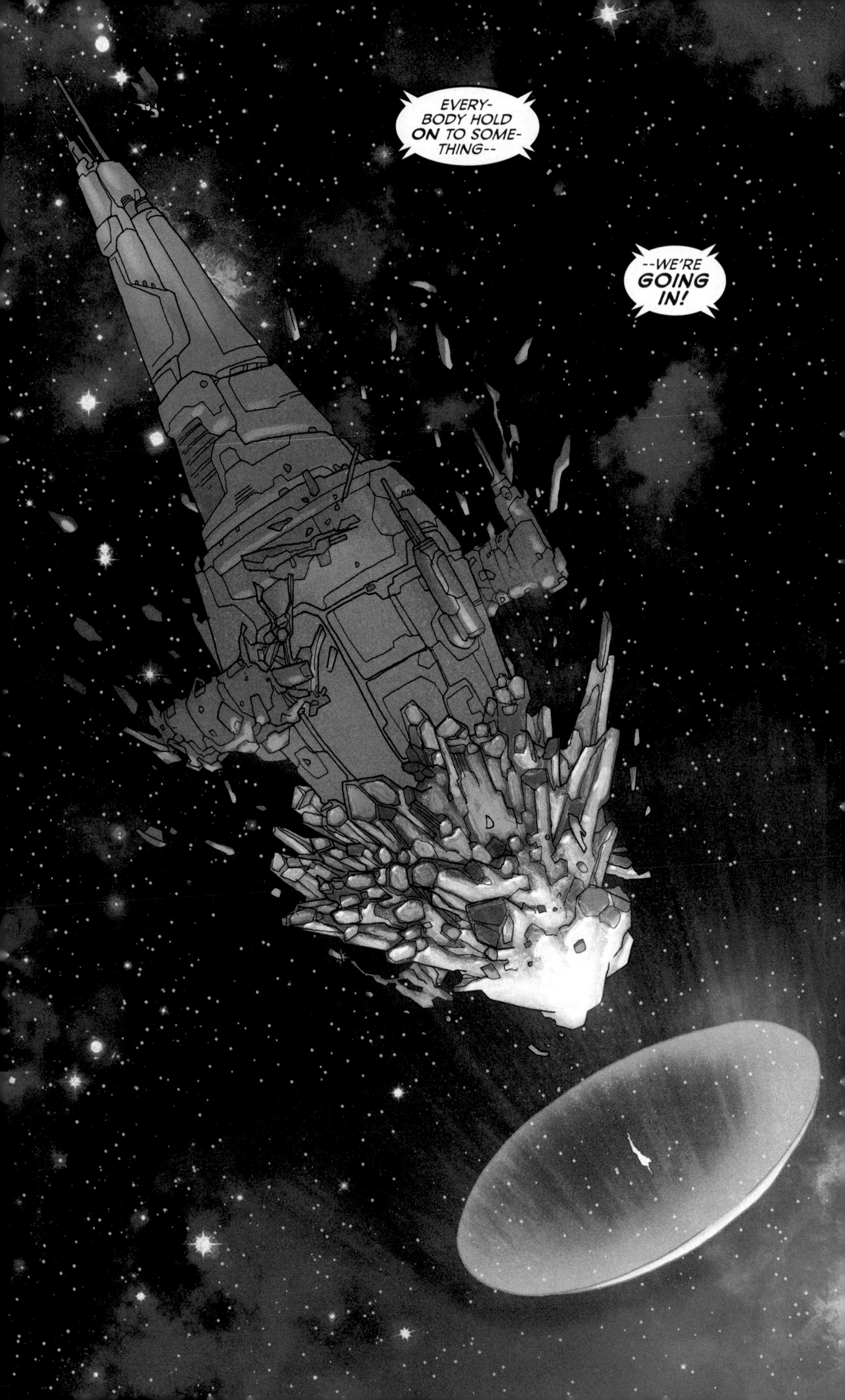
EVERY-BODY HOLD ON TO SOME-THING--
--WE'RE GOING IN!

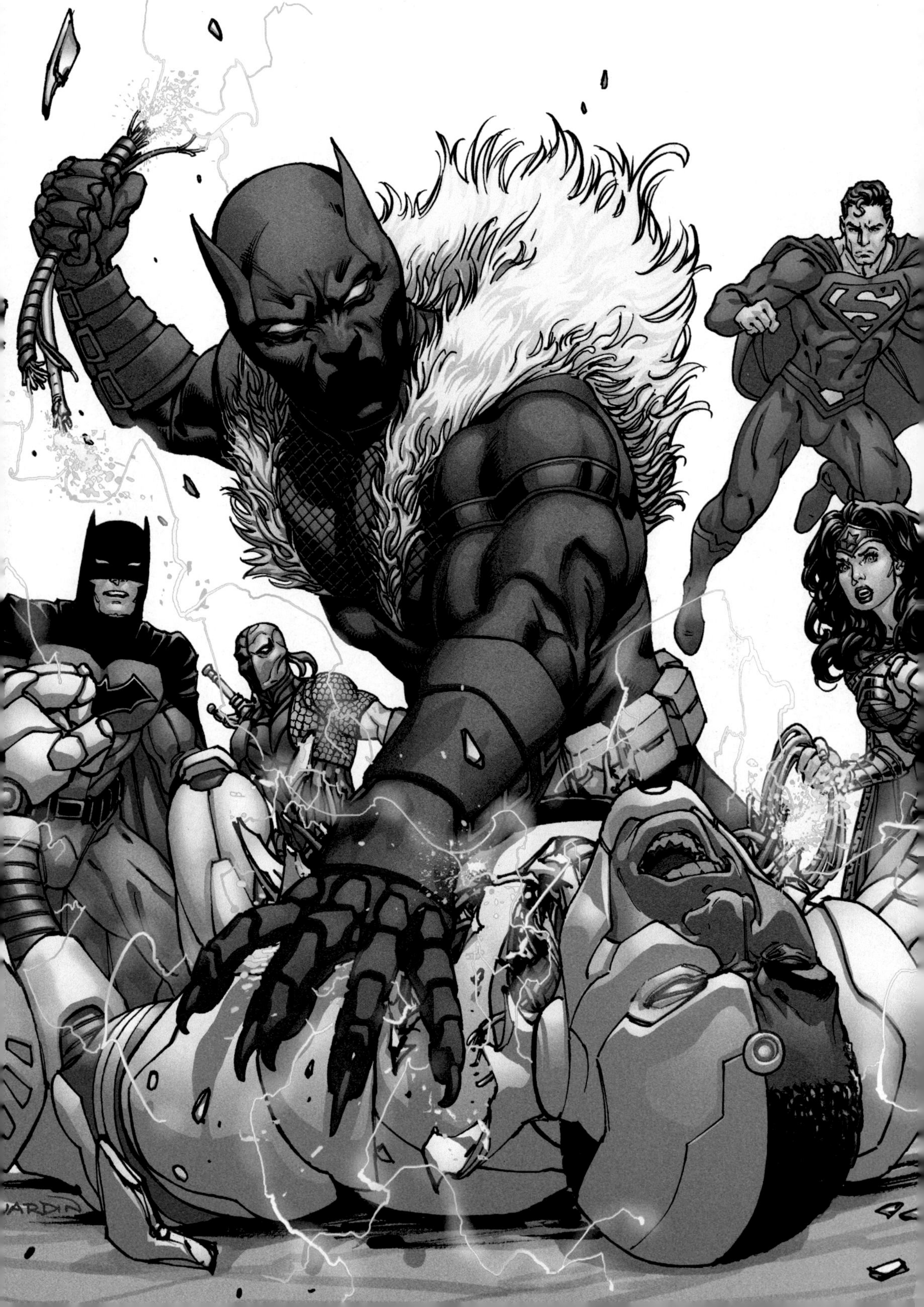

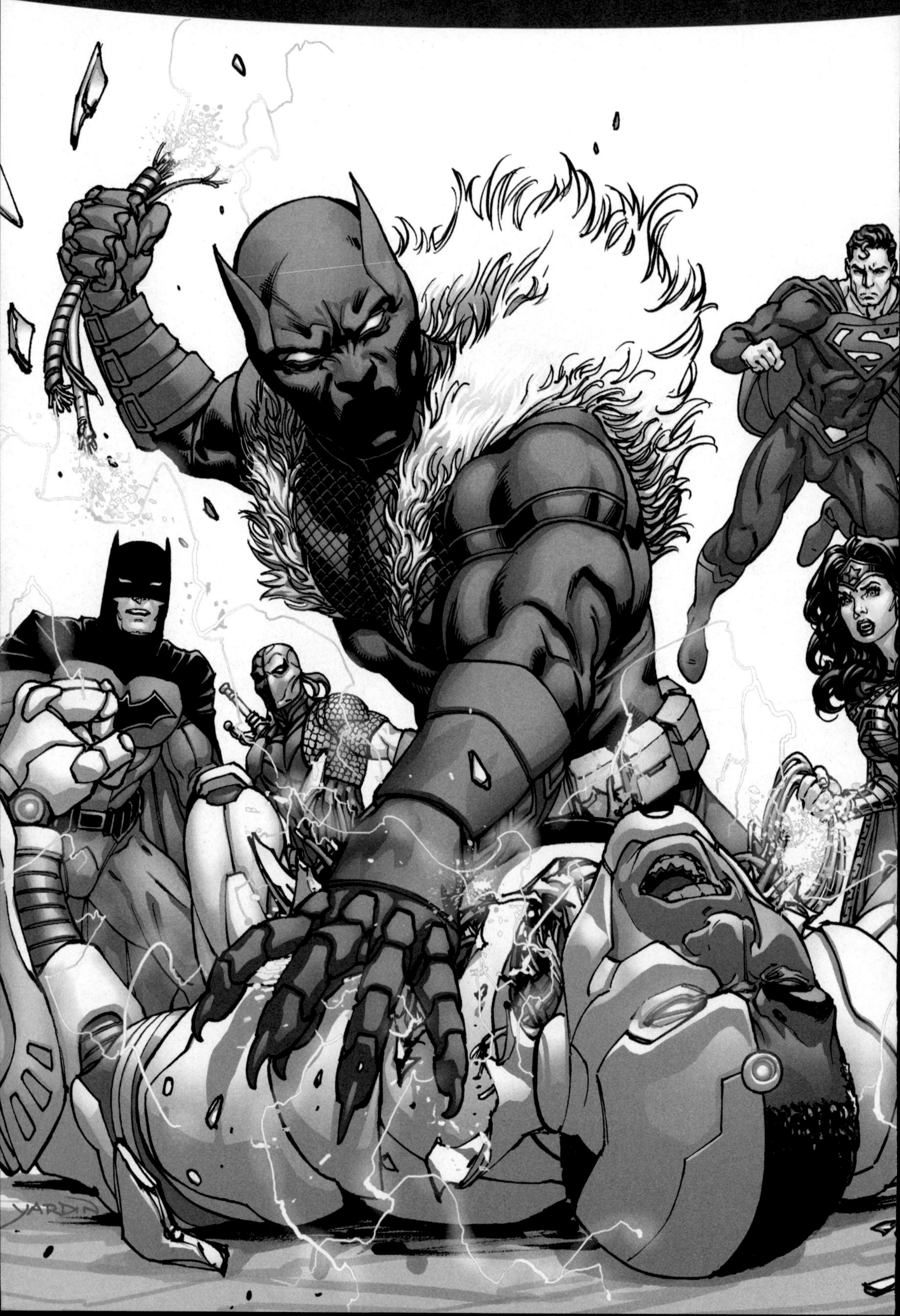

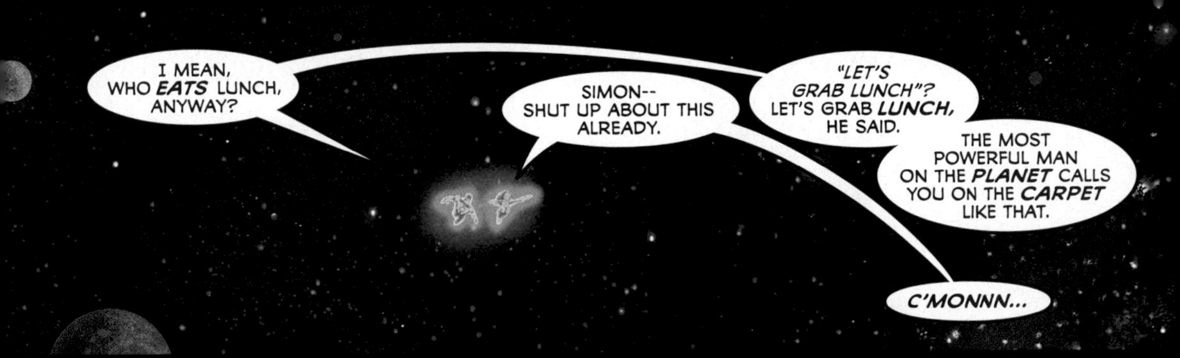
I MEAN, WHO EATS LUNCH, ANYWAY?
"LET'S GRAB LUNCH"? LET'S GRAB LUNCH, HE SAID.
THE MOST POWERFUL MAN ON THE PLANET CALLS YOU ON THE CARPET LIKE THAT.
C'MONNN...
SIMON--SHUT UP ABOUT THIS ALREADY.

"Lunch Break"

VALHALLA VECTOR, 0.83 AU
SPACE SECTOR 2814

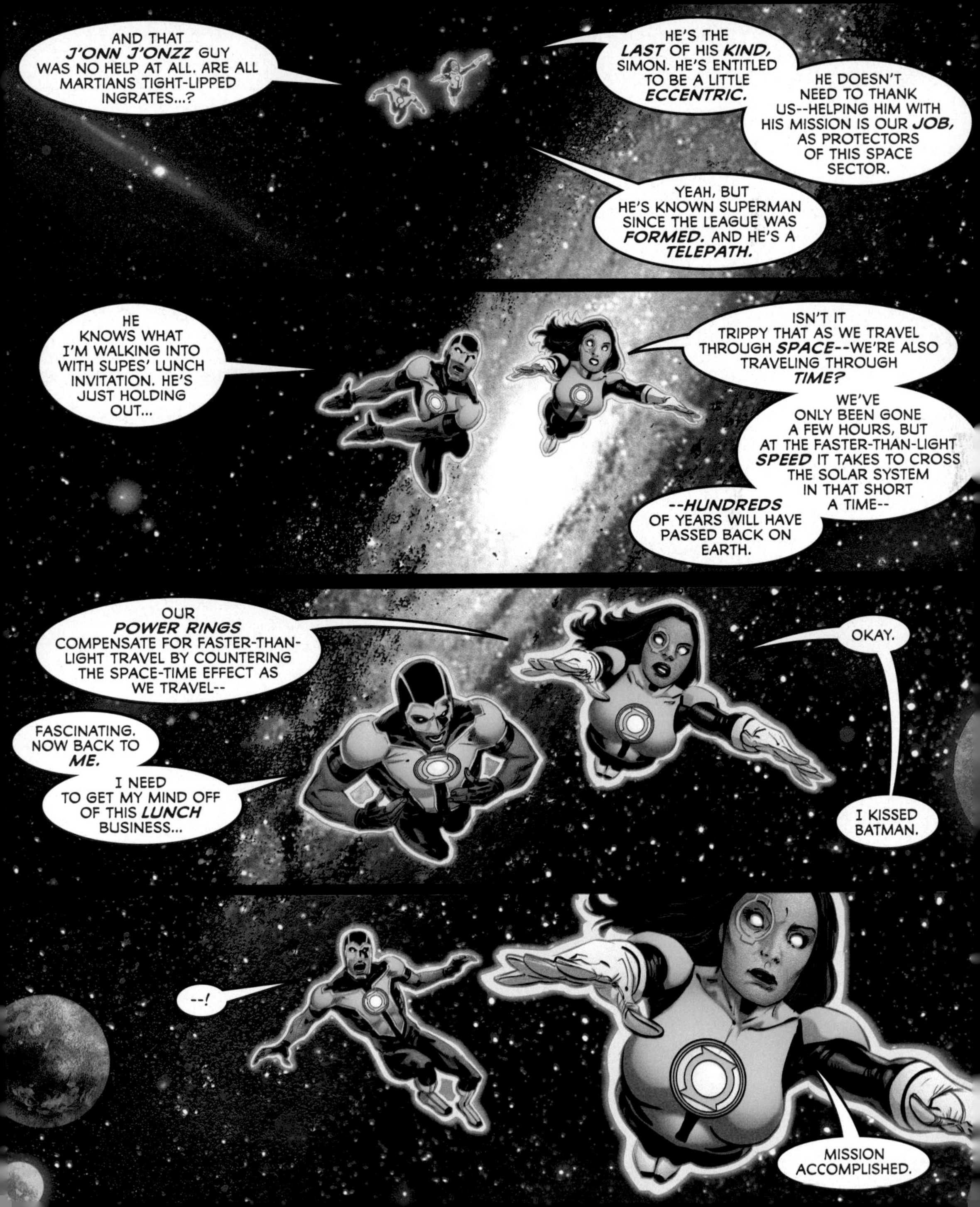
AND THAT J'ONN J'ONZZ GUY WAS NO HELP AT ALL. ARE ALL MARTIANS TIGHT-LIPPED INGRATES...?
HE'S THE LAST OF HIS KIND, SIMON. HE'S ENTITLED TO BE A LITTLE ECCENTRIC.
HE DOESN'T NEED TO THANK US--HELPING HIM WITH HIS MISSION IS OUR JOB, AS PROTECTORS OF THIS SPACE SECTOR.
YEAH, BUT HE'S KNOWN SUPERMAN SINCE THE LEAGUE WAS FORMED. AND HE'S A TELEPATH.
HE KNOWS WHAT I'M WALKING INTO WITH SUPES' LUNCH INVITATION. HE'S JUST HOLDING OUT...
ISN'T IT TRIPPY THAT AS WE TRAVEL THROUGH SPACE--WE'RE ALSO TRAVELING THROUGH TIME?
WE'VE ONLY BEEN GONE A FEW HOURS, BUT AT THE FASTER-THAN-LIGHT SPEED IT TAKES TO CROSS THE SOLAR SYSTEM IN THAT SHORT A TIME--
--HUNDREDS OF YEARS WILL HAVE PASSED BACK ON EARTH.
OUR POWER RINGS COMPENSATE FOR FASTER-THAN-LIGHT TRAVEL BY COUNTERING THE SPACE-TIME EFFECT AS WE TRAVEL--
FASCINATING. NOW BACK TO ME.
I NEED TO GET MY MIND OFF OF THIS LUNCH BUSINESS...
OKAY.
I KISSED BATMAN.
--!
MISSION ACCOMPLISHED.

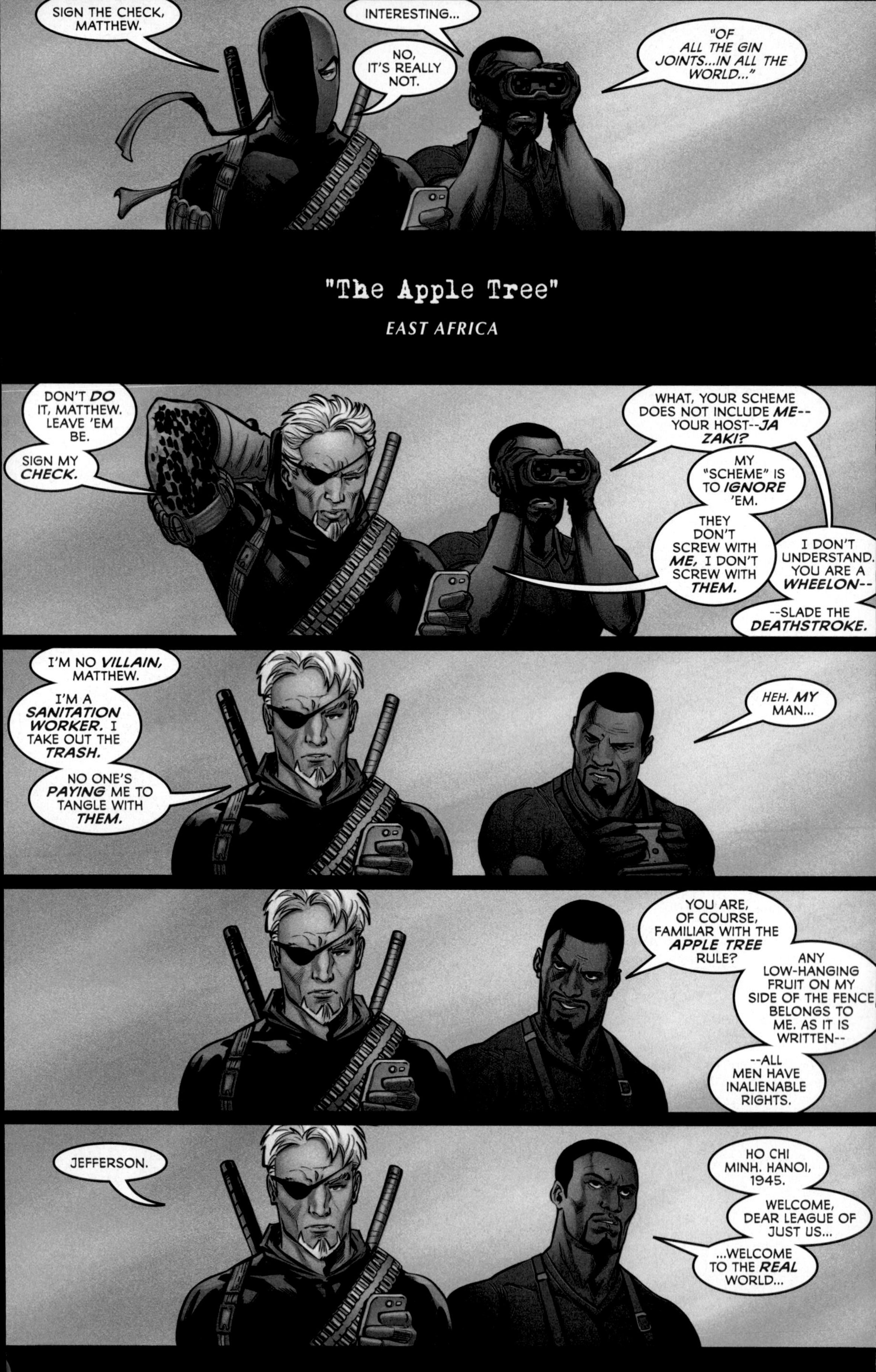
SIGN THE CHECK, MATTHEW.
INTERESTING...
NO, IT'S REALLY NOT.
"OF ALL THE GIN JOINTS...IN ALL THE WORLD..."
"The Apple Tree"
EAST AFRICA
DON'T *DO* IT, MATTHEW. LEAVE 'EM BE.
SIGN MY *CHECK.*
WHAT, YOUR SCHEME DOES NOT INCLUDE *ME*--YOUR HOST--*JA ZAKI?*
MY "SCHEME" IS TO *IGNORE* 'EM.
THEY DON'T SCREW WITH *ME,* I DON'T SCREW WITH *THEM.*
I DON'T UNDERSTAND. YOU ARE A *WHEELON*--
--SLADE THE *DEATHSTROKE.*
I'M NO *VILLAIN,* MATTHEW.
I'M A *SANITATION WORKER.* I TAKE OUT THE *TRASH.*
NO ONE'S *PAYING* ME TO TANGLE WITH *THEM.*
HEH. *MY* MAN...
YOU ARE, OF COURSE, FAMILIAR WITH THE *APPLE TREE* RULE?
ANY LOW-HANGING FRUIT ON MY SIDE OF THE FENCE BELONGS TO ME. AS IT IS WRITTEN--
--ALL MEN HAVE INALIENABLE RIGHTS.
JEFFERSON.
HO CHI MINH. HANOI, 1945.
WELCOME, DEAR LEAGUE OF JUST US...
...WELCOME TO THE *REAL* WORLD...

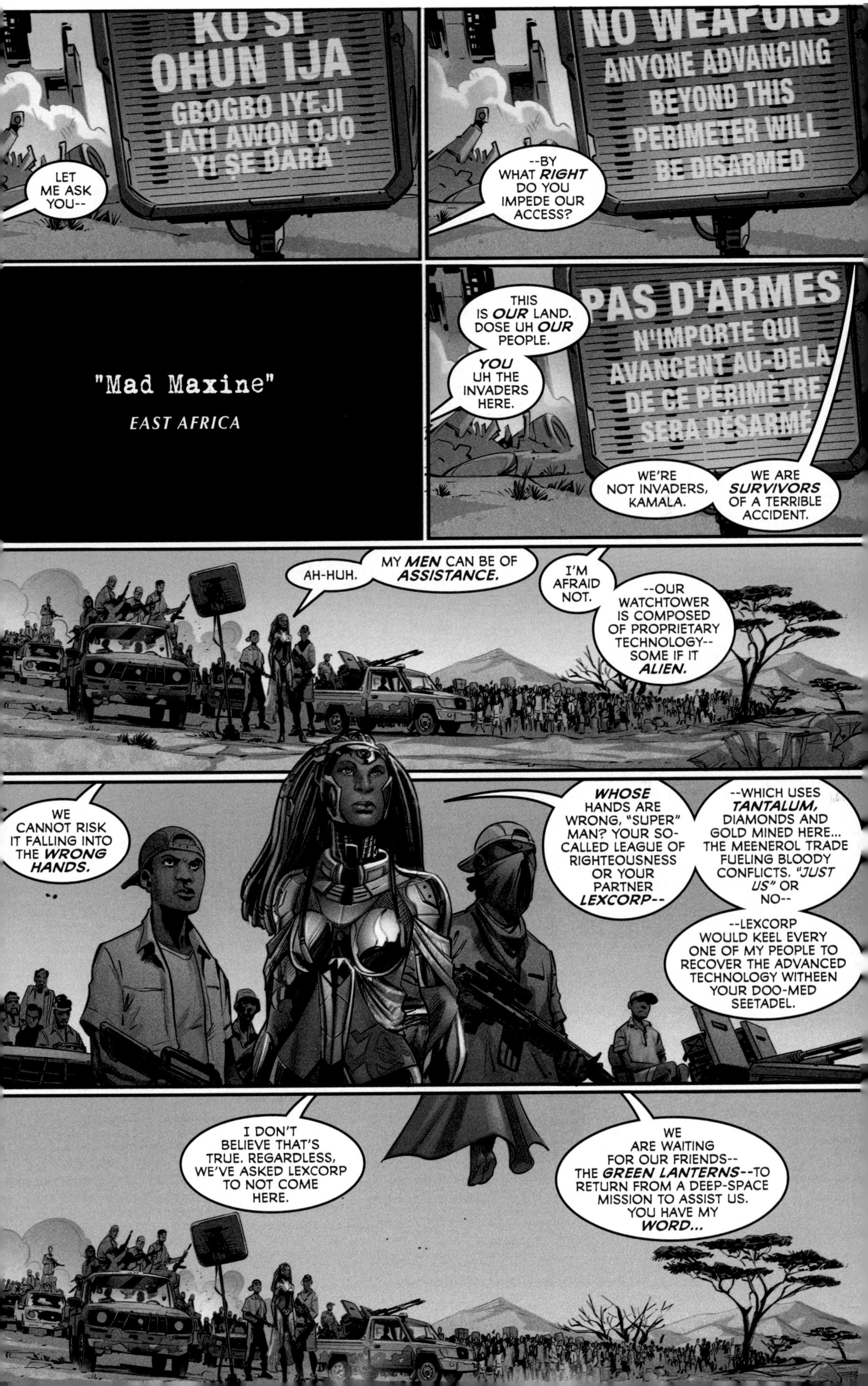
KO SI
OHUN IJA
GBOGBO IYEJI
LATI AWON OJỌ
YI ṢE DARA
LET ME ASK YOU--
NO WEAPONS
ANYONE ADVANCING BEYOND THIS PERIMETER WILL BE DISARMED
--BY WHAT RIGHT DO YOU IMPEDE OUR ACCESS?
"Mad Maxine"
EAST AFRICA
THIS IS OUR LAND. DOSE UH OUR PEOPLE.
YOU UH THE INVADERS HERE.
PAS D'ARMES
N'IMPORTE QUI AVANCENT AU-DELA DE CE PÉRIMÈTRE SERA DÉSARMÉ
WE'RE NOT INVADERS, KAMALA.
WE ARE SURVIVORS OF A TERRIBLE ACCIDENT.
AH-HUH.
MY MEN CAN BE OF ASSISTANCE.
I'M AFRAID NOT.
--OUR WATCHTOWER IS COMPOSED OF PROPRIETARY TECHNOLOGY-- SOME IF IT ALIEN.
WE CANNOT RISK IT FALLING INTO THE WRONG HANDS.
WHOSE HANDS ARE WRONG, "SUPER" MAN? YOUR SO-CALLED LEAGUE OF RIGHTEOUSNESS OR YOUR PARTNER LEXCORP--
--WHICH USES TANTALUM, DIAMONDS AND GOLD MINED HERE... THE MEENEROL TRADE FUELING BLOODY CONFLICTS. "JUST US" OR NO--
--LEXCORP WOULD KEEL EVERY ONE OF MY PEOPLE TO RECOVER THE ADVANCED TECHNOLOGY WITHEEN YOUR DOO-MED SEETADEL.
I DON'T BELIEVE THAT'S TRUE. REGARDLESS, WE'VE ASKED LEXCORP TO NOT COME HERE.
WE ARE WAITING FOR OUR FRIENDS-- THE GREEN LANTERNS--TO RETURN FROM A DEEP-SPACE MISSION TO ASSIST US. YOU HAVE MY WORD...

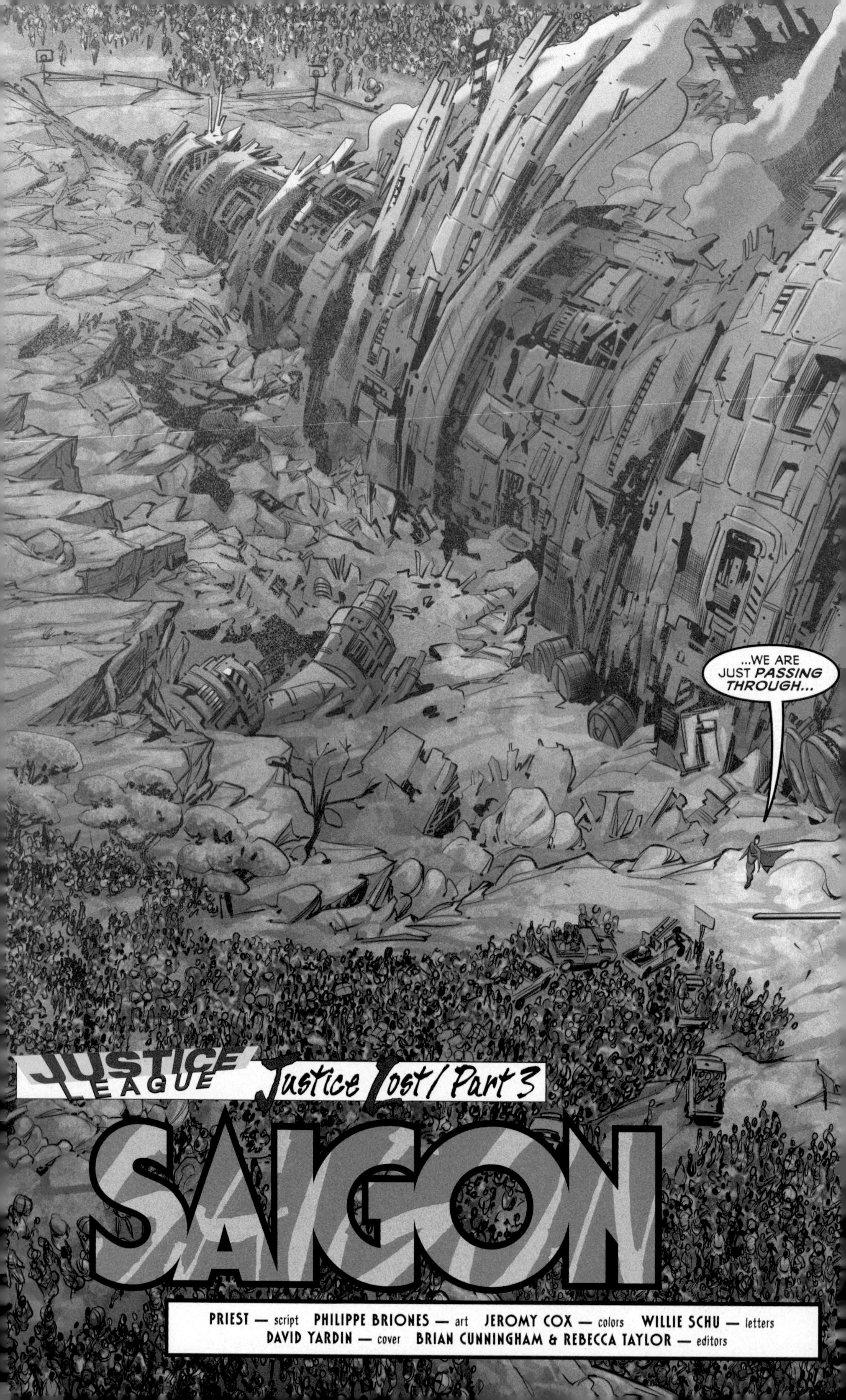
...WE ARE JUST PASSING THROUGH...
JUSTICE LEAGUE
Justice Lost/ Part 3
SAIGON
PRIEST — script PHILIPPE BRIONES — art JEROMY COX — colors WILLIE SCHU — letters
DAVID YARDIN — cover BRIAN CUNNINGHAM & REBECCA TAYLOR — editors

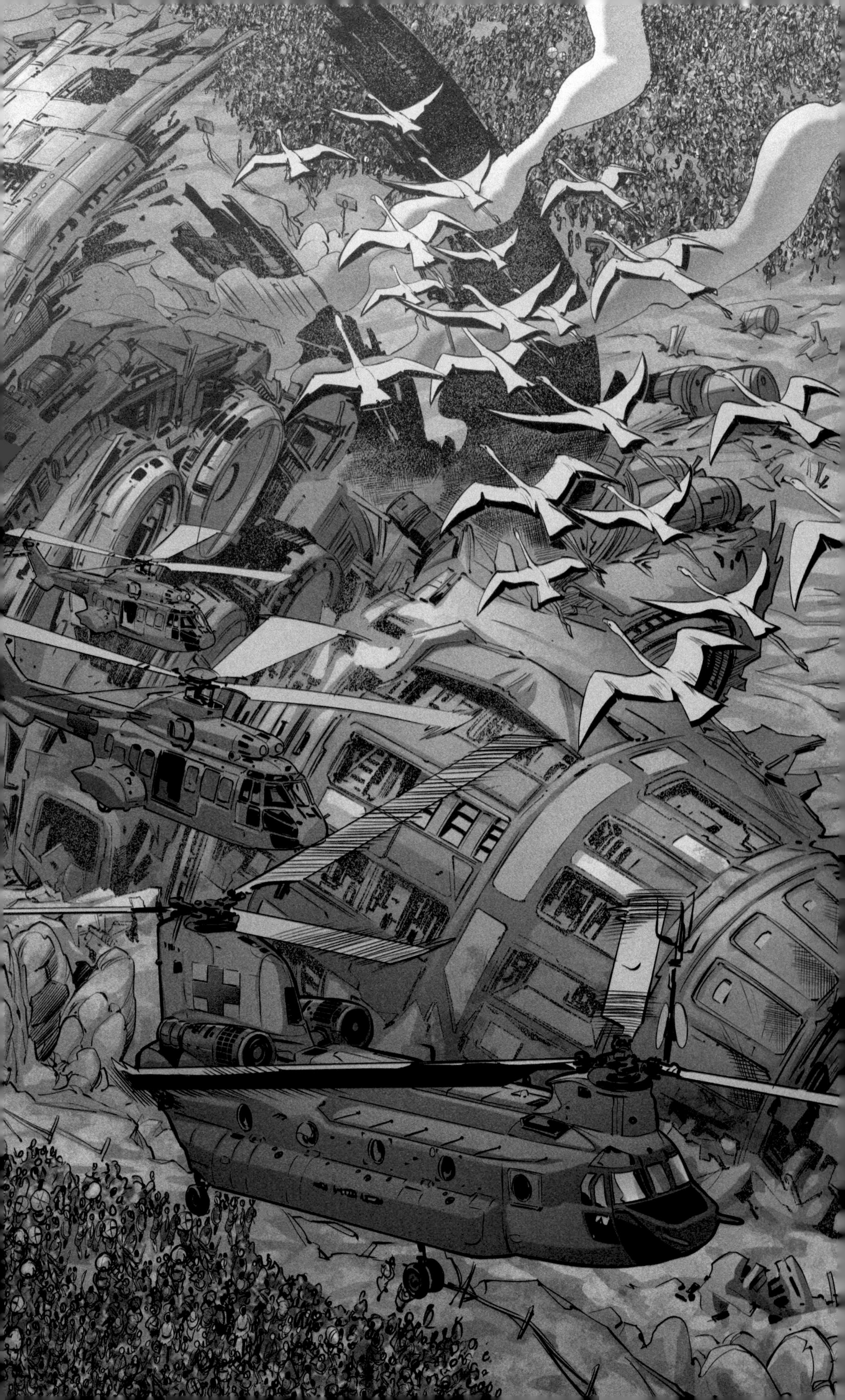

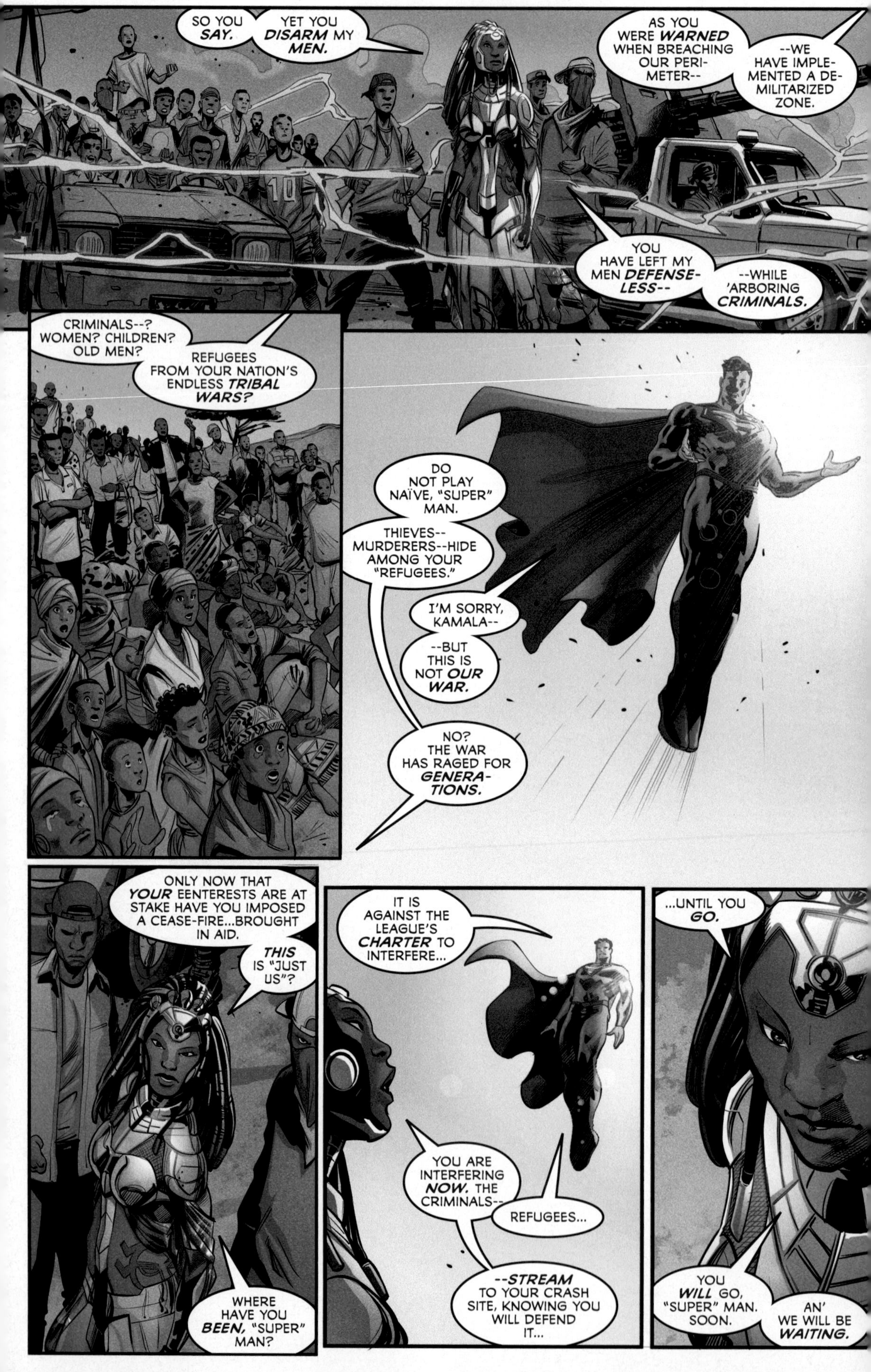
SO YOU SAY.
YET YOU DISARM MY MEN.
AS YOU WERE WARNED WHEN BREACHING OUR PERIMETER--
--WE HAVE IMPLEMENTED A DEMILITARIZED ZONE.
YOU HAVE LEFT MY MEN DEFENSELESS--
--WHILE 'ARBORING CRIMINALS.
CRIMINALS--? WOMEN? CHILDREN? OLD MEN?
REFUGEES FROM YOUR NATION'S ENDLESS TRIBAL WARS?
DO NOT PLAY NAÏVE, "SUPER" MAN.
THIEVES--MURDERERS--HIDE AMONG YOUR "REFUGEES."
I'M SORRY, KAMALA--
--BUT THIS IS NOT OUR WAR.
NO? THE WAR HAS RAGED FOR GENERATIONS.
ONLY NOW THAT YOUR EENTERESTS ARE AT STAKE HAVE YOU IMPOSED A CEASE-FIRE...BROUGHT IN AID.
THIS IS "JUST US"?
WHERE HAVE YOU BEEN, "SUPER" MAN?
IT IS AGAINST THE LEAGUE'S CHARTER TO INTERFERE...
YOU ARE INTERFERING NOW. THE CRIMINALS--
REFUGEES...
--STREAM TO YOUR CRASH SITE, KNOWING YOU WILL DEFEND IT...
...UNTIL YOU GO.
YOU WILL GO, "SUPER" MAN. SOON.
AN' WE WILL BE WAITING.

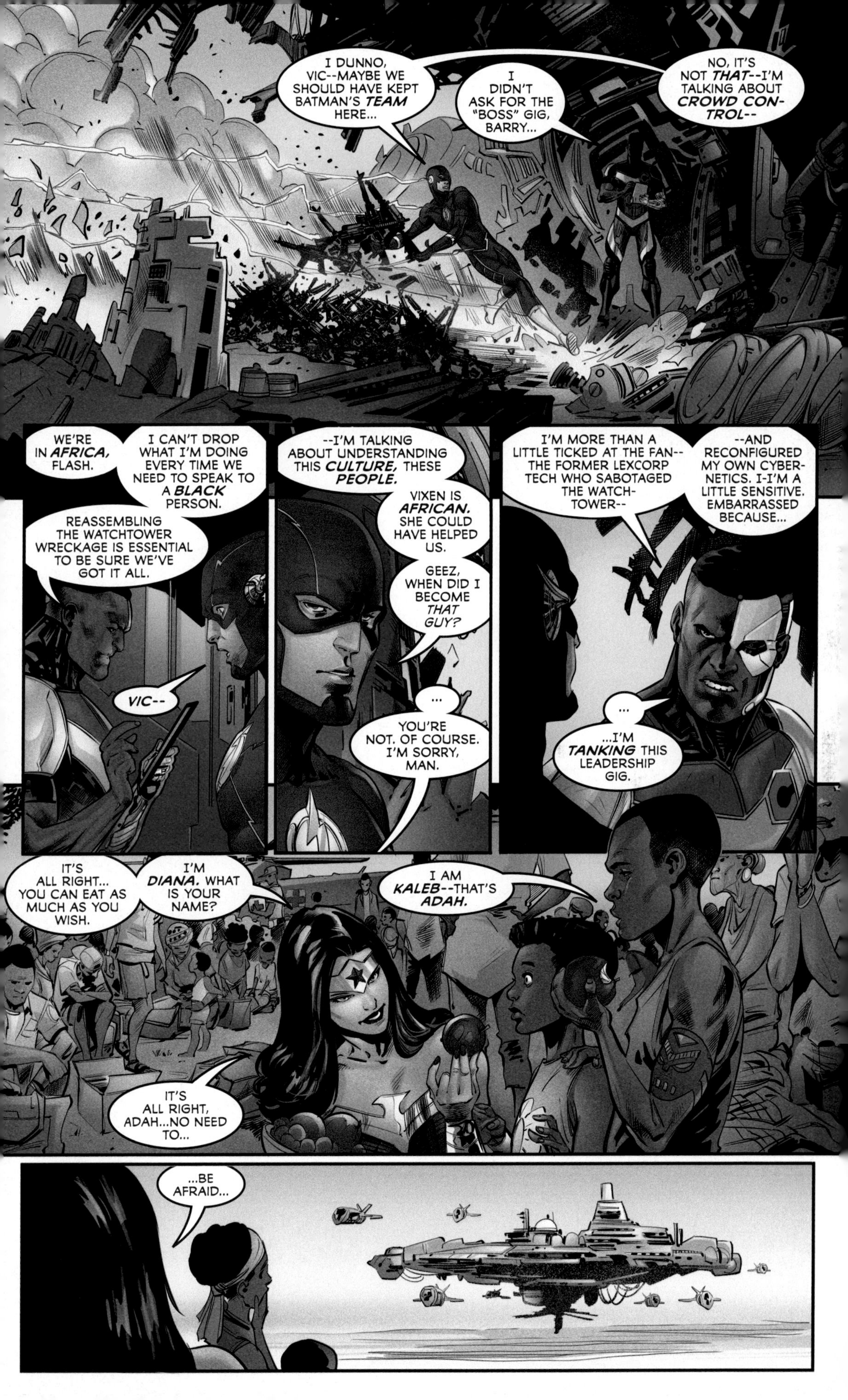
I DUNNO, VIC--MAYBE WE SHOULD HAVE KEPT BATMAN'S TEAM HERE...
I DIDN'T ASK FOR THE "BOSS" GIG, BARRY...
NO, IT'S NOT THAT--I'M TALKING ABOUT CROWD CONTROL--
WE'RE IN AFRICA, FLASH.
I CAN'T DROP WHAT I'M DOING EVERY TIME WE NEED TO SPEAK TO A BLACK PERSON.
REASSEMBLING THE WATCHTOWER WRECKAGE IS ESSENTIAL TO BE SURE WE'VE GOT IT ALL.
VIC--
--I'M TALKING ABOUT UNDERSTANDING THIS CULTURE, THESE PEOPLE.
VIXEN IS AFRICAN. SHE COULD HAVE HELPED US.
GEEZ, WHEN DID I BECOME THAT GUY?
...
YOU'RE NOT. OF COURSE. I'M SORRY, MAN.
I'M MORE THAN A LITTLE TICKED AT THE FAN-- THE FORMER LEXCORP TECH WHO SABOTAGED THE WATCHTOWER--
--AND RECONFIGURED MY OWN CYBERNETICS. I-I'M A LITTLE SENSITIVE. EMBARRASSED BECAUSE...
...
...I'M TANKING THIS LEADERSHIP GIG.
IT'S ALL RIGHT... YOU CAN EAT AS MUCH AS YOU WISH.
I'M DIANA. WHAT IS YOUR NAME?
I AM KALEB--THAT'S ADAH.
IT'S ALL RIGHT, ADAH...NO NEED TO...
...BE AFRAID...

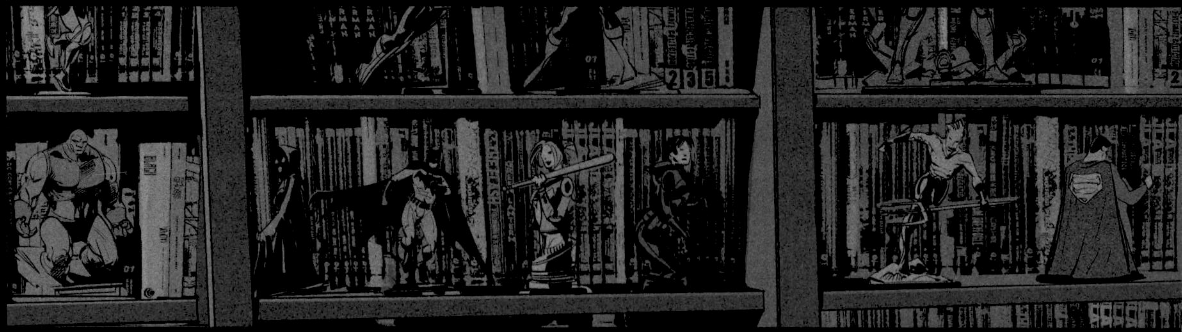

"Spunky"

EAST ST. LOUIS, MO

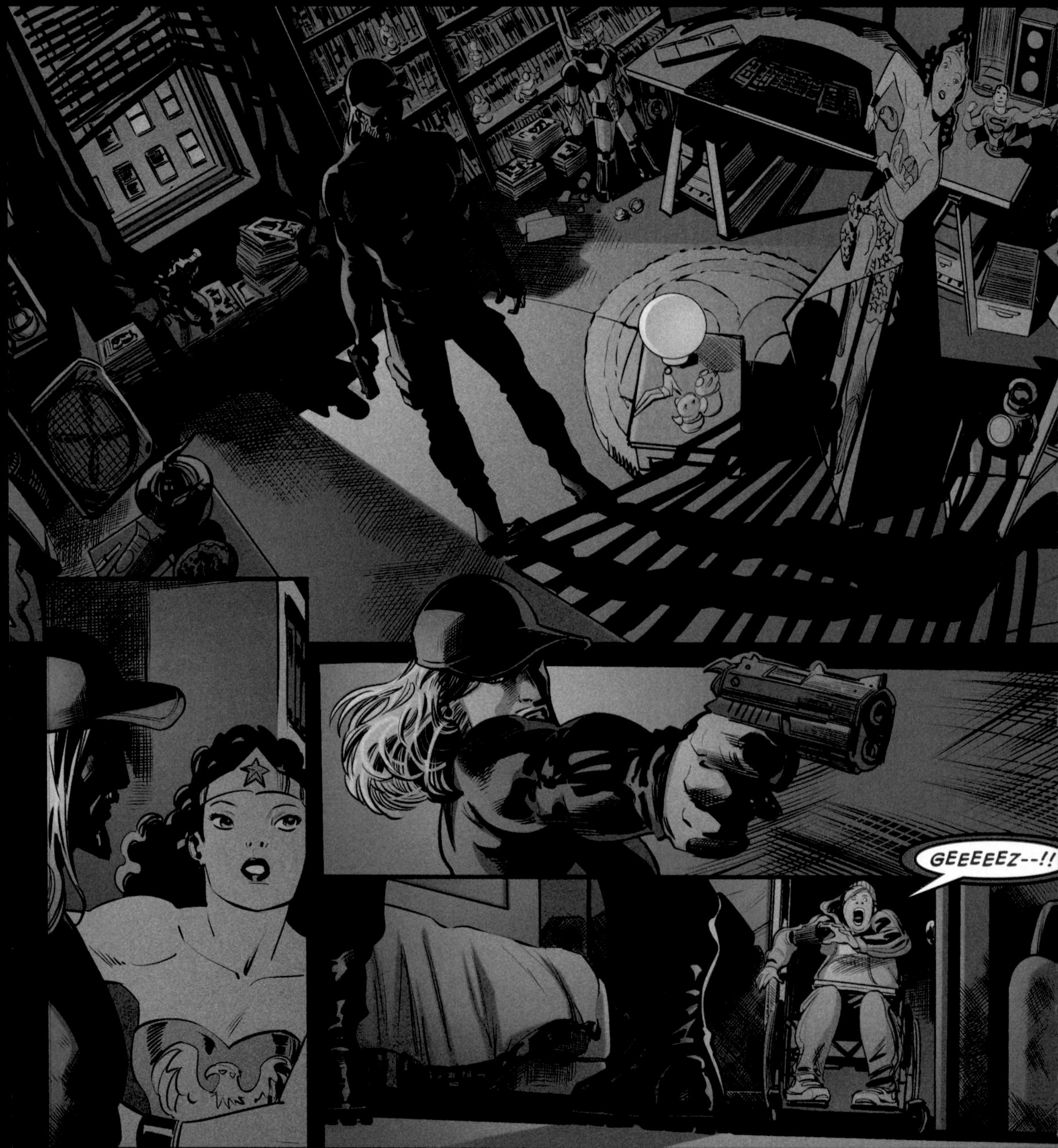
GEEEEEZ--!!

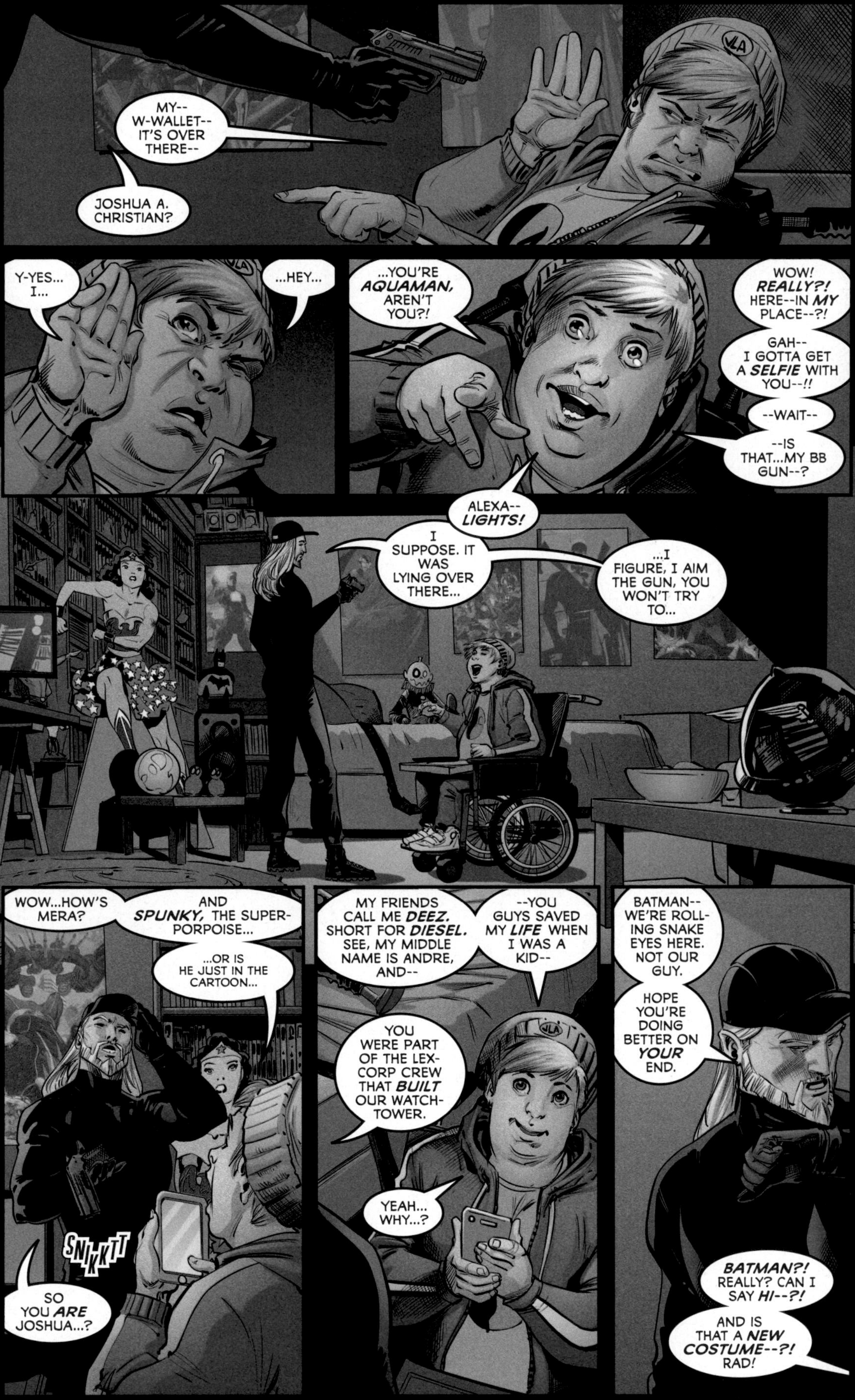

MY-- W-WALLET-- IT'S OVER THERE--
JOSHUA A. CHRISTIAN?
Y-YES... I...
...HEY...
...YOU'RE *AQUAMAN,* AREN'T YOU?!
WOW! *REALLY?!* HERE--IN *MY* PLACE--?!
GAH-- I GOTTA GET A *SELFIE* WITH YOU--!!
--WAIT--
--IS THAT...MY BB GUN--?
ALEXA-- *LIGHTS!*
I SUPPOSE. IT WAS LYING OVER THERE...
...I FIGURE, I AIM THE GUN, YOU WON'T TRY TO...
WOW...HOW'S MERA?
AND *SPUNKY,* THE SUPER-PORPOISE...
...OR IS HE JUST IN THE CARTOON...
SNIKKIT
SO YOU *ARE* JOSHUA...?
MY FRIENDS CALL ME *DEEZ.* SHORT FOR *DIESEL.* SEE, MY MIDDLE NAME IS ANDRE, AND--
--YOU GUYS SAVED MY *LIFE* WHEN I WAS A KID--
YOU WERE PART OF THE LEX-CORP CREW THAT *BUILT* OUR WATCH-TOWER.
YEAH... WHY...?
BATMAN-- WE'RE ROLL-ING SNAKE EYES HERE. NOT OUR GUY.
HOPE YOU'RE DOING BETTER ON *YOUR* END.
BATMAN?! REALLY? CAN I SAY *HI--?!*
AND IS THAT A *NEW COSTUME--?!* RAD!

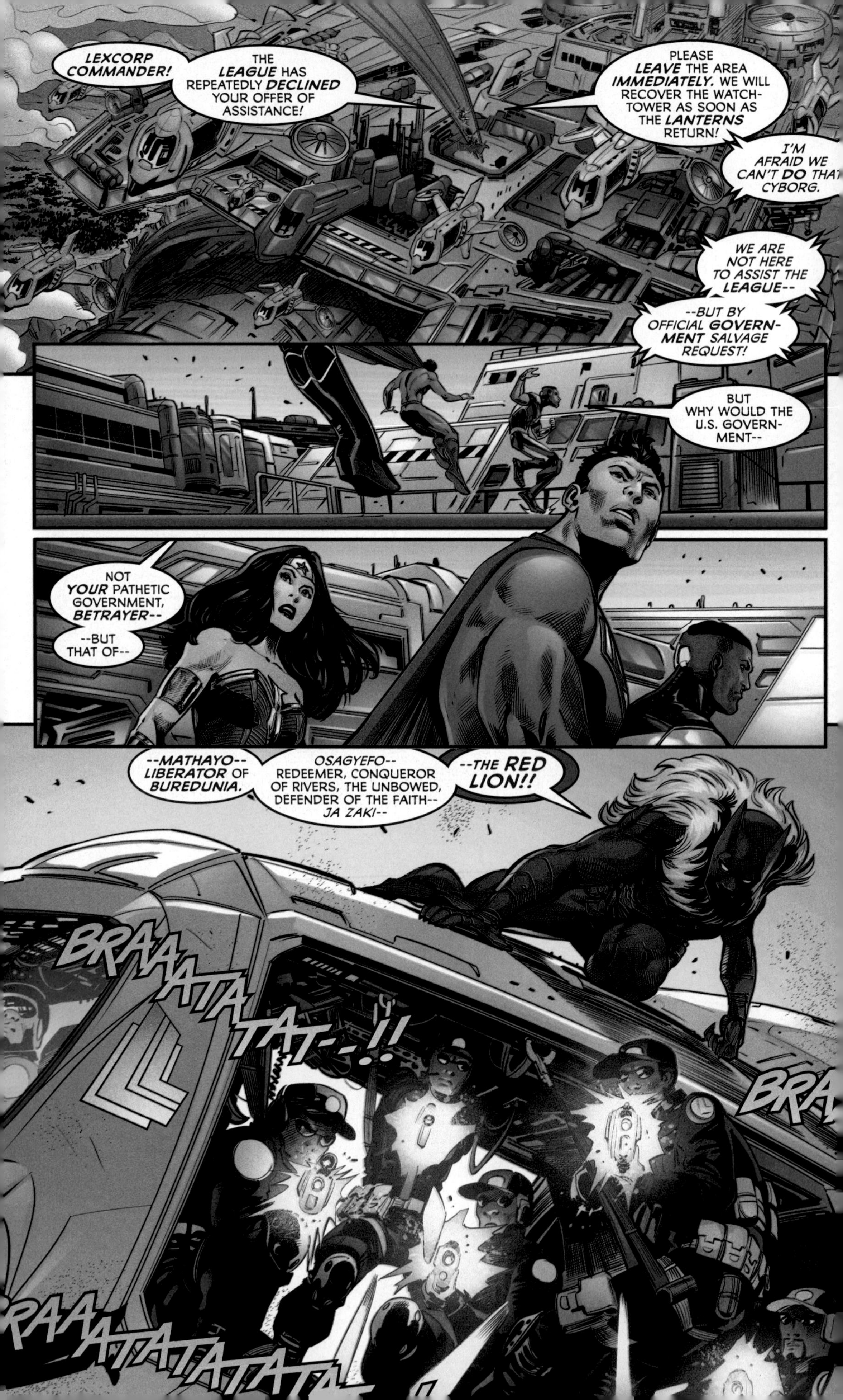
LEXCORP COMMANDER!
THE LEAGUE HAS REPEATEDLY DECLINED YOUR OFFER OF ASSISTANCE!
PLEASE LEAVE THE AREA IMMEDIATELY. WE WILL RECOVER THE WATCH-TOWER AS SOON AS THE LANTERNS RETURN!
I'M AFRAID WE CAN'T DO THAT CYBORG.
WE ARE NOT HERE TO ASSIST THE LEAGUE--
--BUT BY OFFICIAL GOVERN-MENT SALVAGE REQUEST!
BUT WHY WOULD THE U.S. GOVERN-MENT--
NOT YOUR PATHETIC GOVERNMENT, BETRAYER--
--BUT THAT OF--
--MATHAYO--LIBERATOR OF BUREDUNIA.
OSAGYEFO--REDEEMER, CONQUEROR OF RIVERS, THE UNBOWED, DEFENDER OF THE FAITH--JA ZAKI--
--THE RED LION!!
BRAAATATATAT--!!
BRA
RAAATATATATATA

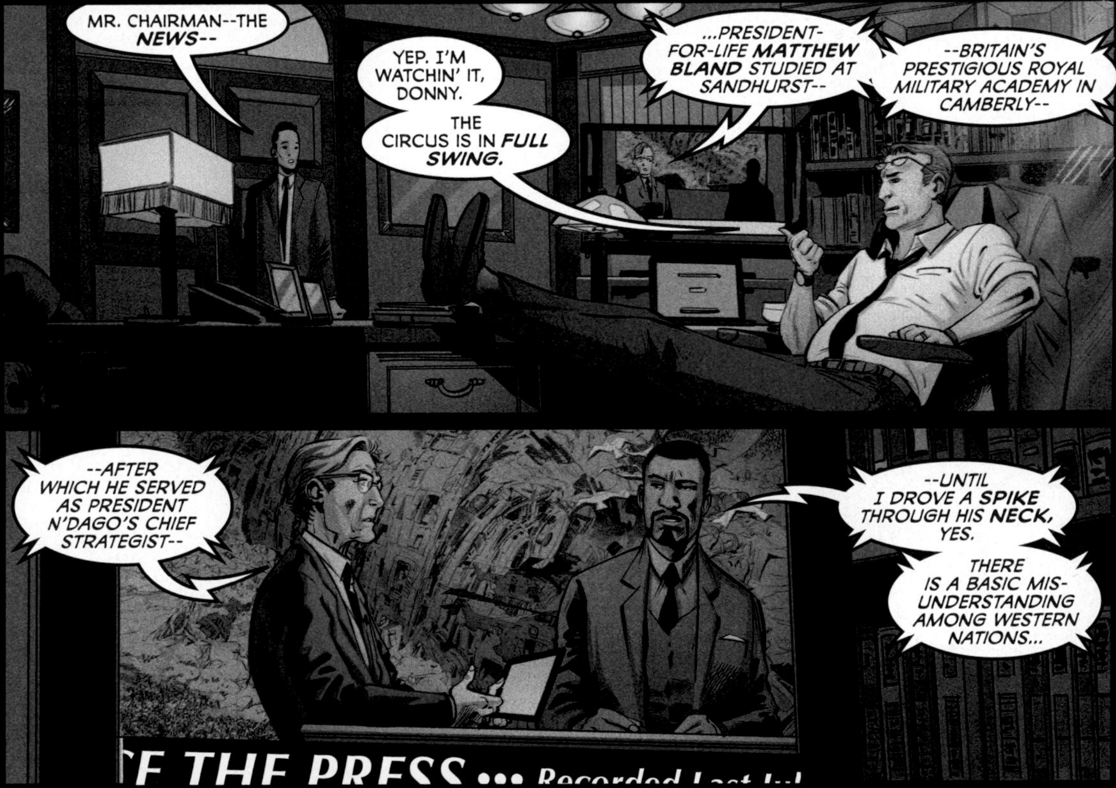

MR. CHAIRMAN--THE NEWS--
YEP. I'M WATCHIN' IT, DONNY.
THE CIRCUS IS IN FULL SWING.
...PRESIDENT-FOR-LIFE MATTHEW BLAND STUDIED AT SANDHURST--
--BRITAIN'S PRESTIGIOUS ROYAL MILITARY ACADEMY IN CAMBERLY--
--AFTER WHICH HE SERVED AS PRESIDENT N'DAGO'S CHIEF STRATEGIST--
--UNTIL I DROVE A SPIKE THROUGH HIS NECK, YES.
THERE IS A BASIC MIS-UNDERSTANDING AMONG WESTERN NATIONS...

"Three Rings"

WASHINGTON, D.C.

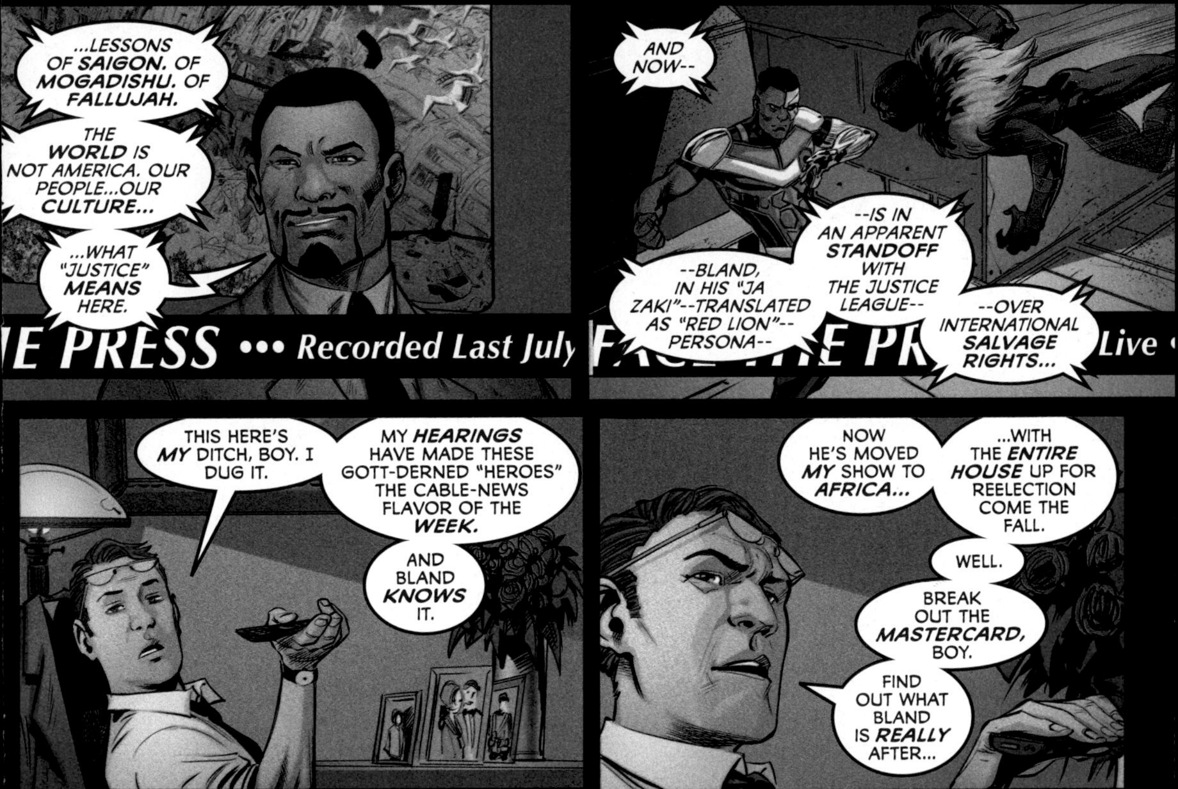

...LESSONS OF SAIGON. OF MOGADISHU. OF FALLUJAH.
THE WORLD IS NOT AMERICA. OUR PEOPLE...OUR CULTURE...
...WHAT "JUSTICE" MEANS HERE.
PRESS ••• Recorded Last July
AND NOW--
--BLAND, IN HIS "JA ZAKI"--TRANSLATED AS "RED LION"--PERSONA--
--IS IN AN APPARENT STANDOFF WITH THE JUSTICE LEAGUE--
--OVER INTERNATIONAL SALVAGE RIGHTS...
Live
THIS HERE'S MY DITCH, BOY. I DUG IT.
MY HEARINGS HAVE MADE THESE GOTT-DERNED "HEROES" THE CABLE-NEWS FLAVOR OF THE WEEK.
AND BLAND KNOWS IT.
NOW HE'S MOVED MY SHOW TO AFRICA...
...WITH THE ENTIRE HOUSE UP FOR REELECTION COME THE FALL.
WELL.
BREAK OUT THE MASTERCARD, BOY.
FIND OUT WHAT BLAND IS REALLY AFTER...

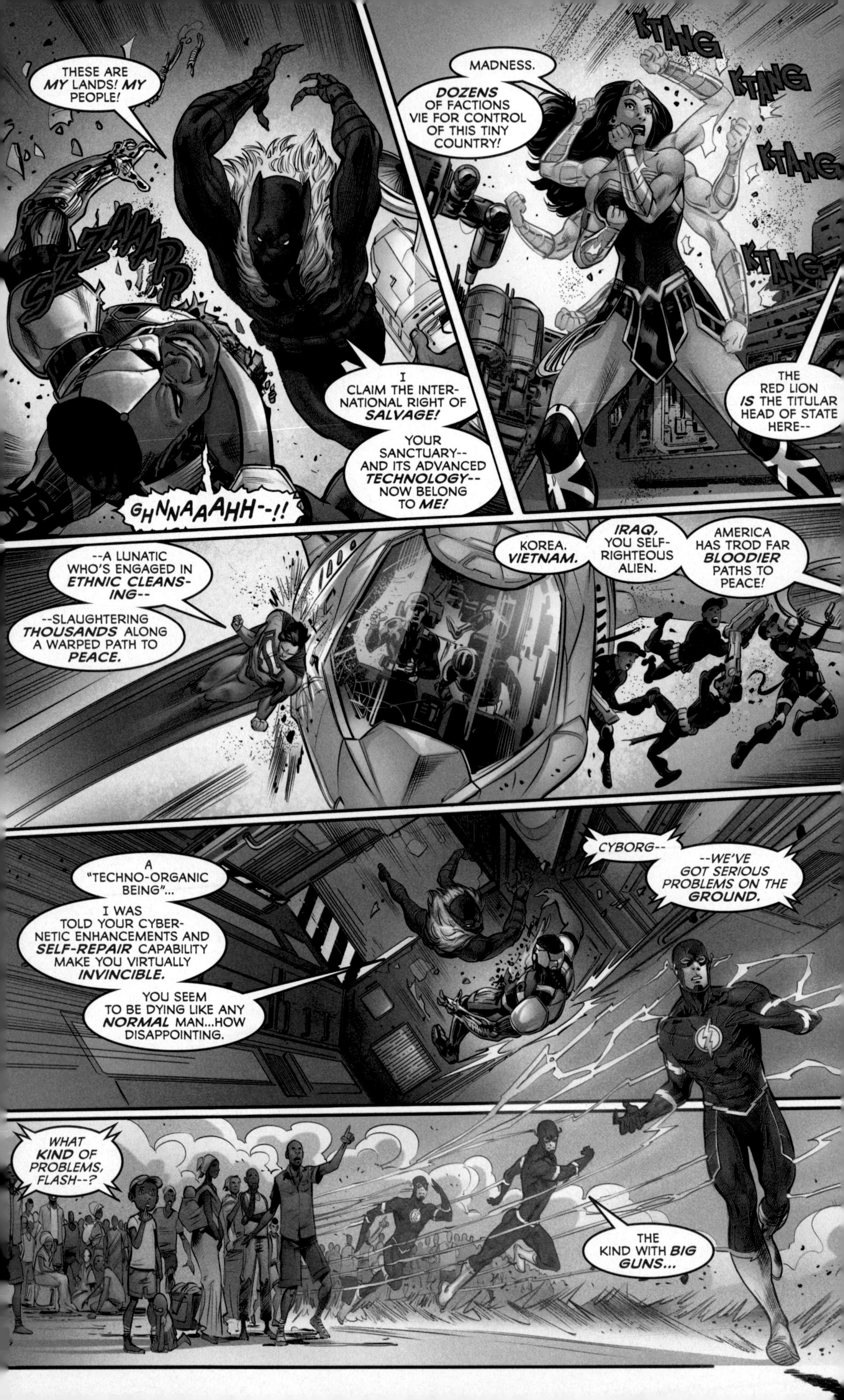

THESE ARE MY LANDS! MY PEOPLE!
SZZAAAPP
I CLAIM THE INTER-NATIONAL RIGHT OF SALVAGE!
YOUR SANCTUARY-- AND ITS ADVANCED TECHNOLOGY-- NOW BELONG TO ME!
GHNNAAAHH--!!
MADNESS.
DOZENS OF FACTIONS VIE FOR CONTROL OF THIS TINY COUNTRY!
KTANG
KTANG
KTANG
KTANG
THE RED LION IS THE TITULAR HEAD OF STATE HERE--
--A LUNATIC WHO'S ENGAGED IN ETHNIC CLEANS-ING--
--SLAUGHTERING THOUSANDS ALONG A WARPED PATH TO PEACE.
KOREA. VIETNAM.
IRAQ, YOU SELF-RIGHTEOUS ALIEN.
AMERICA HAS TROD FAR BLOODIER PATHS TO PEACE!
A "TECHNO-ORGANIC BEING"...
I WAS TOLD YOUR CYBER-NETIC ENHANCEMENTS AND SELF-REPAIR CAPABILITY MAKE YOU VIRTUALLY INVINCIBLE.
YOU SEEM TO BE DYING LIKE ANY NORMAL MAN...HOW DISAPPOINTING.
CYBORG--
--WE'VE GOT SERIOUS PROBLEMS ON THE GROUND.
WHAT KIND OF PROBLEMS, FLASH--?
THE KIND WITH BIG GUNS...

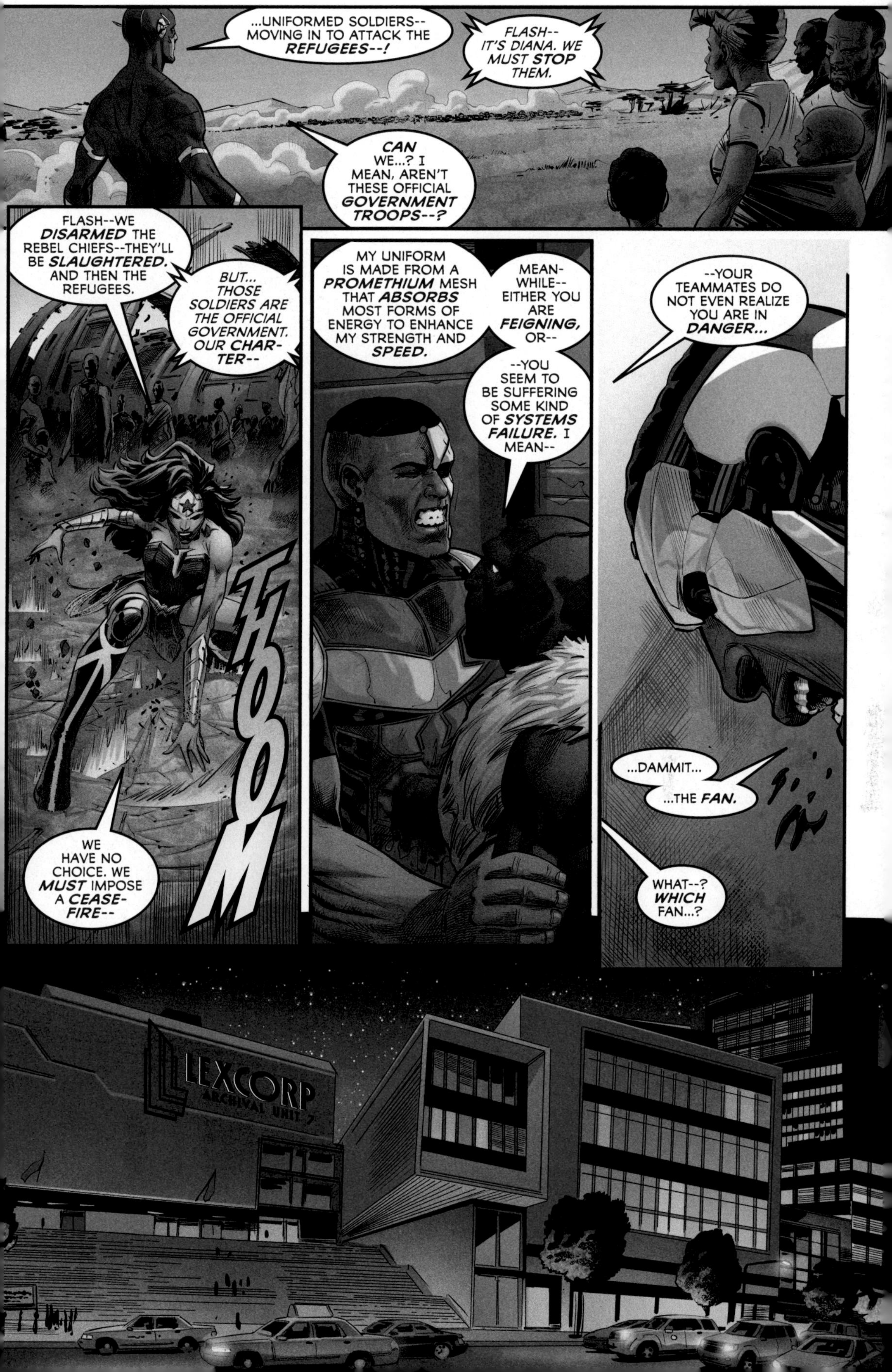
...UNIFORMED SOLDIERS--MOVING IN TO ATTACK THE REFUGEES--!
FLASH--IT'S DIANA. WE MUST STOP THEM.
CAN WE...? I MEAN, AREN'T THESE OFFICIAL GOVERNMENT TROOPS--?
FLASH--WE DISARMED THE REBEL CHIEFS--THEY'LL BE SLAUGHTERED. AND THEN THE REFUGEES.
BUT... THOSE SOLDIERS ARE THE OFFICIAL GOVERNMENT. OUR CHARTER--
WE HAVE NO CHOICE. WE MUST IMPOSE A CEASE-FIRE--
THOOM
MY UNIFORM IS MADE FROM A PROMETHIUM MESH THAT ABSORBS MOST FORMS OF ENERGY TO ENHANCE MY STRENGTH AND SPEED.
MEAN-WHILE--EITHER YOU ARE FEIGNING, OR--
--YOU SEEM TO BE SUFFERING SOME KIND OF SYSTEMS FAILURE. I MEAN--
--YOUR TEAMMATES DO NOT EVEN REALIZE YOU ARE IN DANGER...
...DAMMIT...
...THE FAN.
WHAT--? WHICH FAN...?
LEXCORP
ARCHIVAL UNIT 7

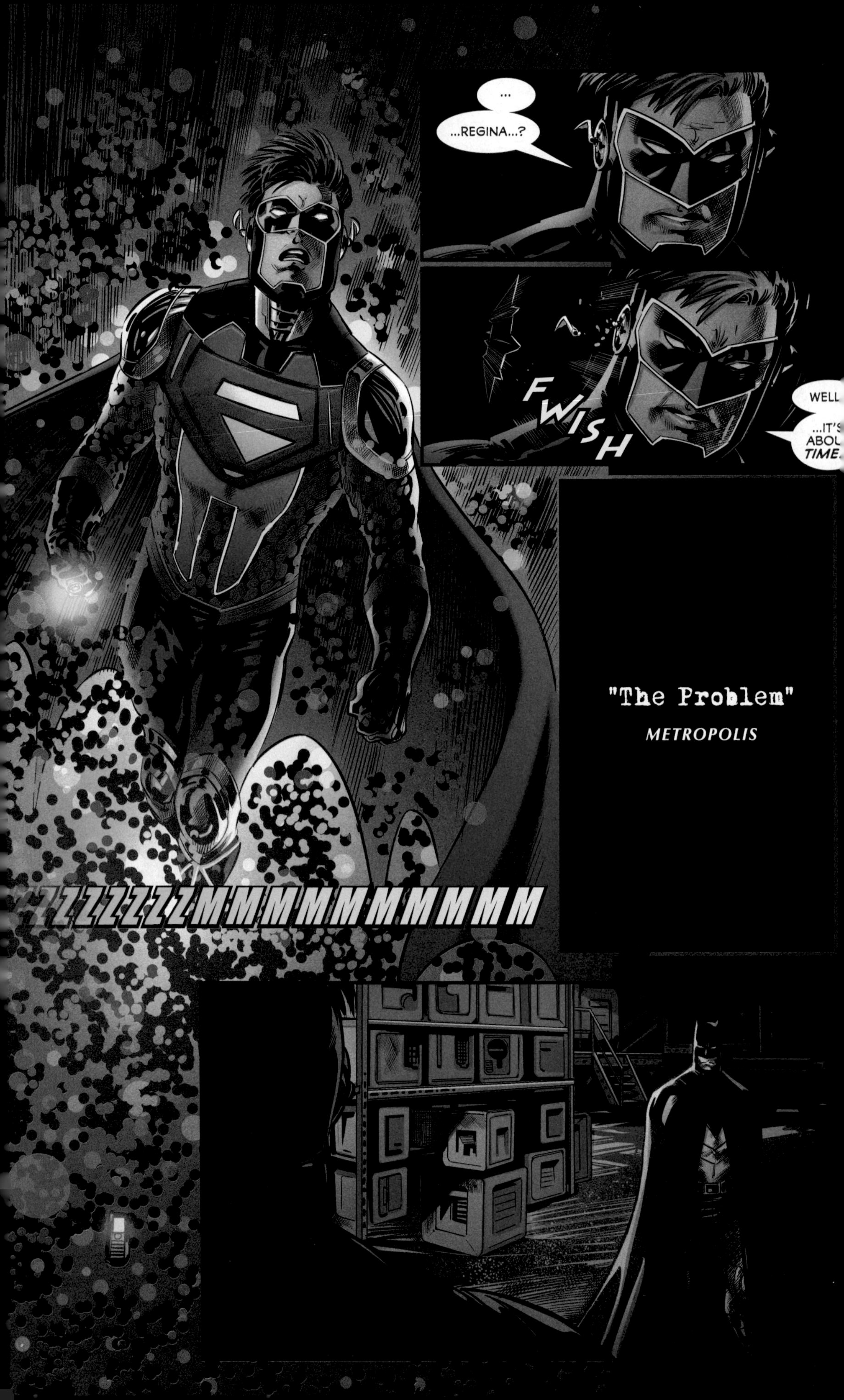
ZZZZZZZZMMMMMMMMMMMMM
...
...REGINA...?
FWISH
WELL
"The Problem"
METROPOLIS

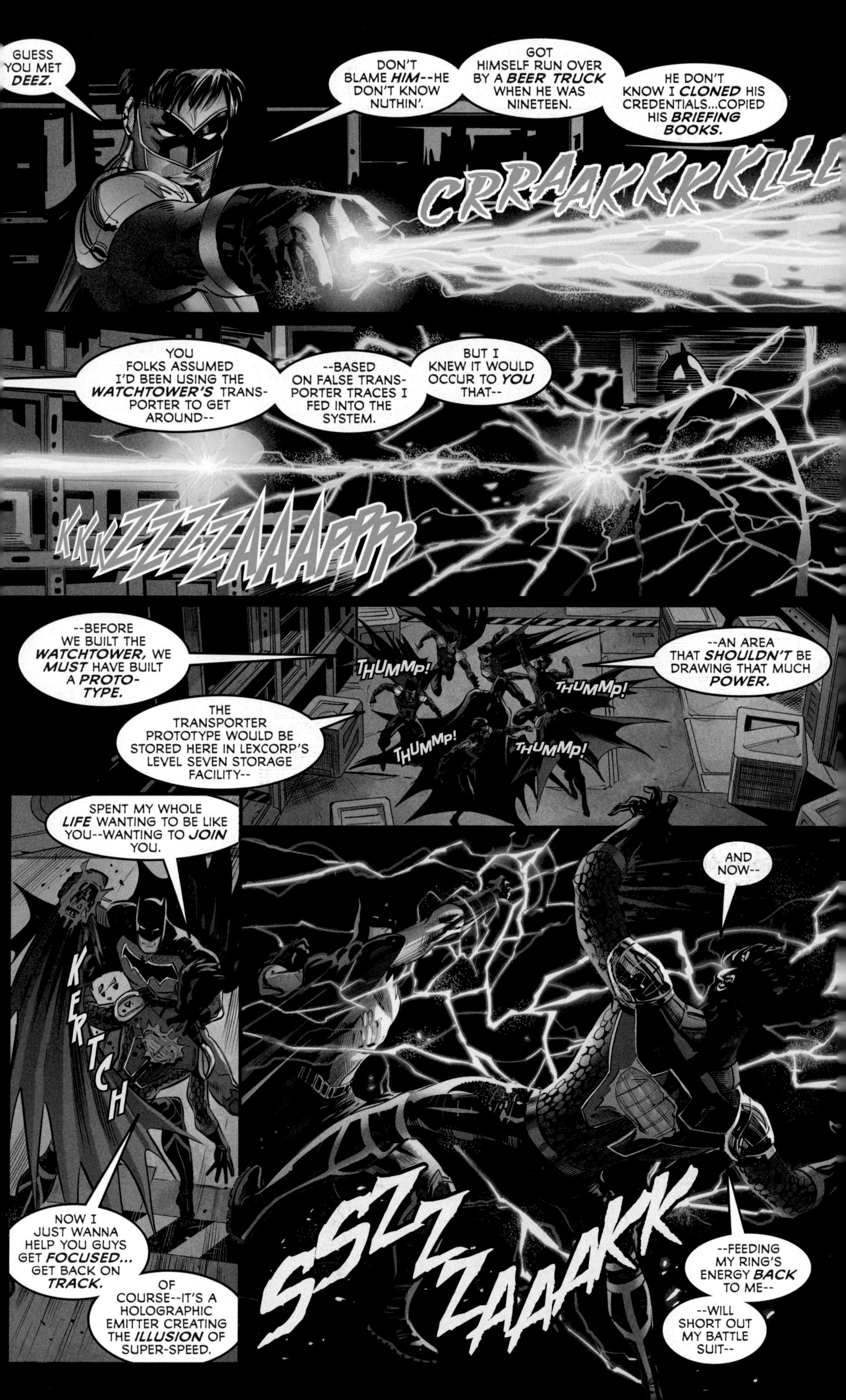
GUESS YOU MET DEEZ.
DON'T BLAME HIM--HE DON'T KNOW NUTHIN'.
GOT HIMSELF RUN OVER BY A BEER TRUCK WHEN HE WAS NINETEEN.
HE DON'T KNOW I CLONED HIS CREDENTIALS...COPIED HIS BRIEFING BOOKS.
CRRAAKKKKLLE
YOU FOLKS ASSUMED I'D BEEN USING THE WATCHTOWER'S TRANSPORTER TO GET AROUND--
--BASED ON FALSE TRANSPORTER TRACES I FED INTO THE SYSTEM.
BUT I KNEW IT WOULD OCCUR TO YOU THAT--
KKKZZZZZAAAAPPPP
--BEFORE WE BUILT THE WATCHTOWER, WE MUST HAVE BUILT A PROTOTYPE.
THE TRANSPORTER PROTOTYPE WOULD BE STORED HERE IN LEXCORP'S LEVEL SEVEN STORAGE FACILITY--
THUMMP!
THUMMP!
THUMMP!
THUMMP!
--AN AREA THAT SHOULDN'T BE DRAWING THAT MUCH POWER.
SPENT MY WHOLE LIFE WANTING TO BE LIKE YOU--WANTING TO JOIN YOU.
KERTCH
NOW I JUST WANNA HELP YOU GUYS GET FOCUSED... GET BACK ON TRACK.
OF COURSE--IT'S A HOLOGRAPHIC EMITTER CREATING THE ILLUSION OF SUPER-SPEED.
AND NOW--
SSZZZAAAKK
--FEEDING MY RING'S ENERGY BACK TO ME--
--WILL SHORT OUT MY BATTLE SUIT--

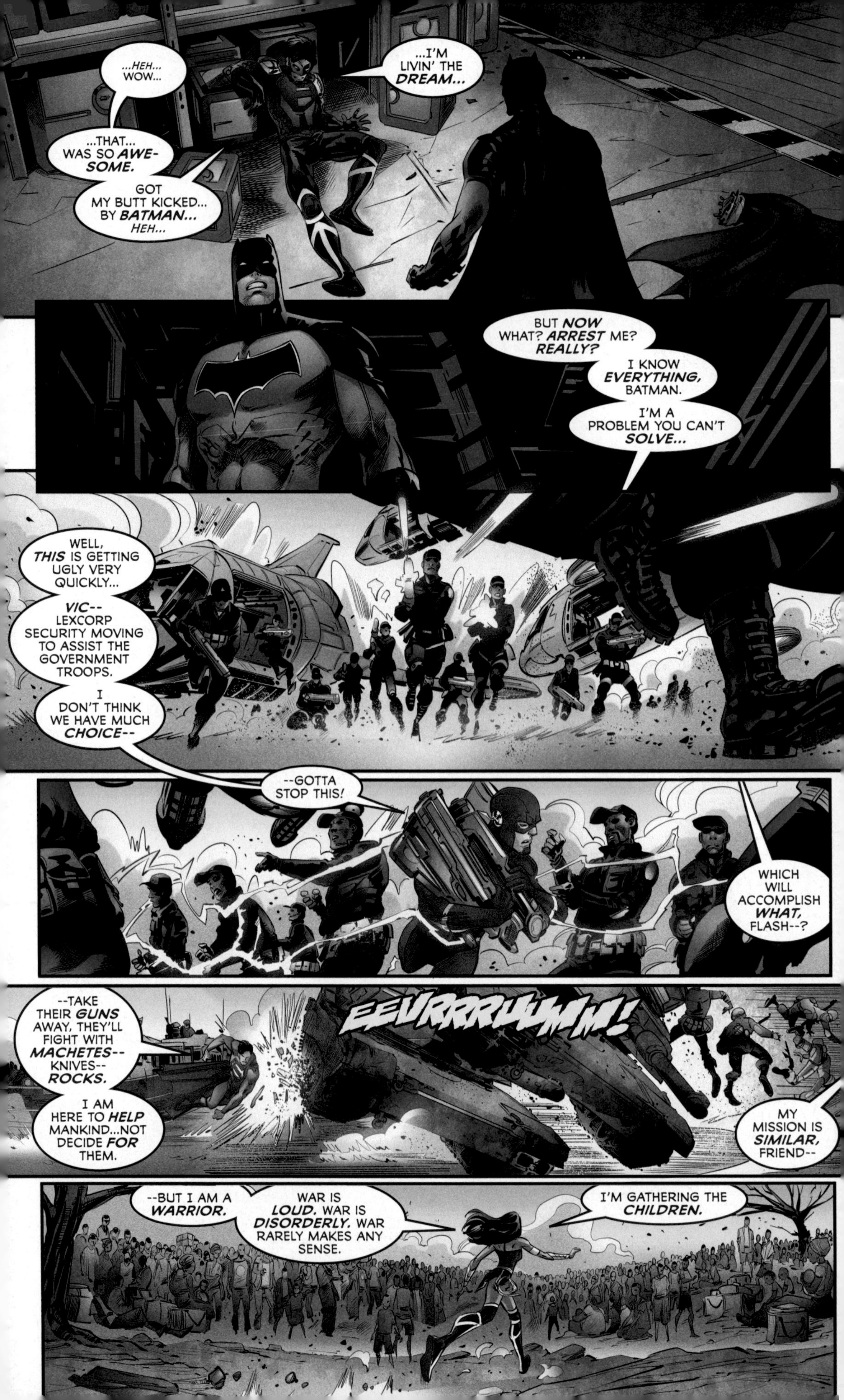

...HEH... WOW...
...THAT... WAS SO AWESOME.
GOT MY BUTT KICKED... BY BATMAN... HEH...
...I'M LIVIN' THE DREAM...
BUT NOW WHAT? ARREST ME? REALLY?
I KNOW EVERYTHING, BATMAN.
I'M A PROBLEM YOU CAN'T SOLVE...
WELL, THIS IS GETTING UGLY VERY QUICKLY...
VIC-- LEXCORP SECURITY MOVING TO ASSIST THE GOVERNMENT TROOPS.
I DON'T THINK WE HAVE MUCH CHOICE--
--GOTTA STOP THIS!
WHICH WILL ACCOMPLISH WHAT, FLASH--?
--TAKE THEIR GUNS AWAY, THEY'LL FIGHT WITH MACHETES-- KNIVES-- ROCKS.
EEURRRRUMM!
I AM HERE TO HELP MANKIND...NOT DECIDE FOR THEM.
MY MISSION IS SIMILAR, FRIEND--
--BUT I AM A WARRIOR.
WAR IS LOUD. WAR IS DISORDERLY. WAR RARELY MAKES ANY SENSE.
I'M GATHERING THE CHILDREN.

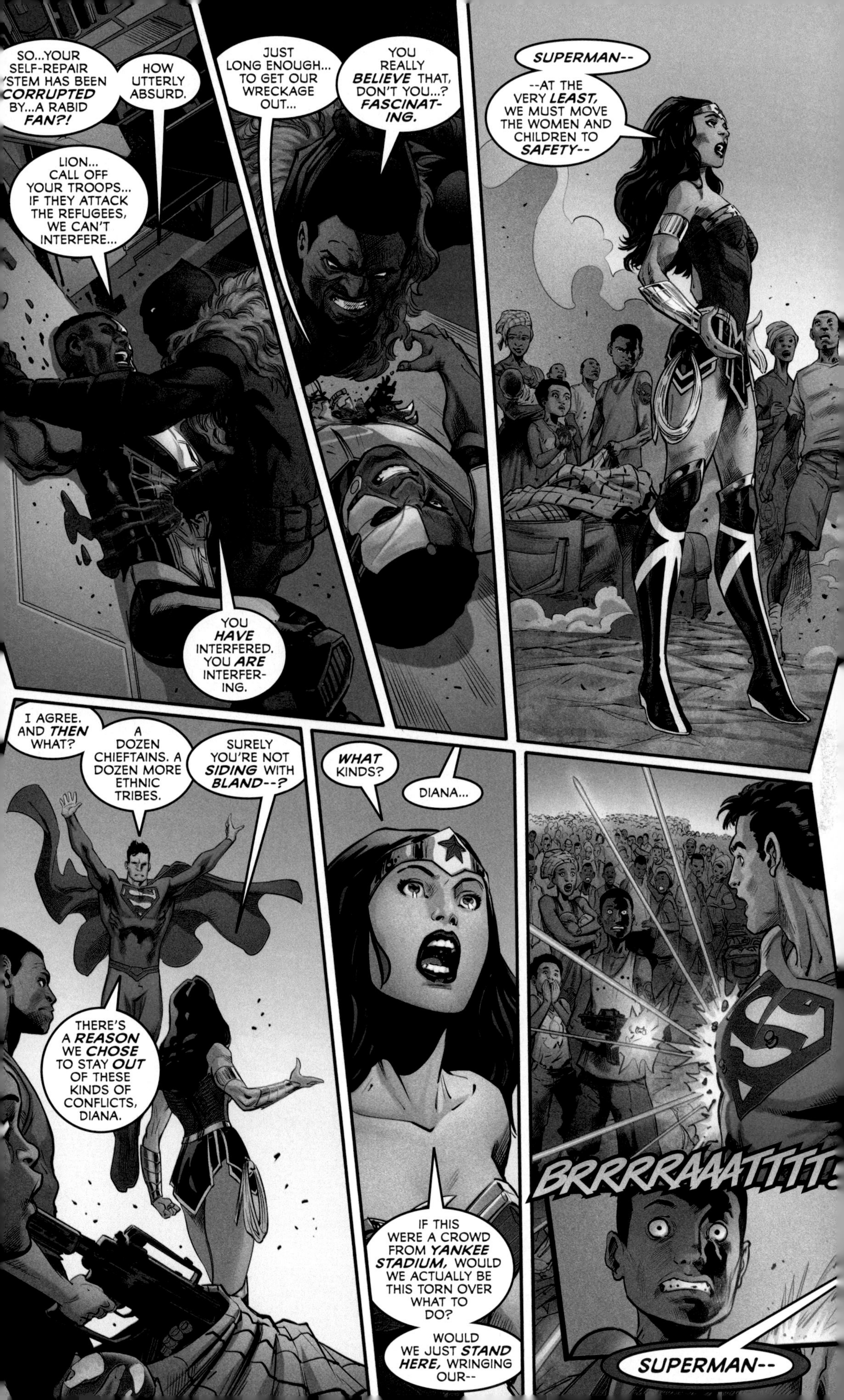
SO...YOUR SELF-REPAIR SYSTEM HAS BEEN CORRUPTED BY...A RABID FAN?!
HOW UTTERLY ABSURD.
LION... CALL OFF YOUR TROOPS... IF THEY ATTACK THE REFUGEES, WE CAN'T INTERFERE...
YOU HAVE INTERFERED. YOU ARE INTERFER-ING.
JUST LONG ENOUGH... TO GET OUR WRECKAGE OUT...
YOU REALLY BELIEVE THAT, DON'T YOU...? FASCINAT-ING.
SUPERMAN--
--AT THE VERY LEAST, WE MUST MOVE THE WOMEN AND CHILDREN TO SAFETY--
I AGREE. AND THEN WHAT?
A DOZEN CHIEFTAINS. A DOZEN MORE ETHNIC TRIBES.
SURELY YOU'RE NOT SIDING WITH BLAND--?
THERE'S A REASON WE CHOSE TO STAY OUT OF THESE KINDS OF CONFLICTS, DIANA.
WHAT KINDS?
DIANA...
IF THIS WERE A CROWD FROM YANKEE STADIUM, WOULD WE ACTUALLY BE THIS TORN OVER WHAT TO DO?
WOULD WE JUST STAND HERE, WRINGING OUR--
BRRRRAAATTTT
SUPERMAN--

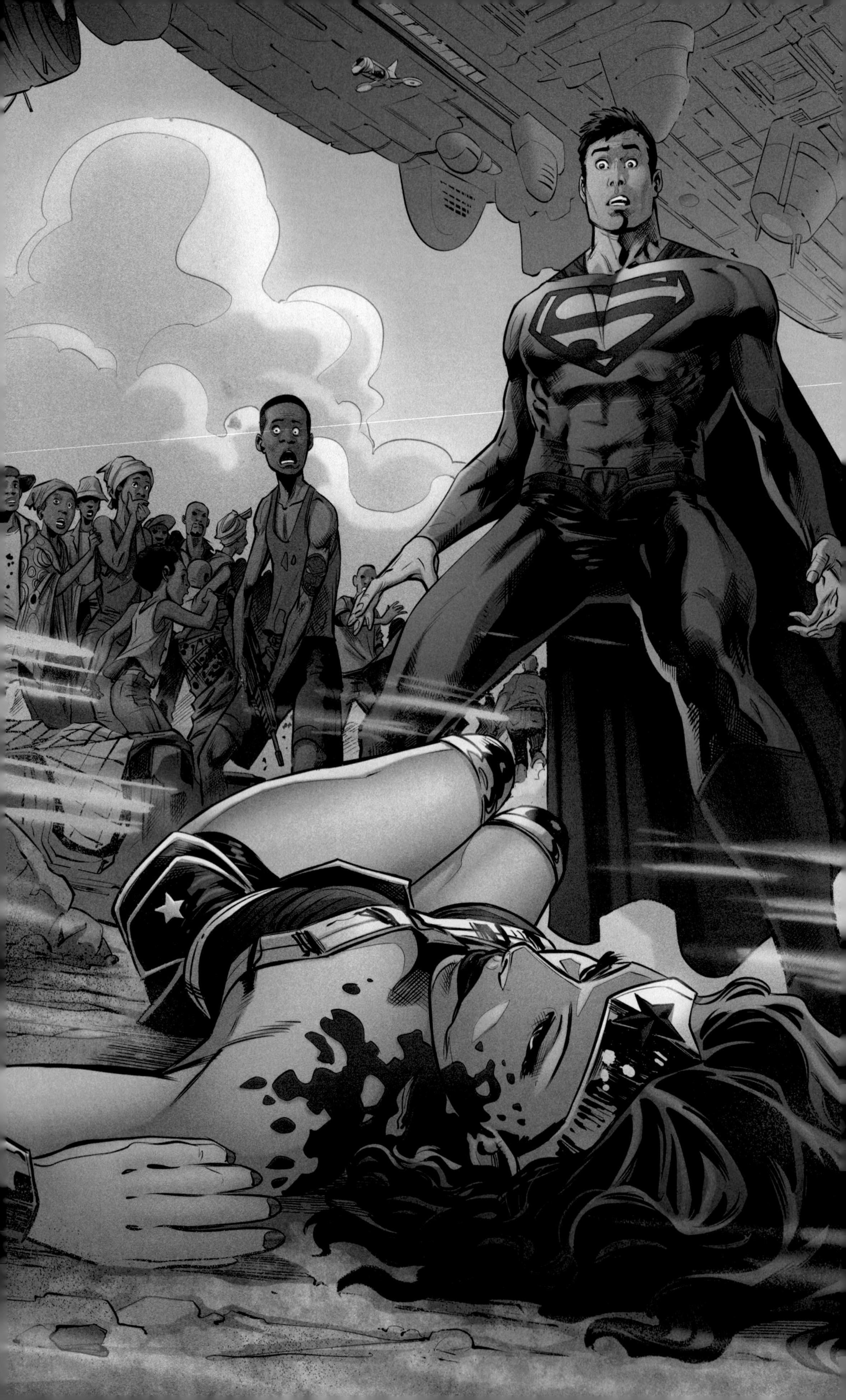

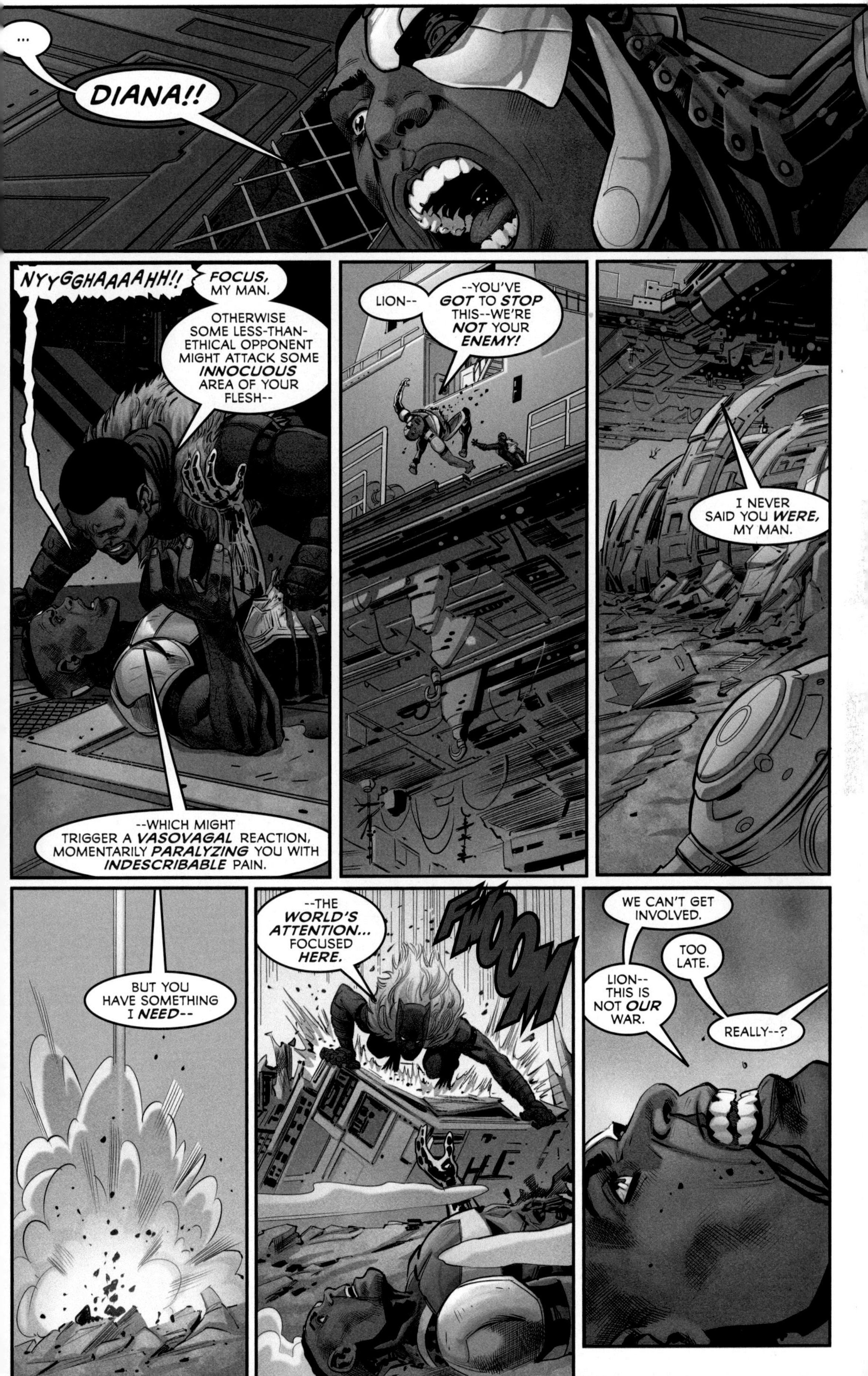
...
DIANA!!
NYYGGHAAAAHH!!
FOCUS, MY MAN.
OTHERWISE SOME LESS-THAN-ETHICAL OPPONENT MIGHT ATTACK SOME INNOCUOUS AREA OF YOUR FLESH--
--WHICH MIGHT TRIGGER A VASOVAGAL REACTION, MOMENTARILY PARALYZING YOU WITH INDESCRIBABLE PAIN.
LION--
--YOU'VE GOT TO STOP THIS--WE'RE NOT YOUR ENEMY!
I NEVER SAID YOU WERE, MY MAN.
BUT YOU HAVE SOMETHING I NEED--
--THE WORLD'S ATTENTION... FOCUSED HERE.
FWOOM
WE CAN'T GET INVOLVED.
LION-- THIS IS NOT OUR WAR.
TOO LATE.
REALLY--?

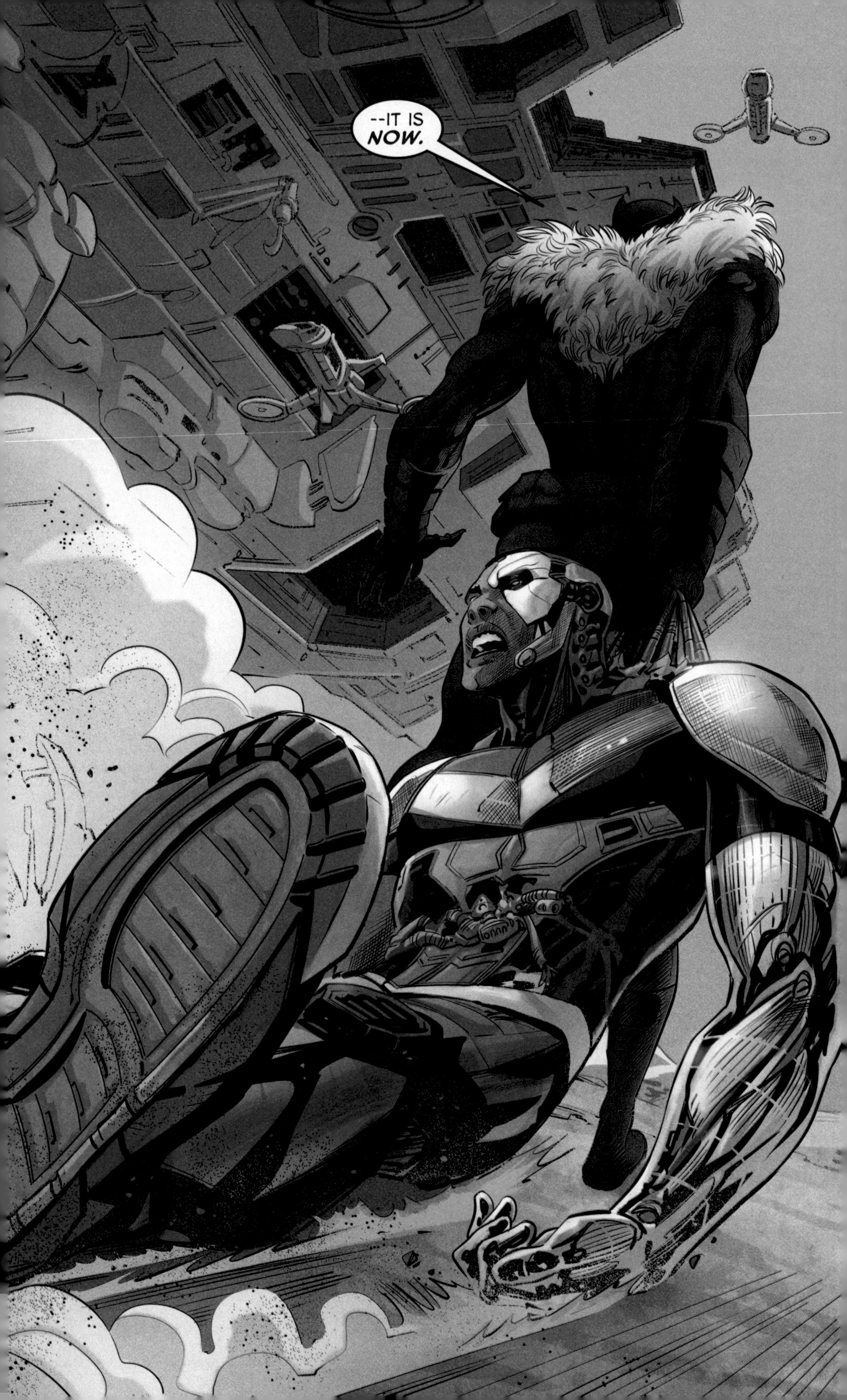
--IT IS NOW.

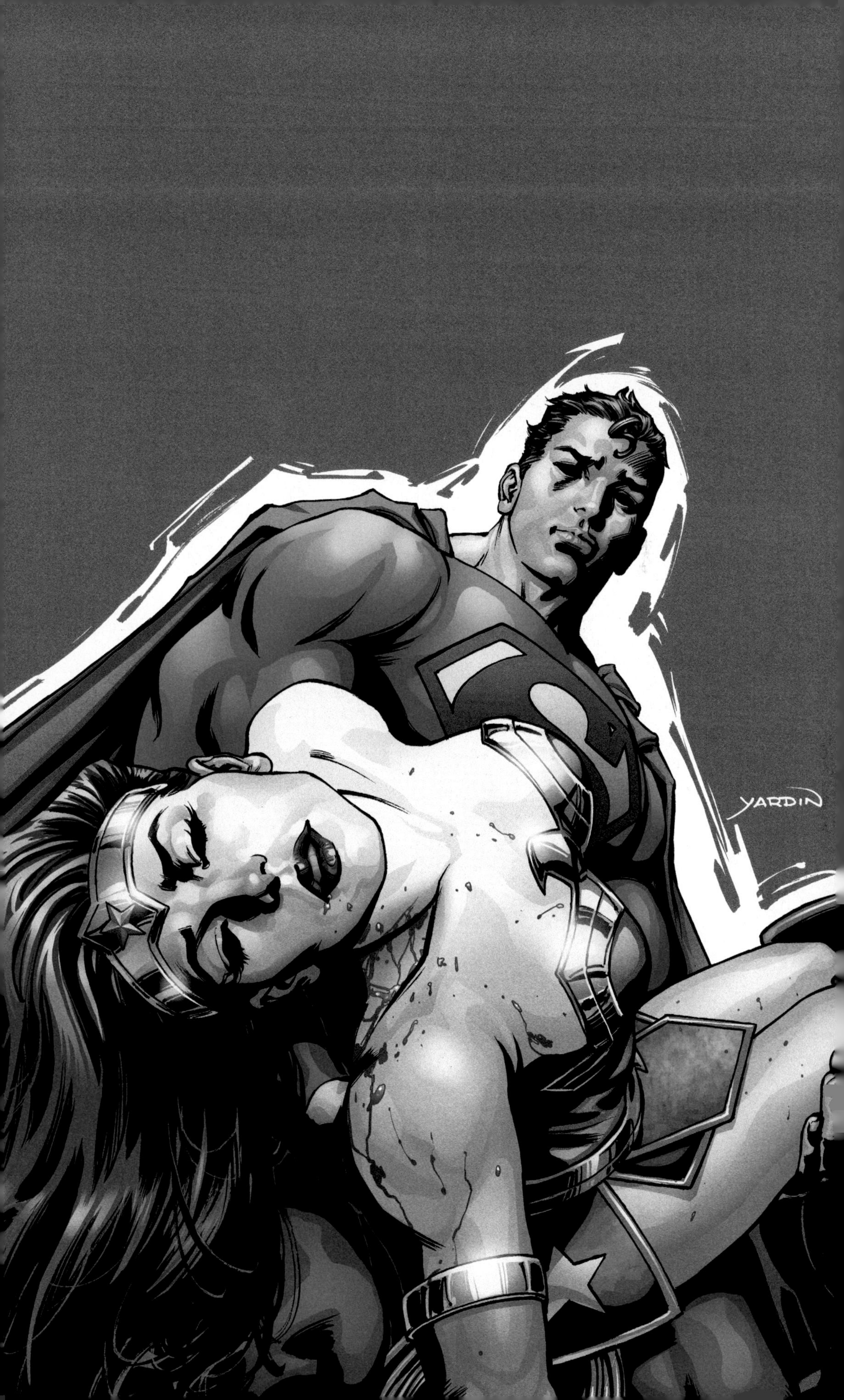
YARDIN

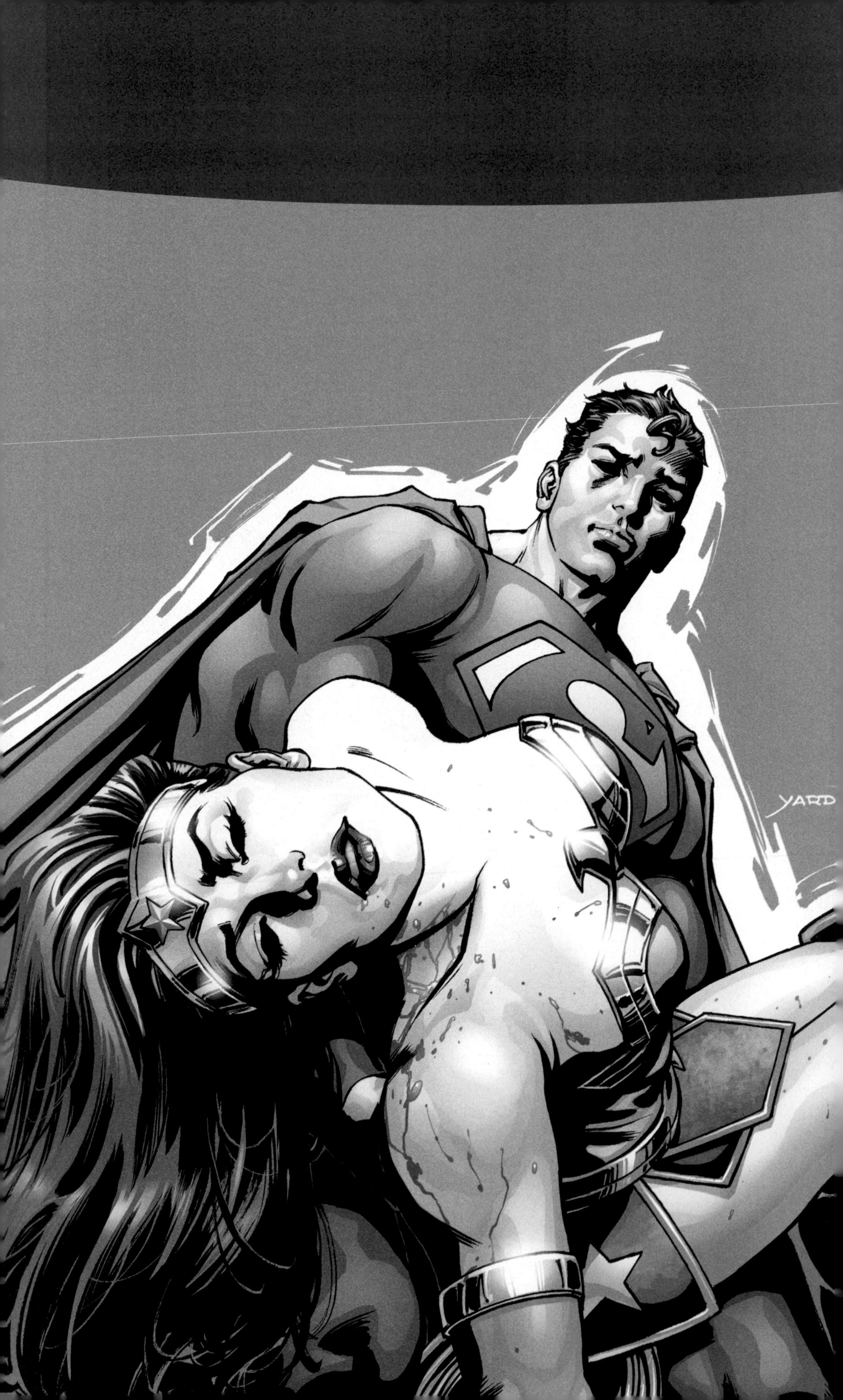
YARD

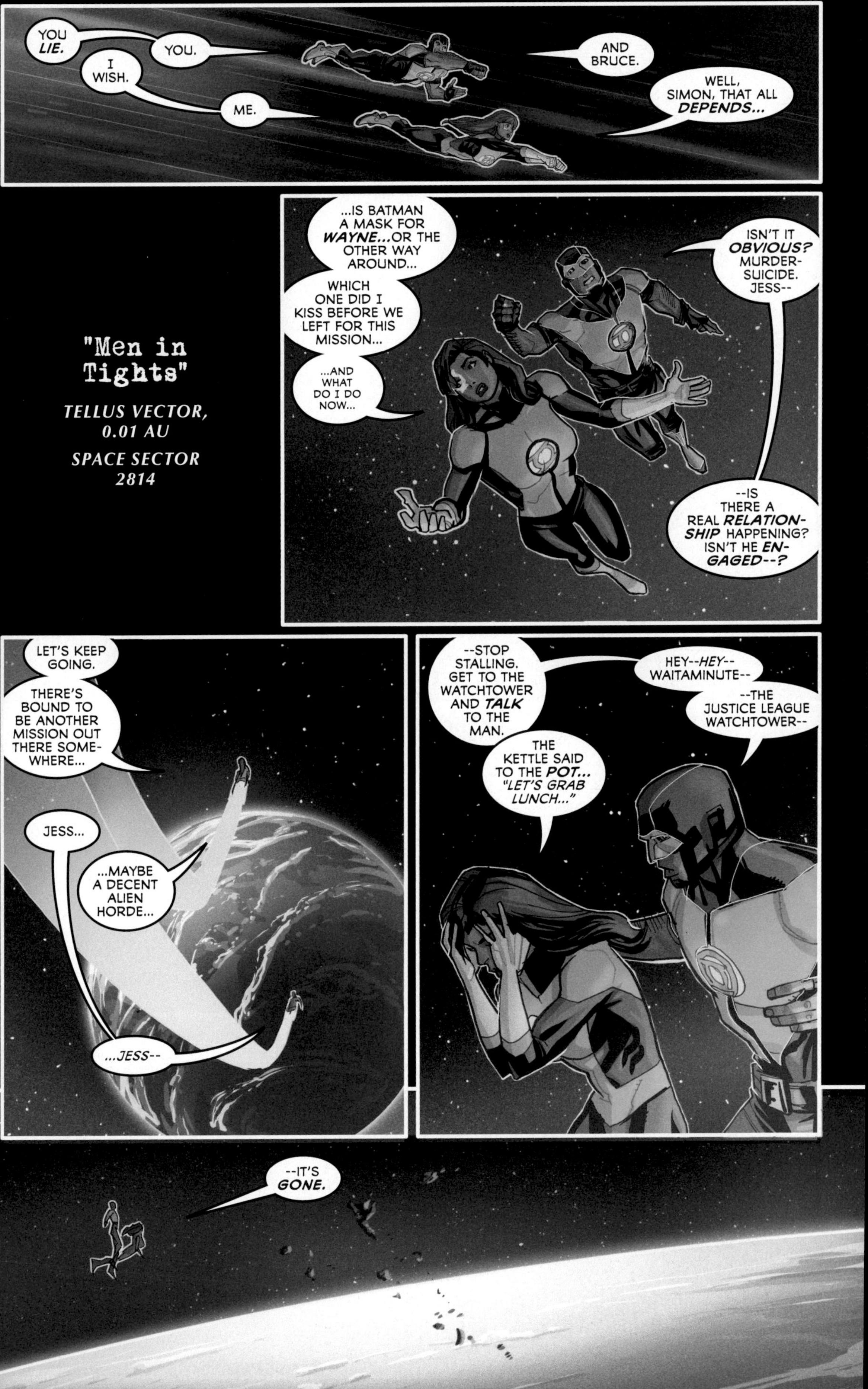
YOU *LIE.*
YOU.
I WISH.
ME.
AND BRUCE.
WELL, SIMON, THAT ALL *DEPENDS...*
"Men in Tights"
TELLUS VECTOR, 0.01 AU
SPACE SECTOR 2814
...IS BATMAN A MASK FOR *WAYNE...*OR THE OTHER WAY AROUND...
WHICH ONE DID I KISS BEFORE WE LEFT FOR THIS MISSION...
...AND WHAT DO I DO NOW...
ISN'T IT *OBVIOUS?* MURDER-SUICIDE. JESS--
--IS THERE A REAL *RELATION-SHIP* HAPPENING? ISN'T HE *EN-GAGED--?*
LET'S KEEP GOING.
THERE'S BOUND TO BE ANOTHER MISSION OUT THERE SOME-WHERE...
JESS...
...MAYBE A DECENT ALIEN HORDE...
...JESS--
--STOP STALLING. GET TO THE WATCHTOWER AND *TALK* TO THE MAN.
HEY--*HEY*-- WAITAMINUTE--
THE KETTLE SAID TO THE *POT... "LET'S GRAB LUNCH..."*
--THE JUSTICE LEAGUE WATCHTOWER--
--IT'S *GONE.*

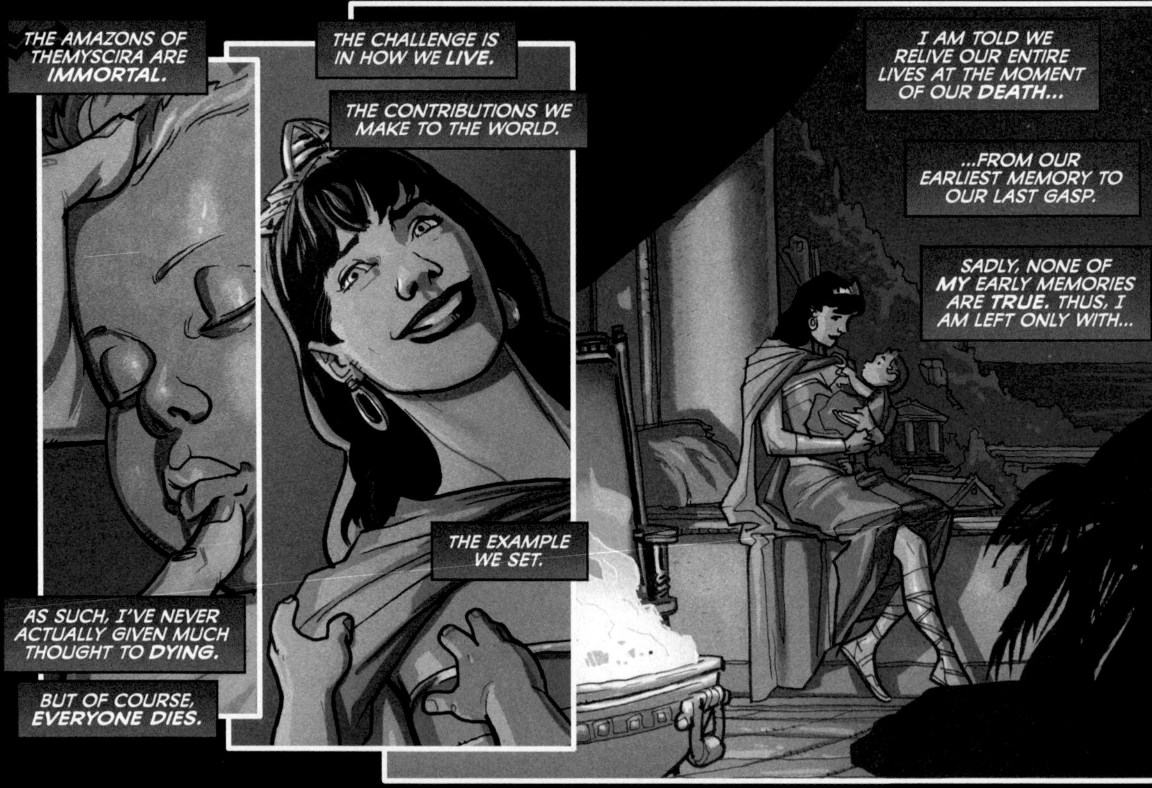
THE AMAZONS OF THEMYSCIRA ARE IMMORTAL.
AS SUCH, I'VE NEVER ACTUALLY GIVEN MUCH THOUGHT TO DYING.
BUT OF COURSE, EVERYONE DIES.
THE CHALLENGE IS IN HOW WE LIVE.
THE CONTRIBUTIONS WE MAKE TO THE WORLD.
THE EXAMPLE WE SET.
I AM TOLD WE RELIVE OUR ENTIRE LIVES AT THE MOMENT OF OUR DEATH...
...FROM OUR EARLIEST MEMORY TO OUR LAST GASP.
SADLY, NONE OF MY EARLY MEMORIES ARE TRUE. THUS, I AM LEFT ONLY WITH...

"Lies My Mother Told Me"

EAST AFRICA

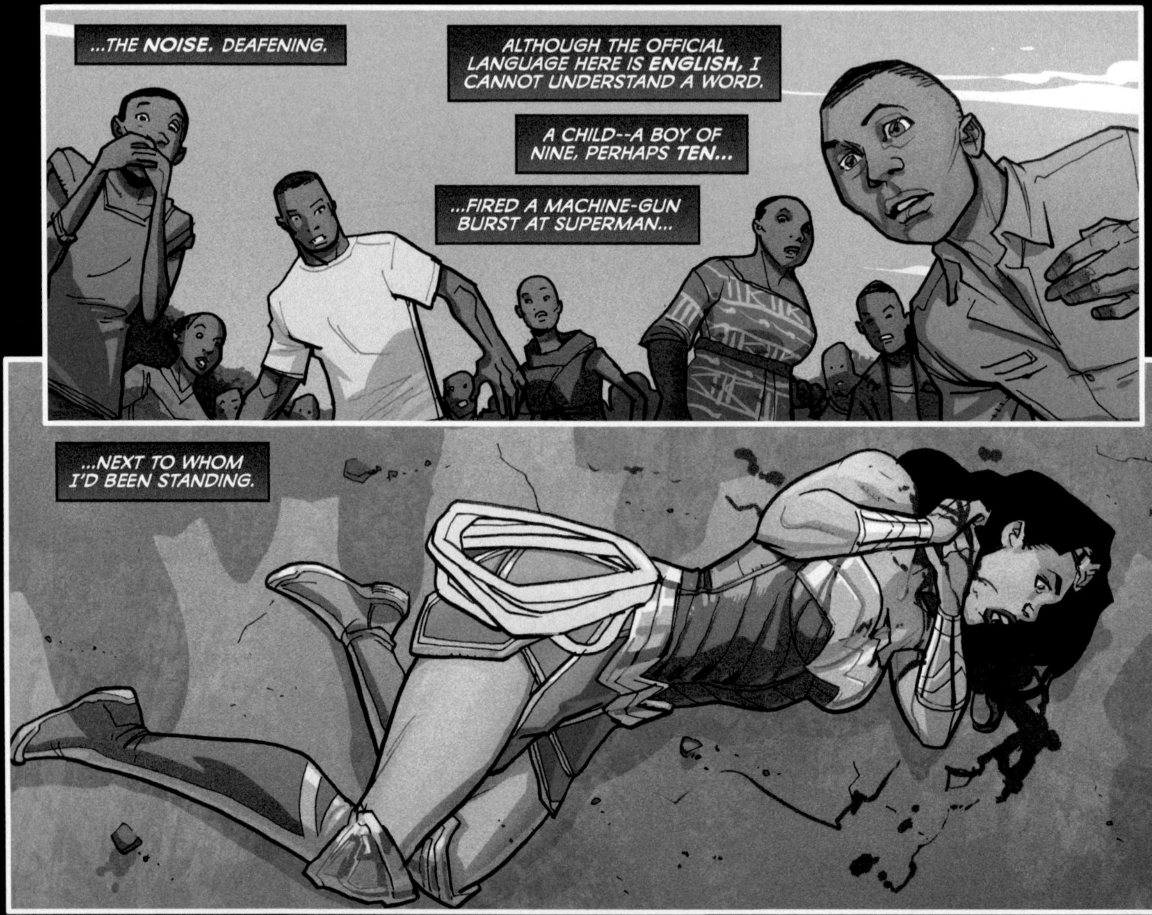
...THE NOISE. DEAFENING.
ALTHOUGH THE OFFICIAL LANGUAGE HERE IS ENGLISH, I CANNOT UNDERSTAND A WORD.
A CHILD--A BOY OF NINE, PERHAPS TEN...
...FIRED A MACHINE-GUN BURST AT SUPERMAN...
...NEXT TO WHOM I'D BEEN STANDING.

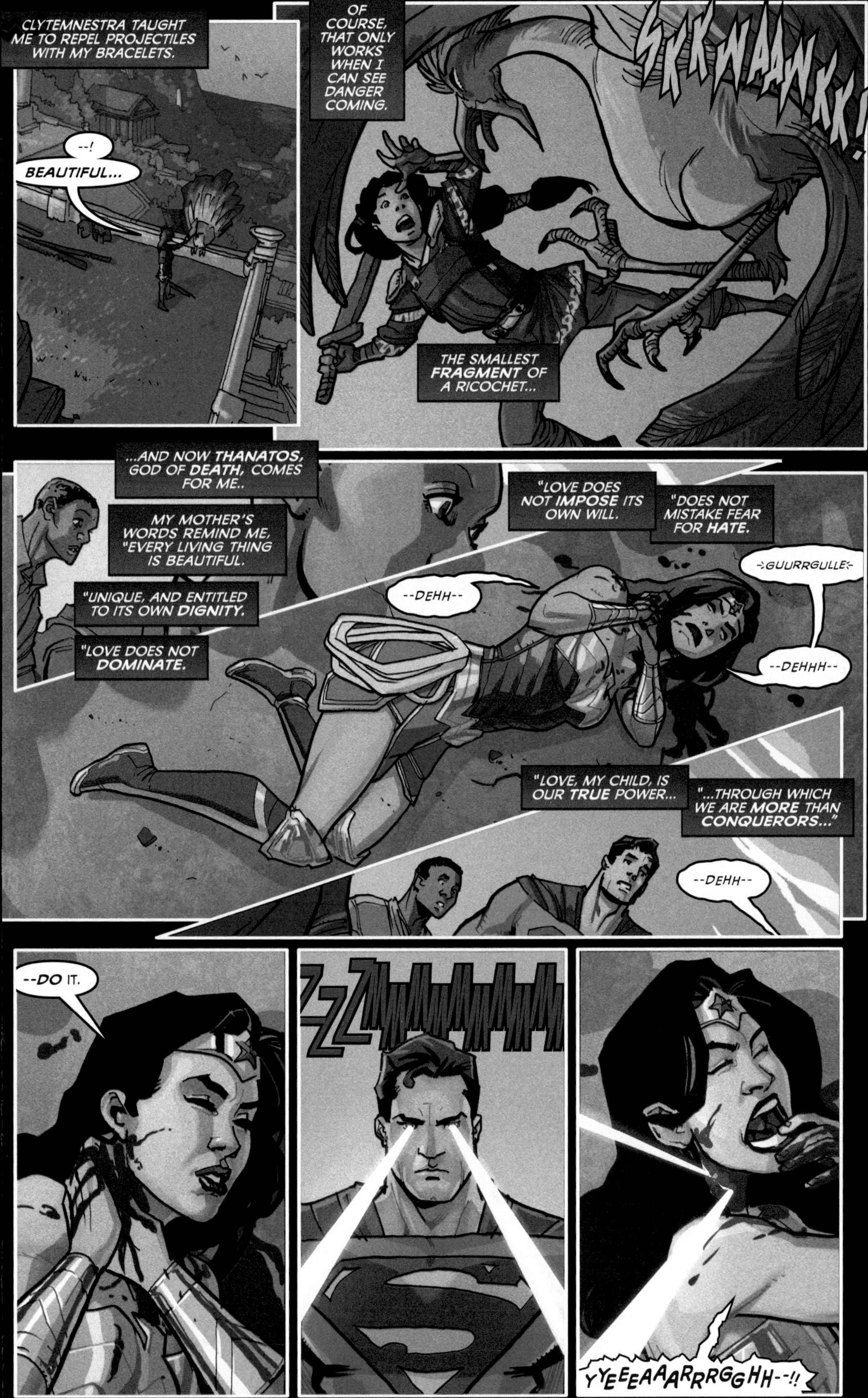
CLYTEMNESTRA TAUGHT ME TO REPEL PROJECTILES WITH MY BRACELETS.
--!
BEAUTIFUL...
OF COURSE, THAT ONLY WORKS WHEN I CAN SEE DANGER COMING.
SKKWAANKK!!
THE SMALLEST FRAGMENT OF A RICOCHET...
...AND NOW THANATOS, GOD OF DEATH, COMES FOR ME..
MY MOTHER'S WORDS REMIND ME, "EVERY LIVING THING IS BEAUTIFUL.
"UNIQUE, AND ENTITLED TO ITS OWN DIGNITY.
"LOVE DOES NOT DOMINATE.
"LOVE DOES NOT IMPOSE ITS OWN WILL.
"DOES NOT MISTAKE FEAR FOR HATE.
GUURRGULLE
--DEHH--
--DEHHH--
"LOVE, MY CHILD, IS OUR TRUE POWER...
"...THROUGH WHICH WE ARE MORE THAN CONQUERORS..."
--DEHH--
--DO IT.
ZZZWWWWWWWWW
YYEEEAAARRRGGHH--!!

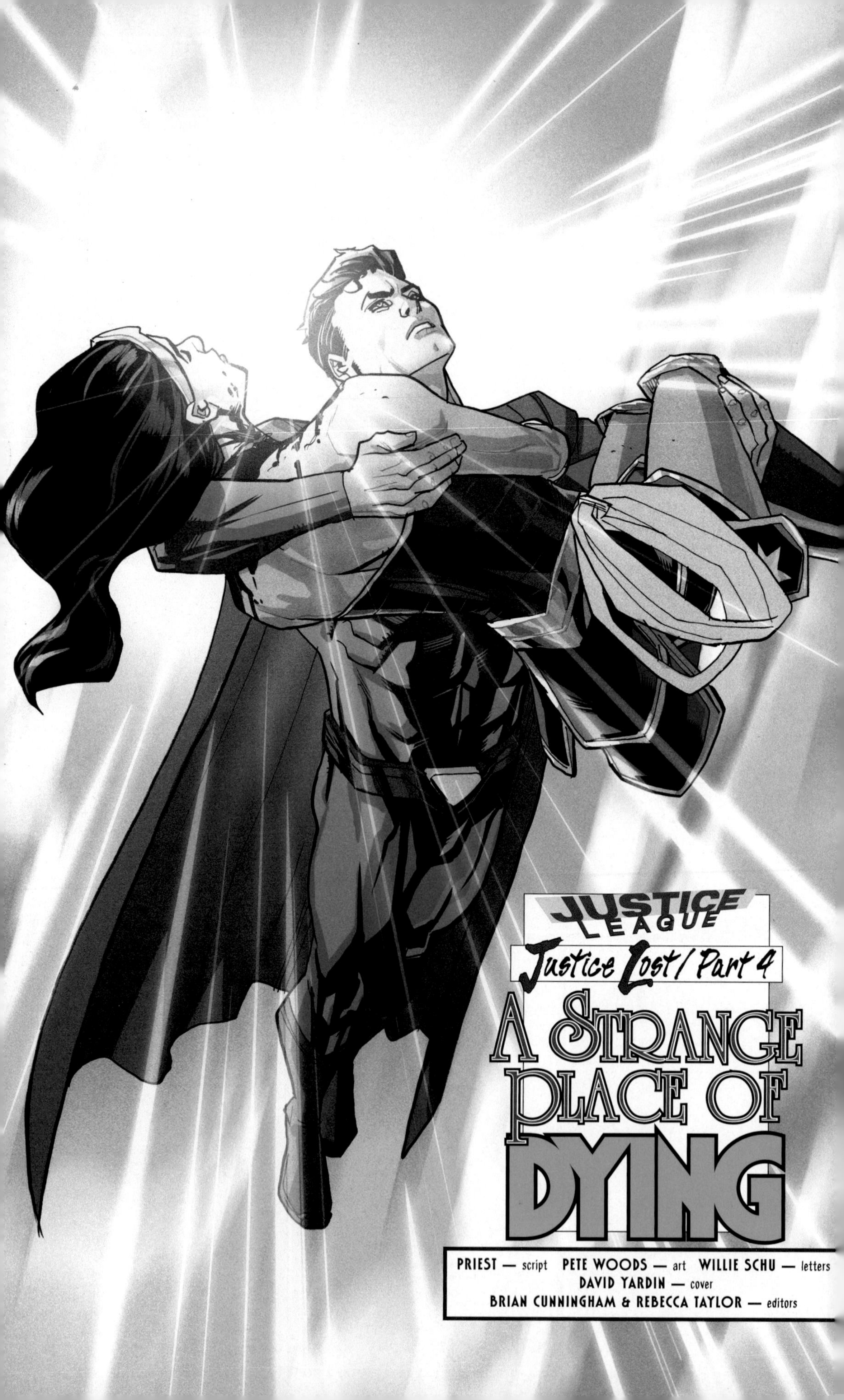
JUSTICE LEAGUE
Justice Lost / Part 4
A STRANGE PLACE OF DYING
PRIEST — script PETE WOODS — art WILLIE SCHU — letters
DAVID YARDIN — cover
BRIAN CUNNINGHAM & REBECCA TAYLOR — editors

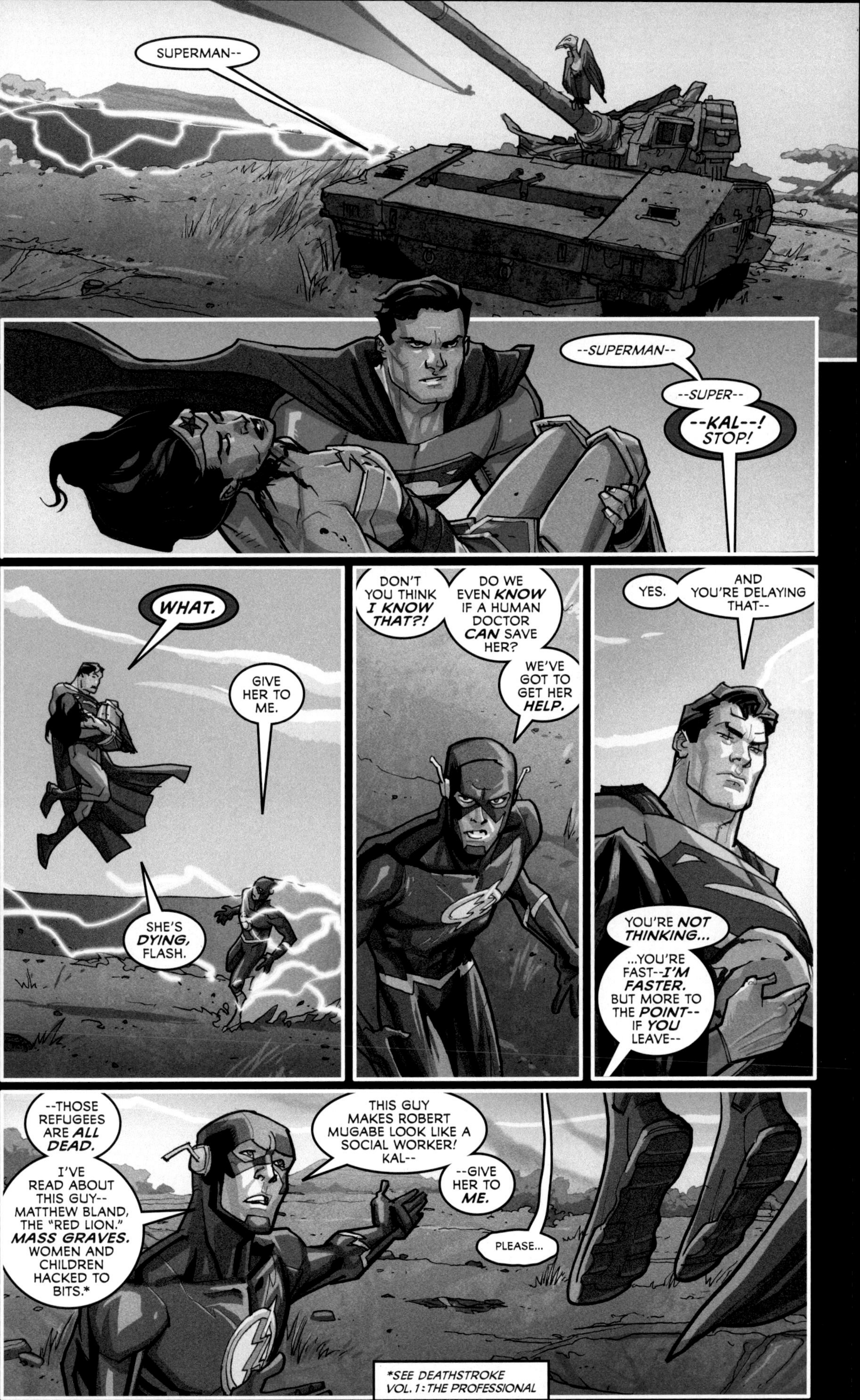

SUPERMAN--
--SUPERMAN--
--SUPER--
--KAL--! STOP!
WHAT.
GIVE HER TO ME.
SHE'S DYING, FLASH.
DON'T YOU THINK I KNOW THAT?!
DO WE EVEN KNOW IF A HUMAN DOCTOR CAN SAVE HER?
WE'VE GOT TO GET HER HELP.
YES.
AND YOU'RE DELAYING THAT--
YOU'RE NOT THINKING...
...YOU'RE FAST--I'M FASTER. BUT MORE TO THE POINT-- IF YOU LEAVE--
--THOSE REFUGEES ARE ALL DEAD.
I'VE READ ABOUT THIS GUY-- MATTHEW BLAND, THE "RED LION." MASS GRAVES. WOMEN AND CHILDREN HACKED TO BITS.*
THIS GUY MAKES ROBERT MUGABE LOOK LIKE A SOCIAL WORKER! KAL--
--GIVE HER TO ME.
PLEASE...
*SEE DEATHSTROKE VOL. 1: THE PROFESSIONAL

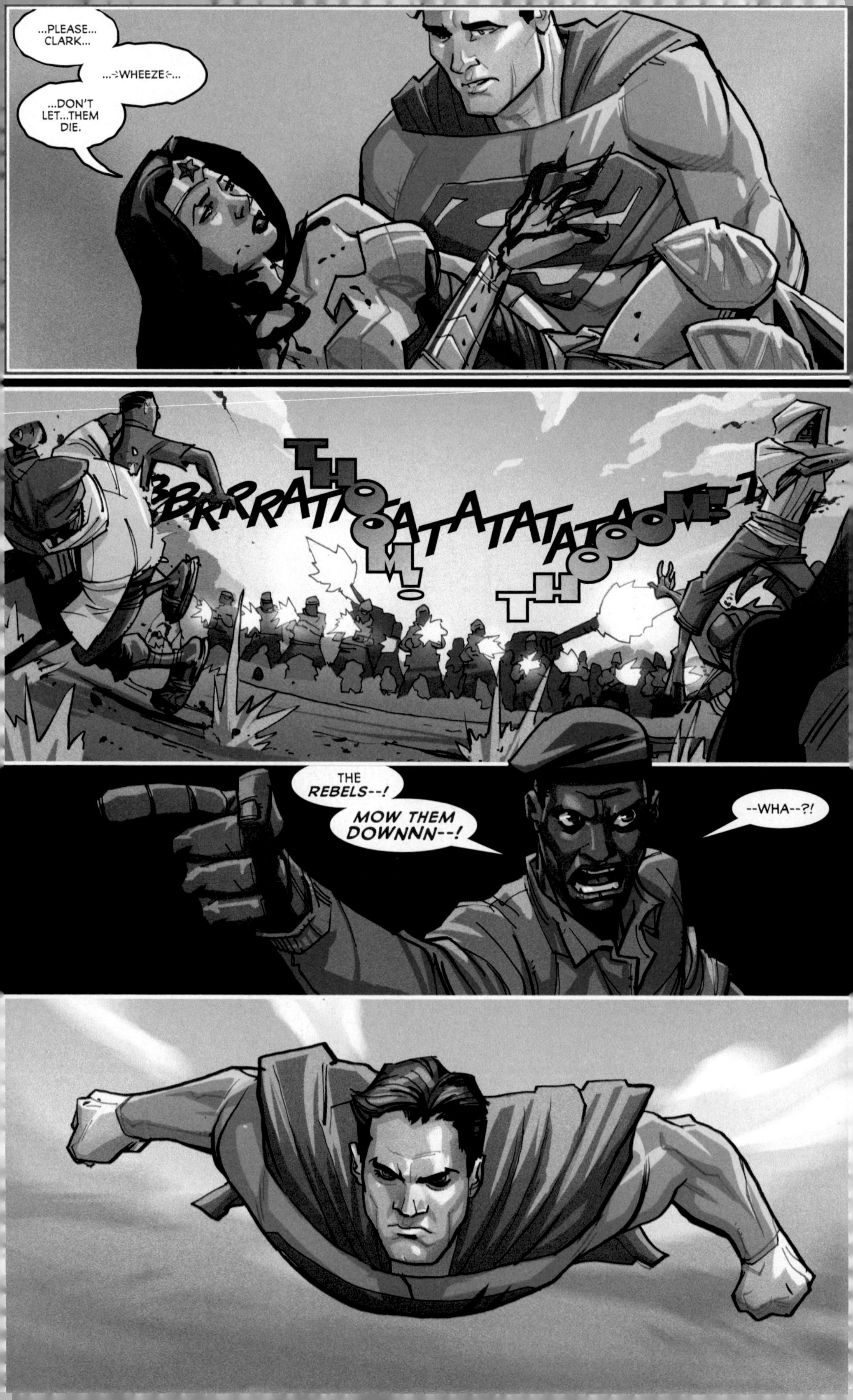
...PLEASE... CLARK...
...⇒WHEEZE⇐...
...DON'T LET...THEM DIE.
THOOM!
BBRRRRATTATATATATATAT
THOOOOOM!
THE REBELS--!
MOW THEM DOWNNN--!
--WHA--?!

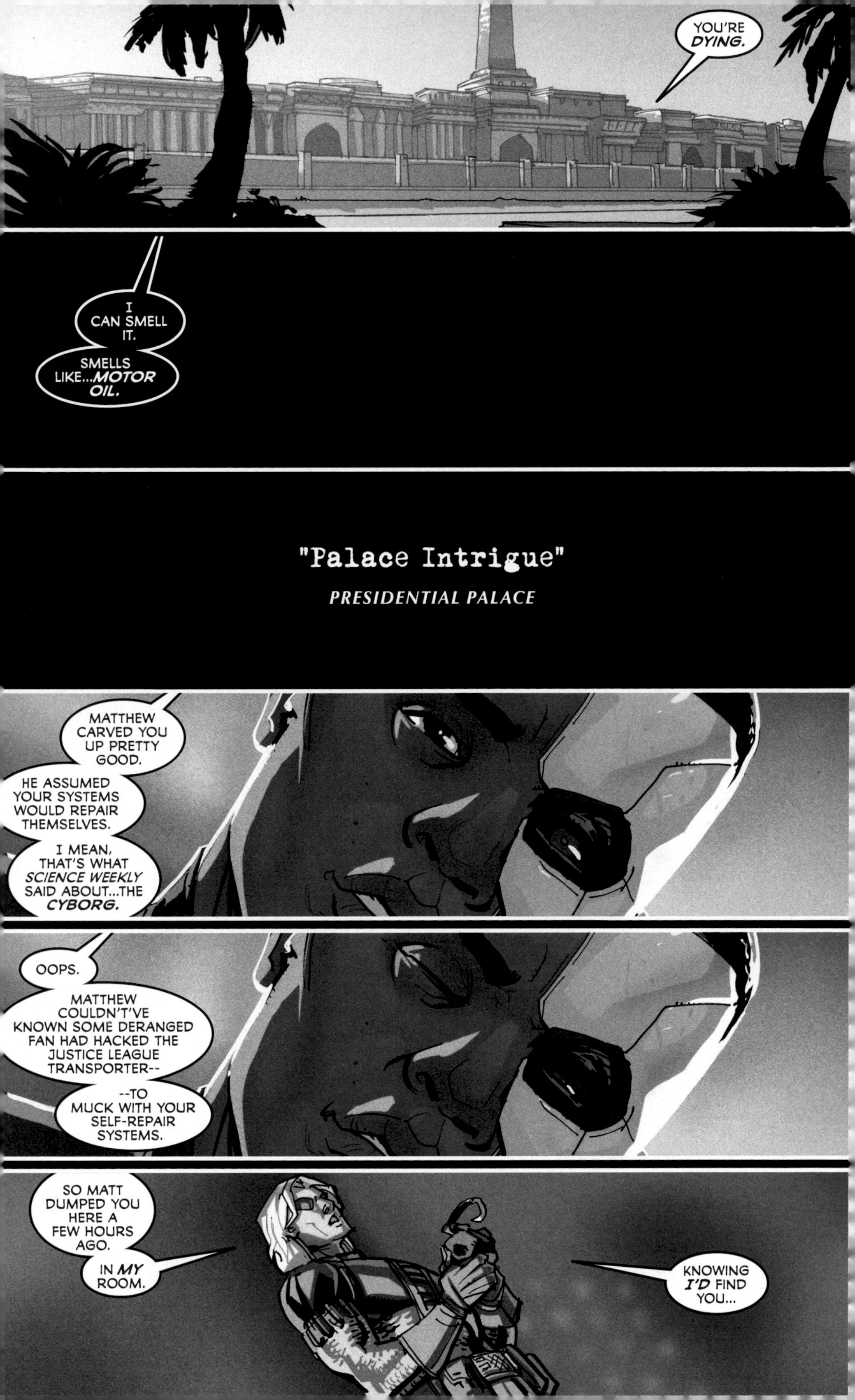
YOU'RE *DYING.*
I CAN SMELL IT.
SMELLS LIKE...*MOTOR OIL.*
"Palace Intrigue"
PRESIDENTIAL PALACE
MATTHEW CARVED YOU UP PRETTY GOOD.
HE ASSUMED YOUR SYSTEMS WOULD REPAIR THEMSELVES.
I MEAN, THAT'S WHAT *SCIENCE WEEKLY* SAID ABOUT...THE *CYBORG.*
OOPS.
MATTHEW COULDN'T'VE KNOWN SOME DERANGED FAN HAD HACKED THE JUSTICE LEAGUE TRANSPORTER--
--TO MUCK WITH YOUR SELF-REPAIR SYSTEMS.
SO MATT DUMPED YOU HERE A FEW HOURS AGO.
IN *MY* ROOM.
KNOWING *I'D* FIND YOU...

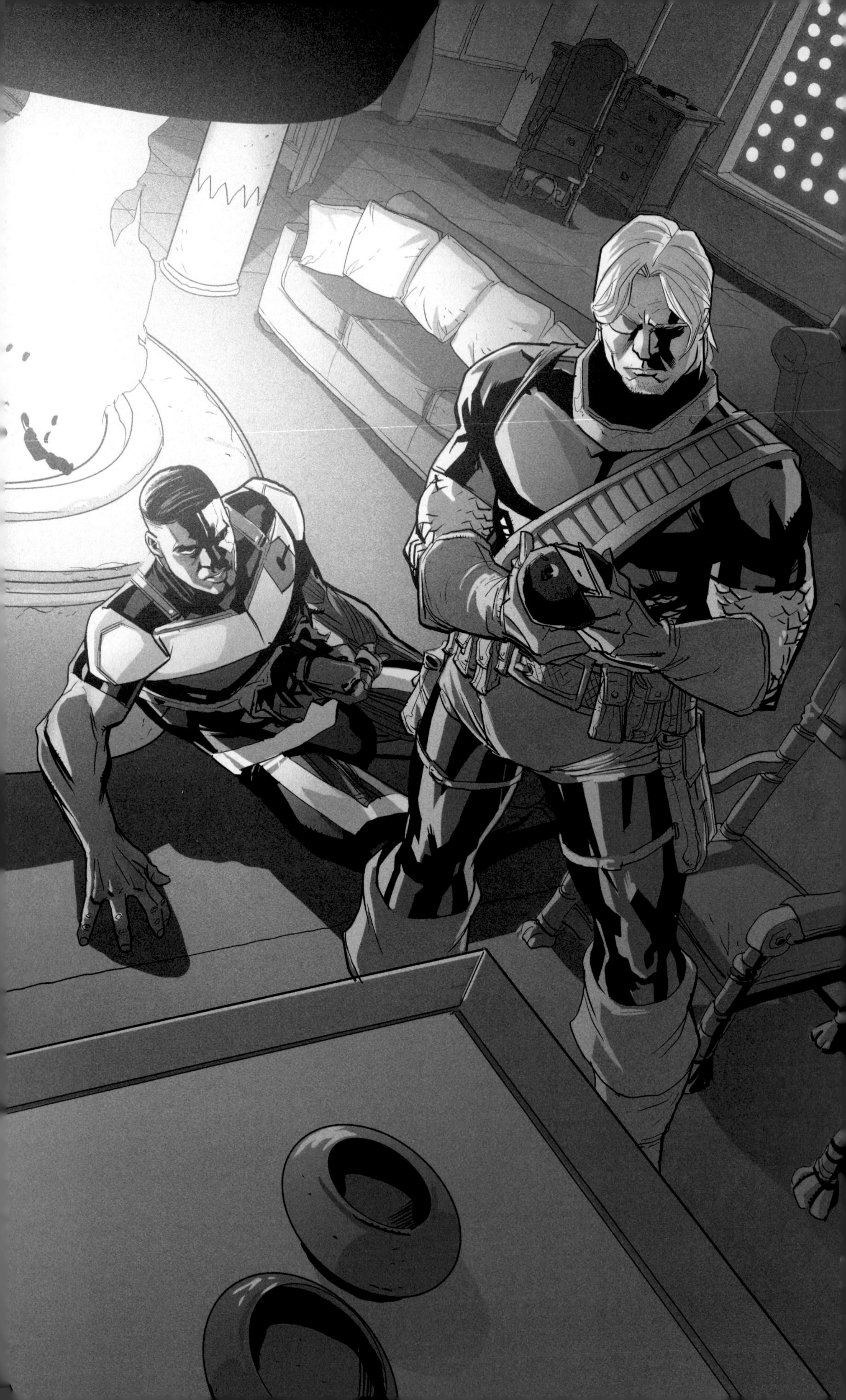

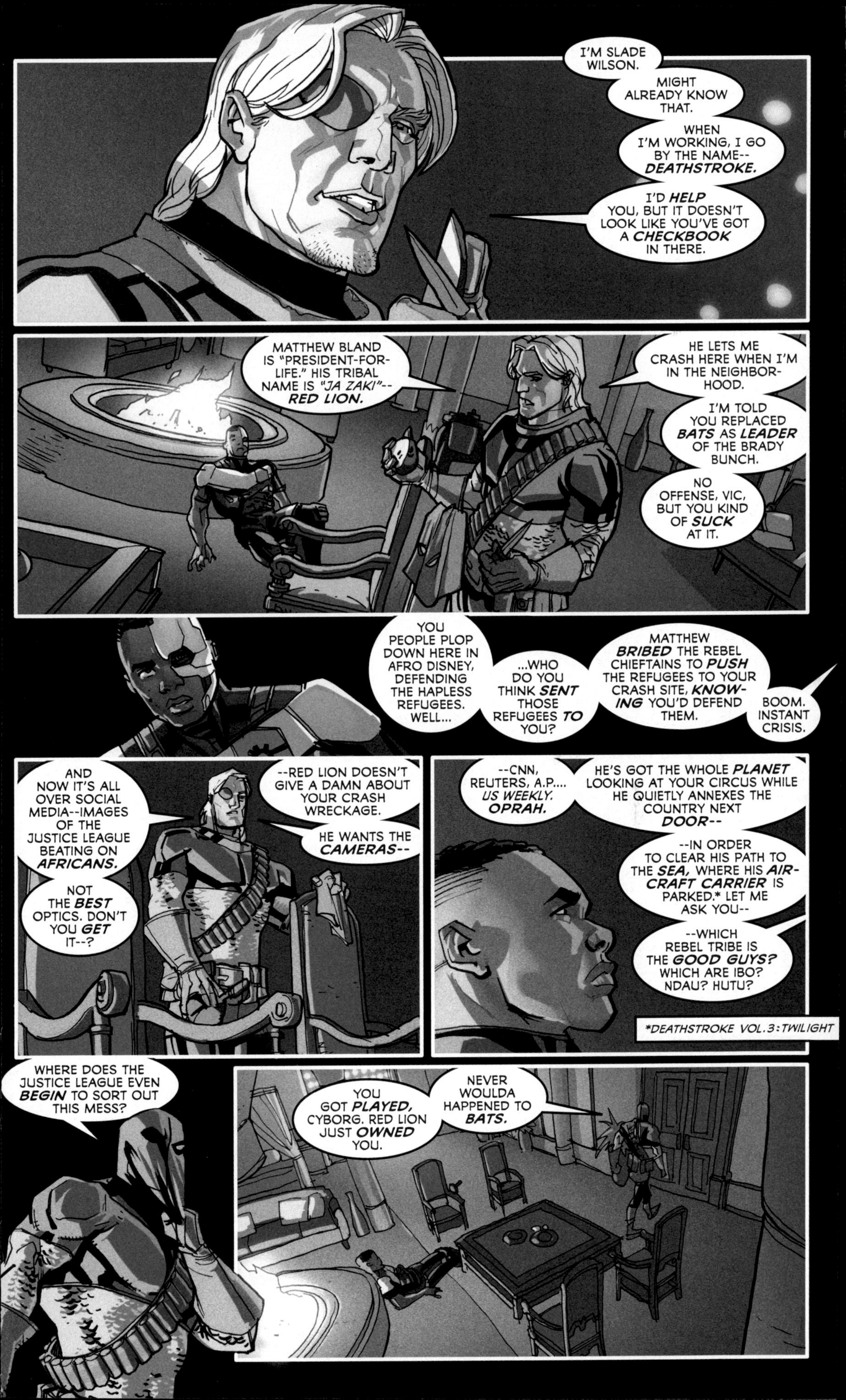
I'M SLADE WILSON.
MIGHT ALREADY KNOW THAT.
WHEN I'M WORKING, I GO BY THE NAME-- DEATHSTROKE.
I'D HELP YOU, BUT IT DOESN'T LOOK LIKE YOU'VE GOT A CHECKBOOK IN THERE.
MATTHEW BLAND IS "PRESIDENT-FOR-LIFE." HIS TRIBAL NAME IS "JA ZAKI"-- RED LION.
HE LETS ME CRASH HERE WHEN I'M IN THE NEIGHBOR-HOOD.
I'M TOLD YOU REPLACED BATS AS LEADER OF THE BRADY BUNCH.
NO OFFENSE, VIC, BUT YOU KIND OF SUCK AT IT.
YOU PEOPLE PLOP DOWN HERE IN AFRO DISNEY, DEFENDING THE HAPLESS REFUGEES. WELL...
...WHO DO YOU THINK SENT THOSE REFUGEES TO YOU?
MATTHEW BRIBED THE REBEL CHIEFTAINS TO PUSH THE REFUGEES TO YOUR CRASH SITE, KNOW-ING YOU'D DEFEND THEM.
BOOM. INSTANT CRISIS.
AND NOW IT'S ALL OVER SOCIAL MEDIA--IMAGES OF THE JUSTICE LEAGUE BEATING ON AFRICANS.
NOT THE BEST OPTICS. DON'T YOU GET IT--?
--RED LION DOESN'T GIVE A DAMN ABOUT YOUR CRASH WRECKAGE.
HE WANTS THE CAMERAS--
--CNN, REUTERS, A.P.... US WEEKLY. OPRAH.
HE'S GOT THE WHOLE PLANET LOOKING AT YOUR CIRCUS WHILE HE QUIETLY ANNEXES THE COUNTRY NEXT DOOR--
--IN ORDER TO CLEAR HIS PATH TO THE SEA, WHERE HIS AIR-CRAFT CARRIER IS PARKED.* LET ME ASK YOU--
--WHICH REBEL TRIBE IS THE GOOD GUYS? WHICH ARE IBO? NDAU? HUTU?
*DEATHSTROKE VOL.3: TWILIGHT
WHERE DOES THE JUSTICE LEAGUE EVEN BEGIN TO SORT OUT THIS MESS?
YOU GOT PLAYED, CYBORG. RED LION JUST OWNED YOU.
NEVER WOULDA HAPPENED TO BATS.

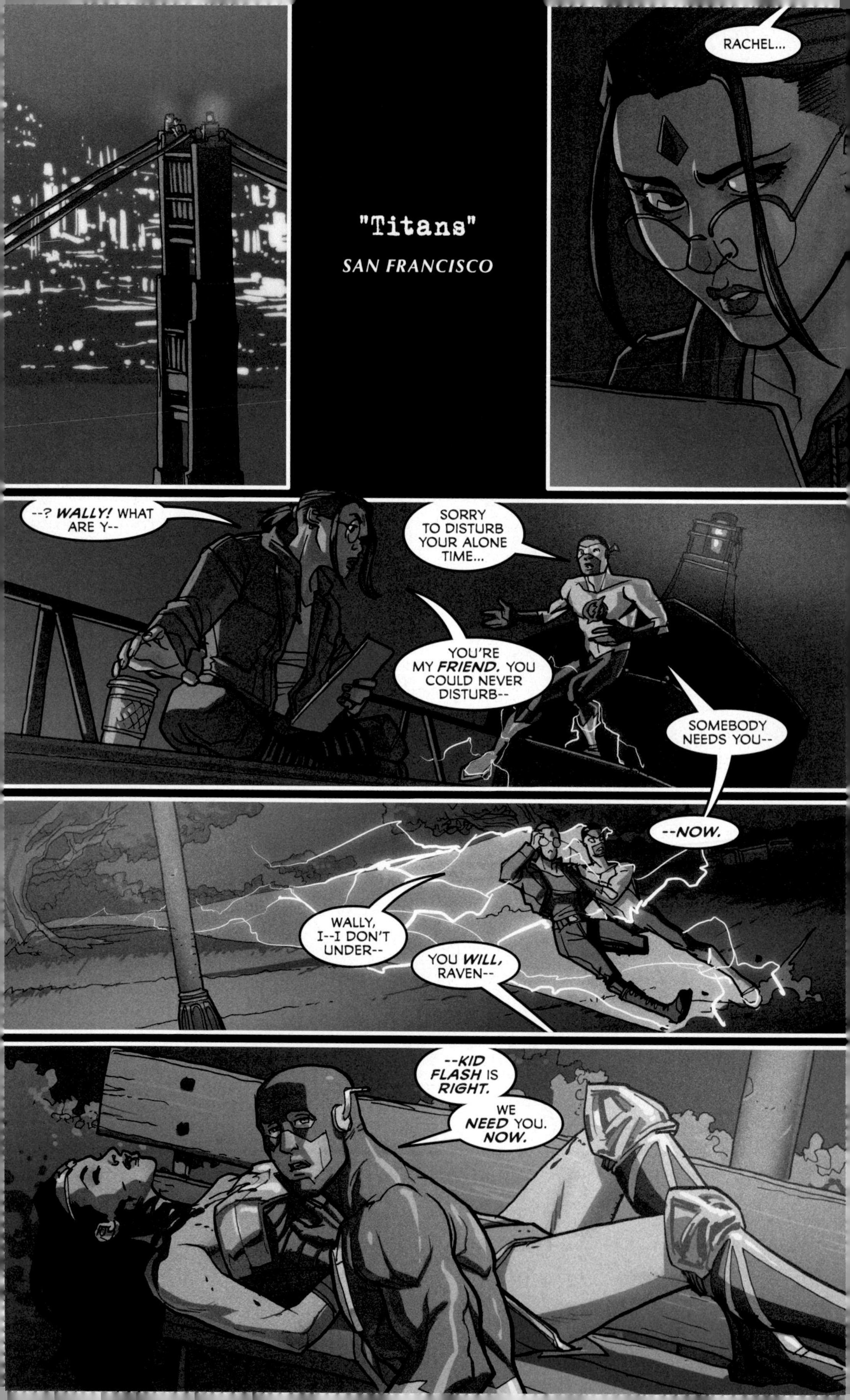
"Titans"
SAN FRANCISCO
RACHEL...
--? WALLY! WHAT ARE Y--
SORRY TO DISTURB YOUR ALONE TIME...
YOU'RE MY FRIEND. YOU COULD NEVER DISTURB--
SOMEBODY NEEDS YOU--
--NOW.
WALLY, I--I DON'T UNDER--
YOU WILL, RAVEN--
--KID FLASH IS RIGHT.
WE NEED YOU. NOW.

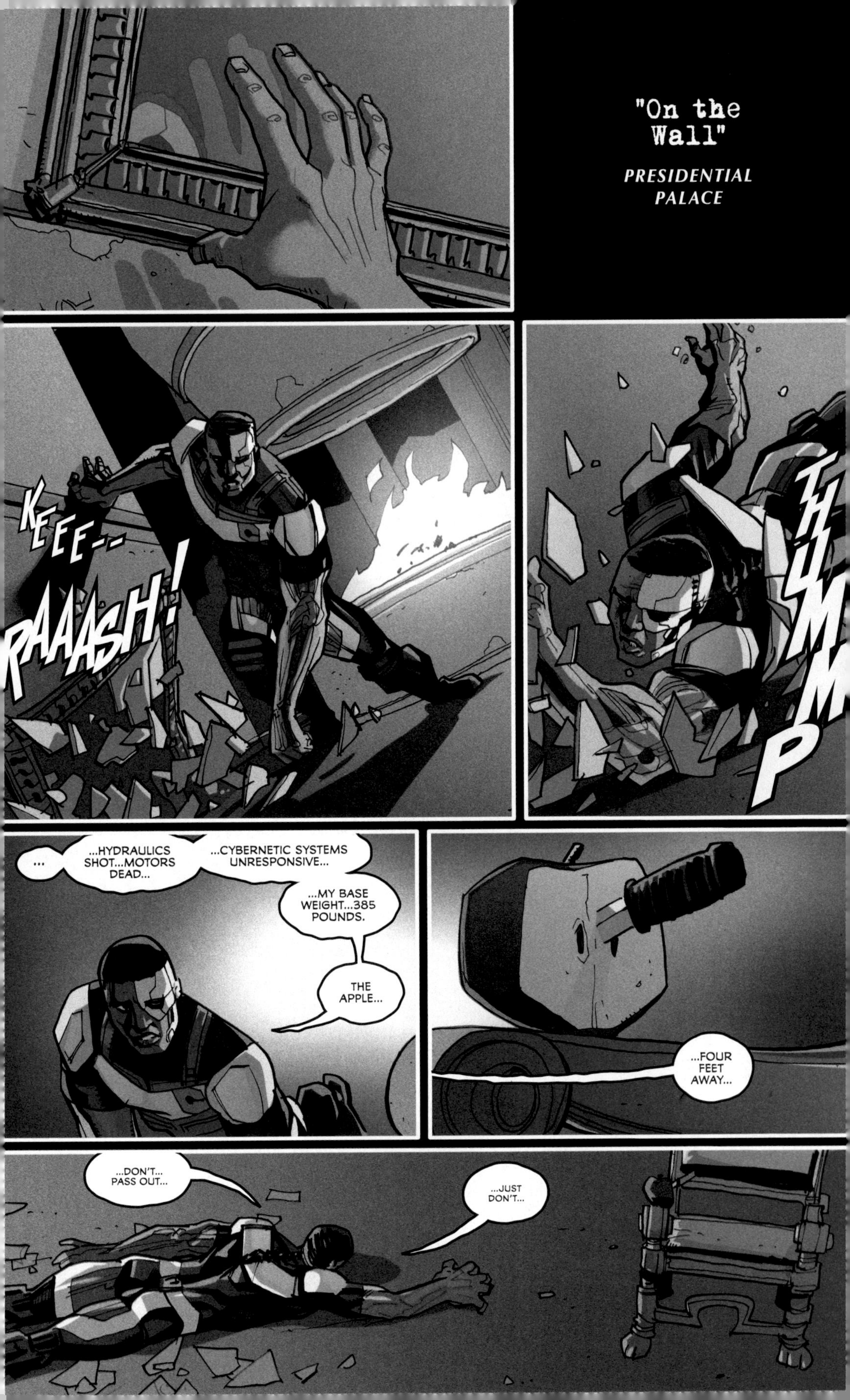
"On the Wall"
PRESIDENTIAL PALACE
KEEE--RAAASH!
THUMMP
...
...HYDRAULICS SHOT...MOTORS DEAD...
...CYBERNETIC SYSTEMS UNRESPONSIVE...
...MY BASE WEIGHT...385 POUNDS.
THE APPLE...
...FOUR FEET AWAY...
...DON'T... PASS OUT...
...JUST DON'T...

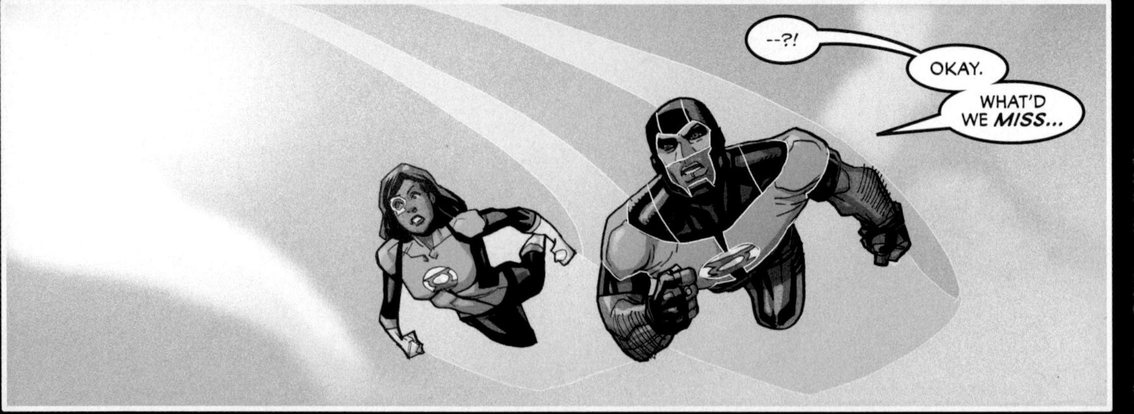
--?!
OKAY.
WHAT'D WE *MISS*...

"Better Never Than Late"

EAST AFRICA

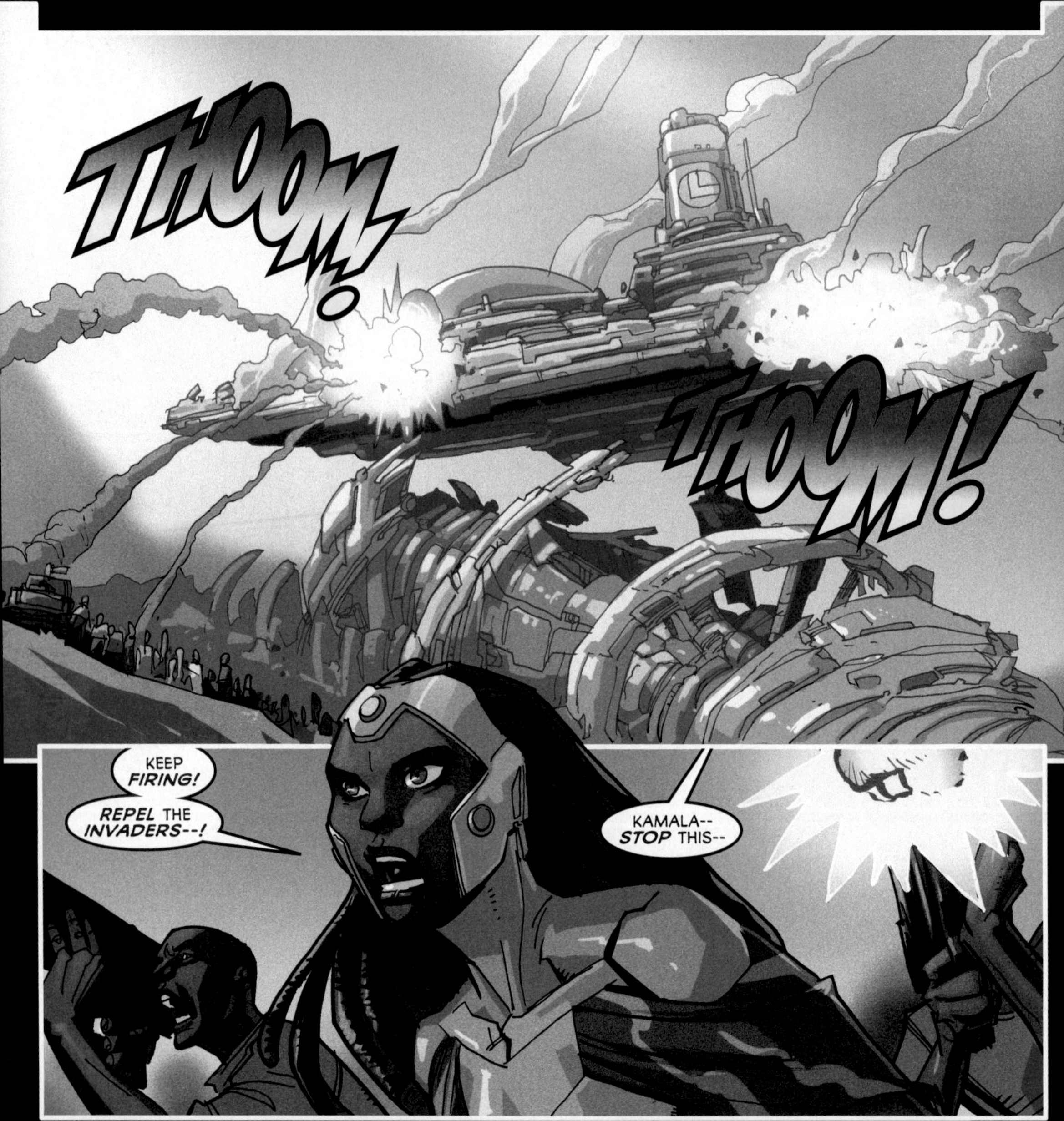
THOOM!
THOOM!
KEEP *FIRING!*
REPEL THE *INVADERS*--!
KAMALA-- *STOP* THIS--

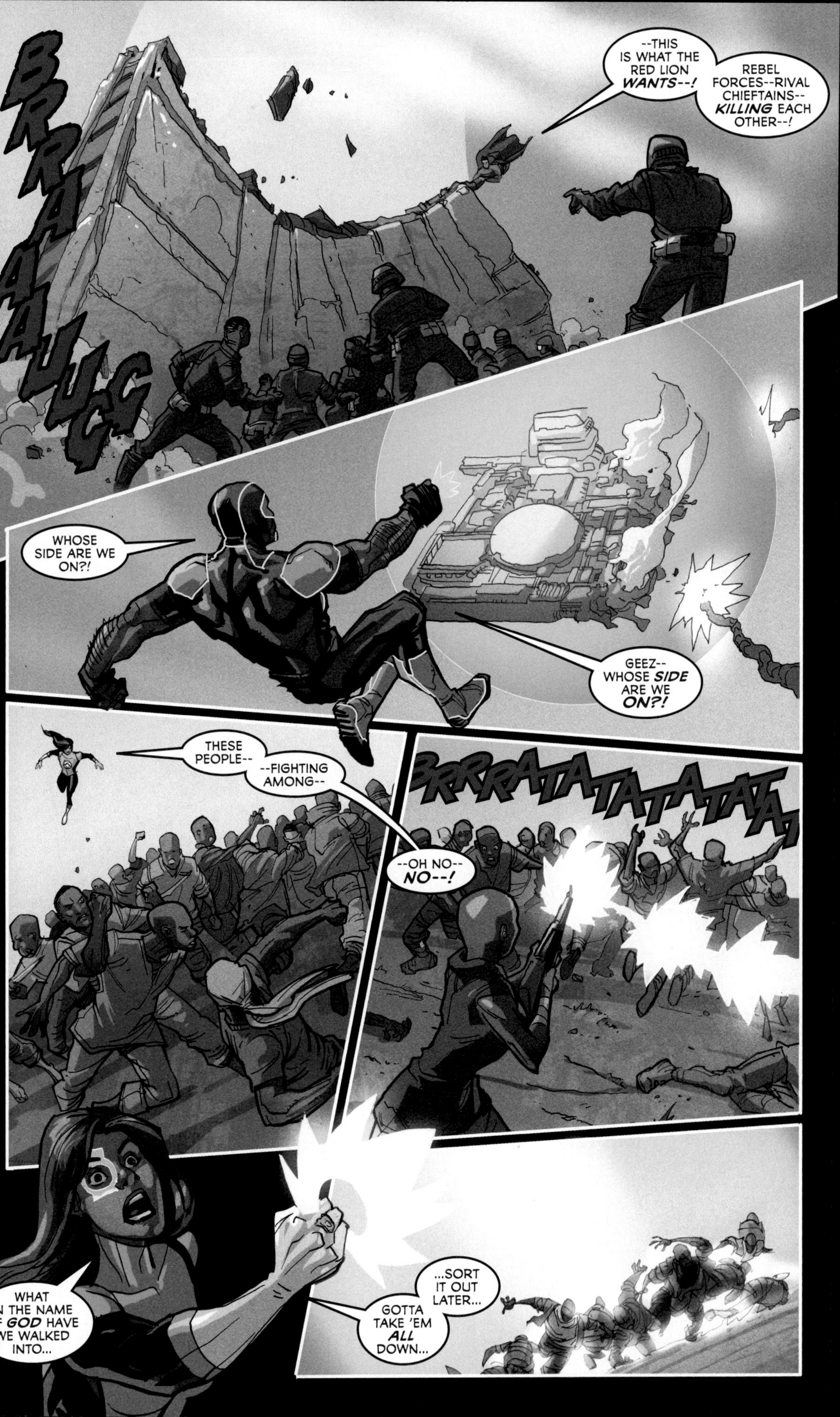
BRRAAAAUUGG
--THIS IS WHAT THE RED LION *WANTS*--!
REBEL FORCES--RIVAL CHIEFTAINS--*KILLING* EACH OTHER--!
WHOSE SIDE ARE WE ON?!
GEEZ-- WHOSE *SIDE* ARE WE *ON?!*
THESE PEOPLE--
--FIGHTING AMONG--
--OH NO-- *NO*--!
BRRRATATATATATATAT
WHAT IN THE NAME OF *GOD* HAVE WE WALKED INTO...
...SORT IT OUT LATER...
GOTTA TAKE 'EM *ALL* DOWN...

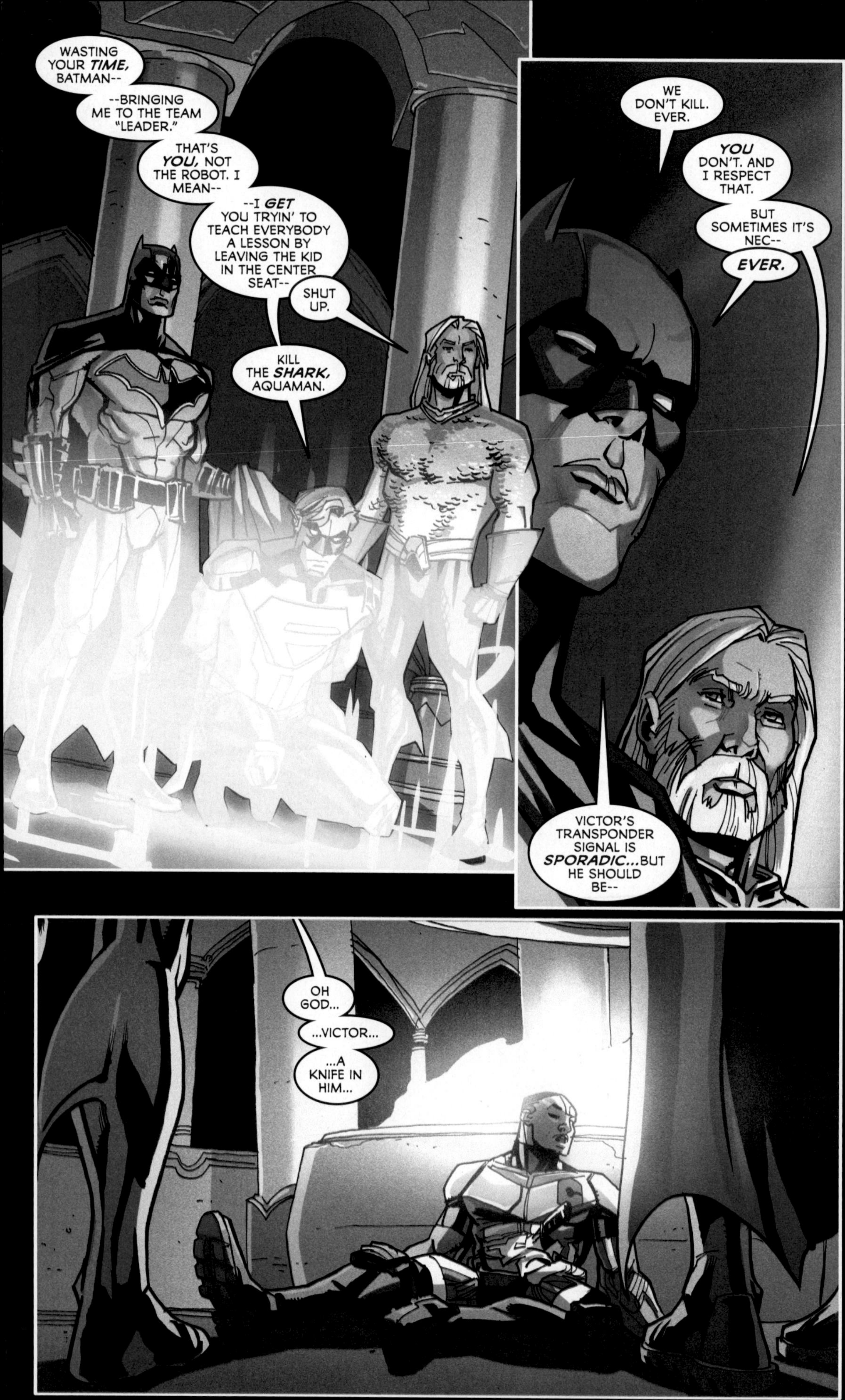

WASTING YOUR *TIME,* BATMAN--
--BRINGING ME TO THE TEAM "LEADER."
THAT'S *YOU,* NOT THE ROBOT. I MEAN--
--I *GET* YOU TRYIN' TO TEACH EVERYBODY A LESSON BY LEAVING THE KID IN THE CENTER SEAT--
SHUT UP.
KILL THE *SHARK,* AQUAMAN.
WE DON'T KILL. EVER.
YOU DON'T. AND I RESPECT THAT.
BUT SOMETIMES IT'S NEC--
EVER.
VICTOR'S TRANSPONDER SIGNAL IS *SPORADIC...*BUT HE SHOULD BE--
OH GOD...
...VICTOR...
...A KNIFE IN HIM...

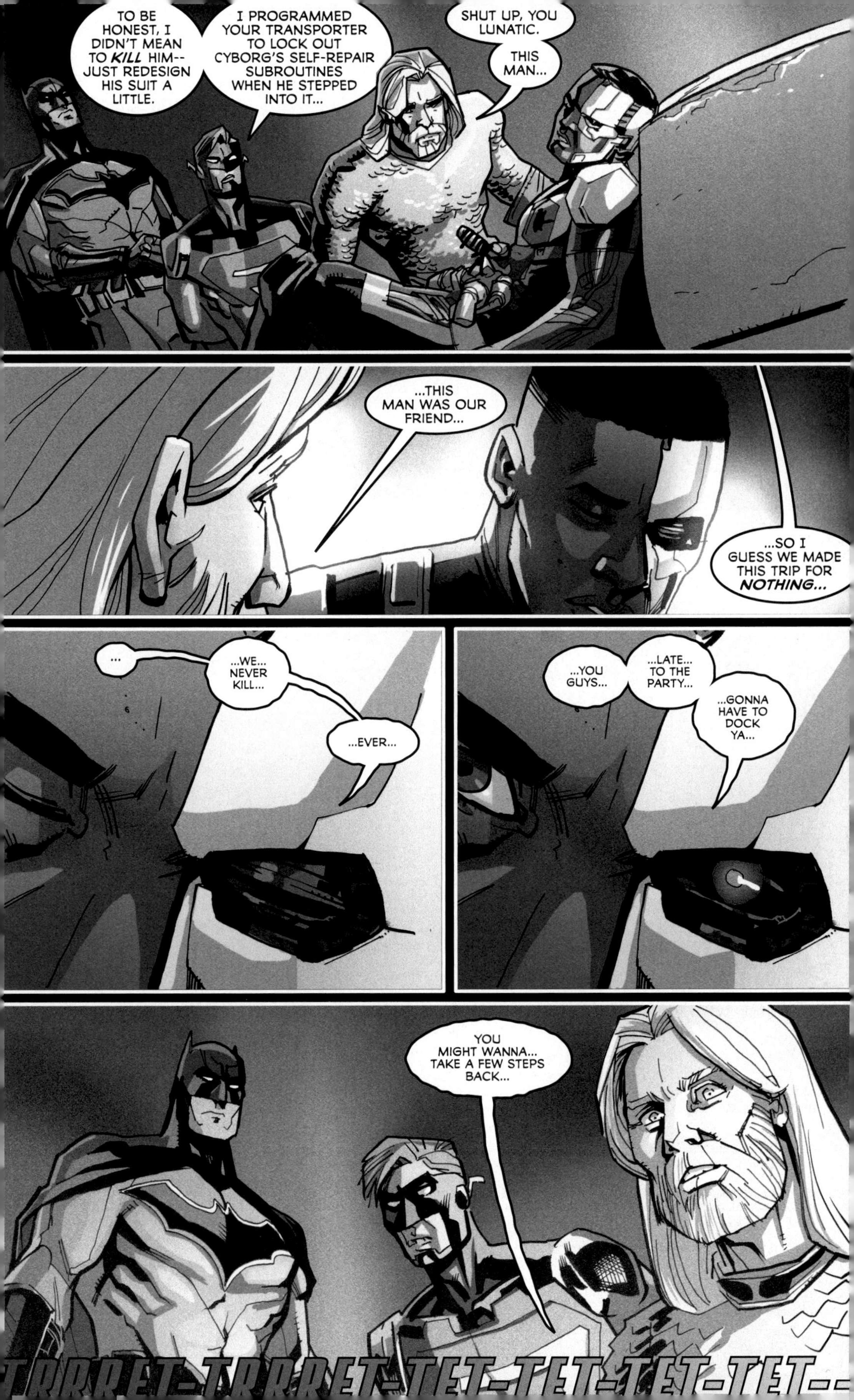

TO BE HONEST, I DIDN'T MEAN TO *KILL* HIM-- JUST REDESIGN HIS SUIT A LITTLE.
I PROGRAMMED YOUR TRANSPORTER TO LOCK OUT CYBORG'S SELF-REPAIR SUBROUTINES WHEN HE STEPPED INTO IT...
SHUT UP, YOU LUNATIC.
THIS MAN...
...THIS MAN WAS OUR FRIEND...
...SO I GUESS WE MADE THIS TRIP FOR *NOTHING...*
...
...WE... NEVER KILL...
...EVER...
...YOU GUYS...
...LATE... TO THE PARTY...
...GONNA HAVE TO DOCK YA...
YOU MIGHT WANNA... TAKE A FEW STEPS BACK...
TRRRET-TRRRET-TET-TET-TET-TET--

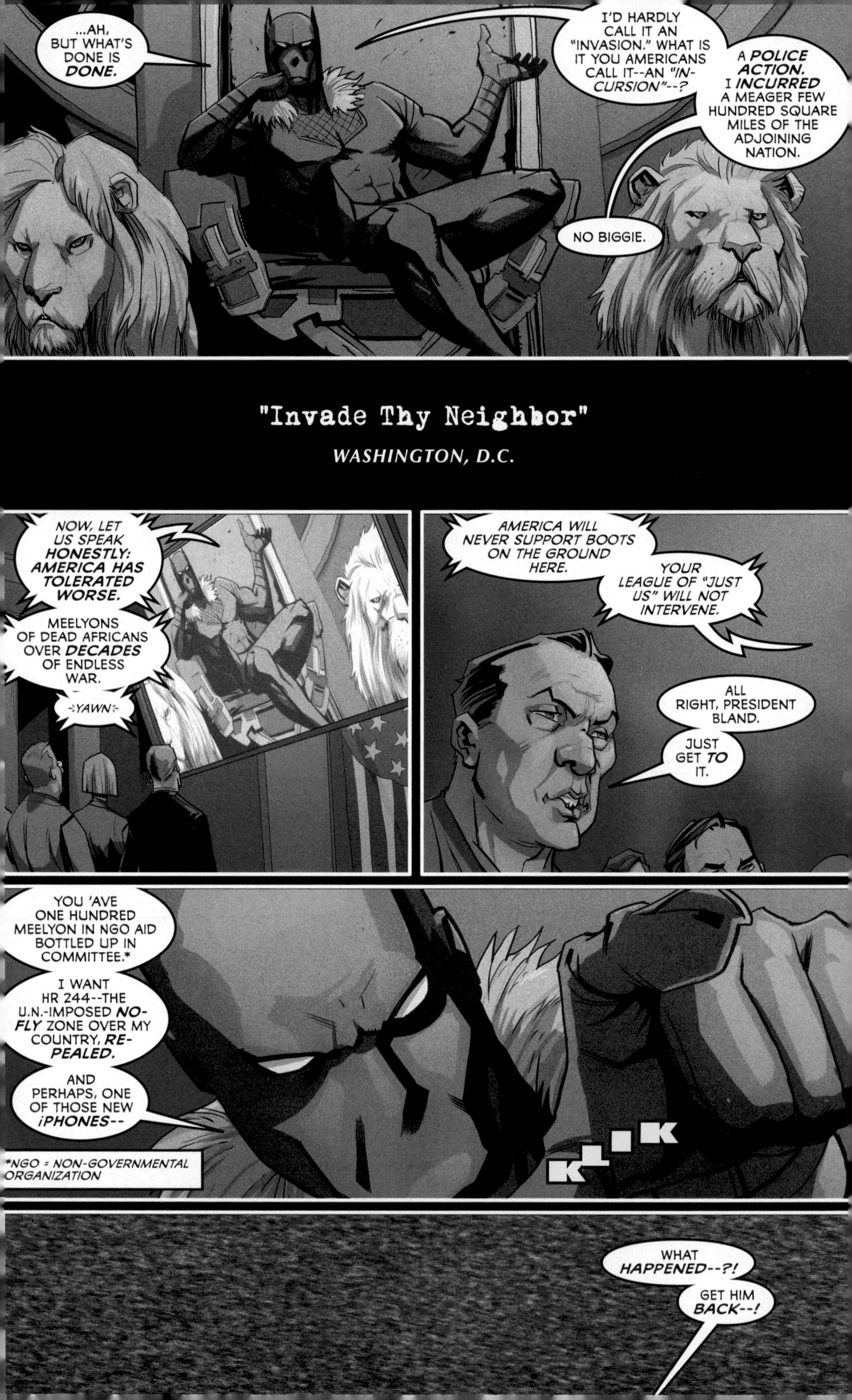
...AH, BUT WHAT'S DONE IS DONE.
I'D HARDLY CALL IT AN "INVASION." WHAT IS IT YOU AMERICANS CALL IT--AN "INCURSION"--?
A POLICE ACTION. I INCURRED A MEAGER FEW HUNDRED SQUARE MILES OF THE ADJOINING NATION.
NO BIGGIE.
"Invade Thy Neighbor"
WASHINGTON, D.C.
NOW, LET US SPEAK HONESTLY: AMERICA HAS TOLERATED WORSE.
MEELYONS OF DEAD AFRICANS OVER DECADES OF ENDLESS WAR.
YAWN
AMERICA WILL NEVER SUPPORT BOOTS ON THE GROUND HERE.
YOUR LEAGUE OF "JUST US" WILL NOT INTERVENE.
ALL RIGHT, PRESIDENT BLAND.
JUST GET TO IT.
YOU 'AVE ONE HUNDRED MEELYON IN NGO AID BOTTLED UP IN COMMITTEE.*
I WANT HR 244--THE U.N.-IMPOSED NO-FLY ZONE OVER MY COUNTRY, REPEALED.
AND PERHAPS, ONE OF THOSE NEW iPHONES--
*NGO = NON-GOVERNMENTAL ORGANIZATION
KLIK
WHAT HAPPENED--?!
GET HIM BACK--!

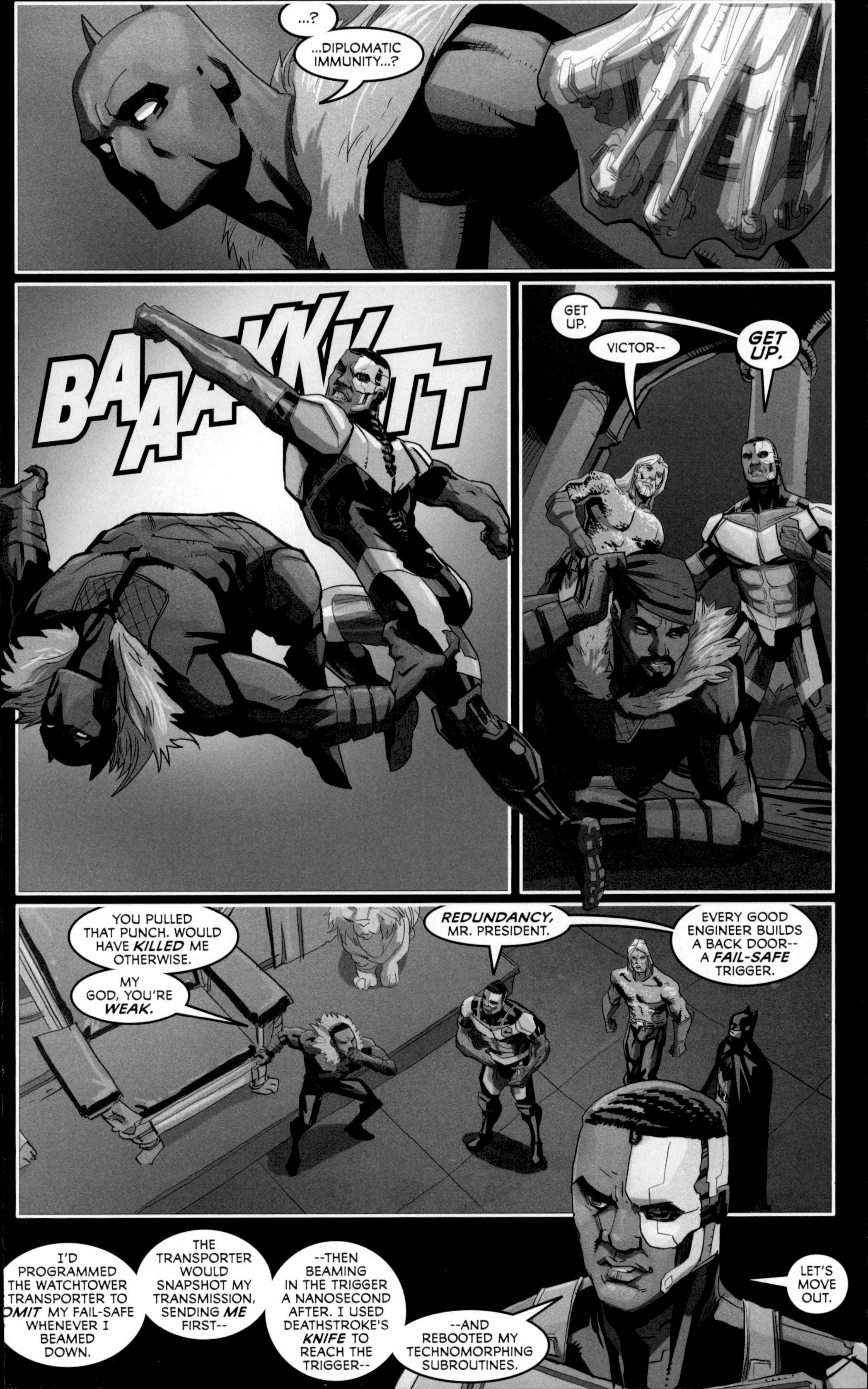
...?
...DIPLOMATIC IMMUNITY...?
BAAAKKKTT
GET UP.
VICTOR--
GET UP.
YOU PULLED THAT PUNCH. WOULD HAVE KILLED ME OTHERWISE.
MY GOD, YOU'RE WEAK.
REDUNDANCY, MR. PRESIDENT.
EVERY GOOD ENGINEER BUILDS A BACK DOOR-- A FAIL-SAFE TRIGGER.
I'D PROGRAMMED THE WATCHTOWER TRANSPORTER TO OMIT MY FAIL-SAFE WHENEVER I BEAMED DOWN.
THE TRANSPORTER WOULD SNAPSHOT MY TRANSMISSION, SENDING ME FIRST--
--THEN BEAMING IN THE TRIGGER A NANOSECOND AFTER. I USED DEATHSTROKE'S KNIFE TO REACH THE TRIGGER--
--AND REBOOTED MY TECHNOMORPHING SUBROUTINES.
LET'S MOVE OUT.

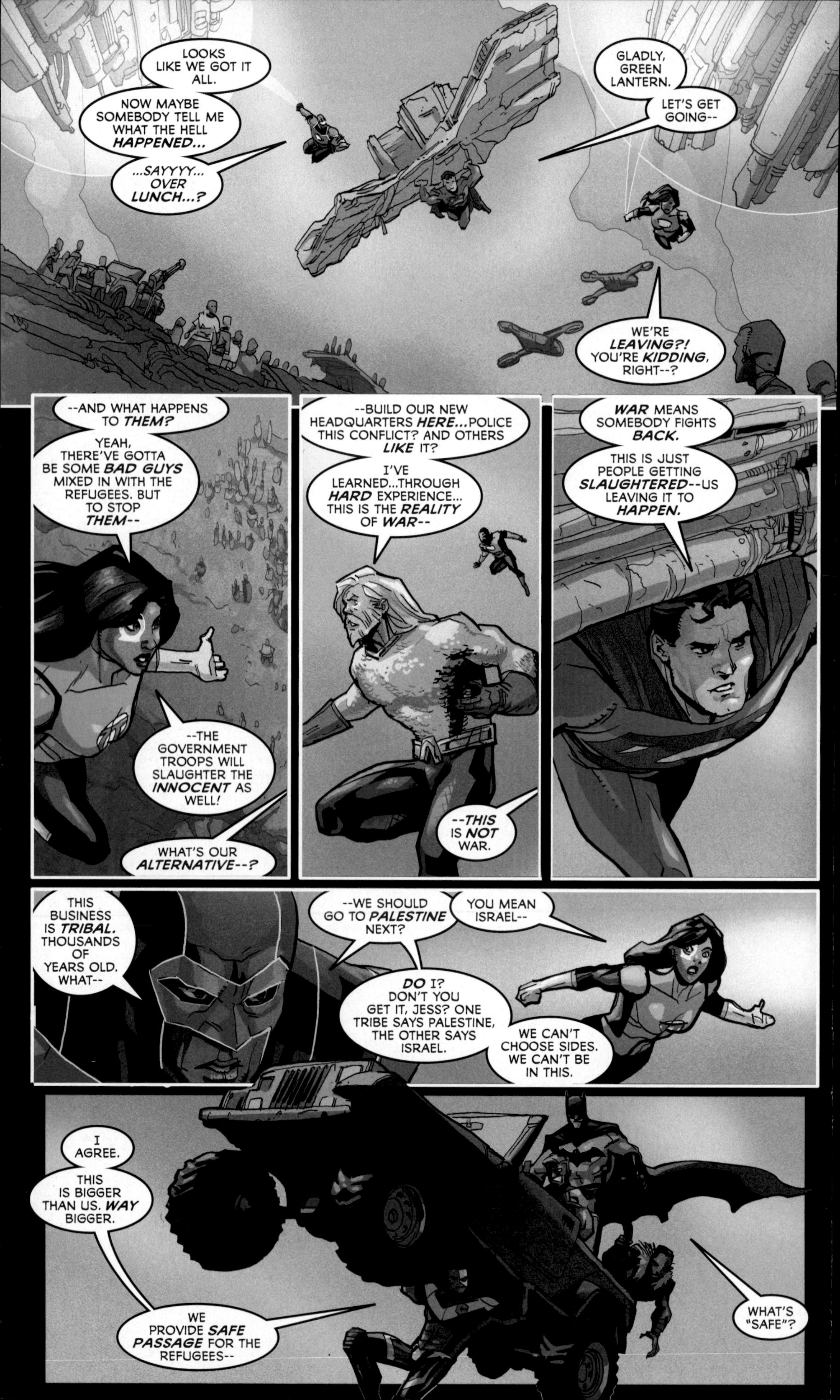

LOOKS LIKE WE GOT IT ALL.
NOW MAYBE SOMEBODY TELL ME WHAT THE HELL *HAPPENED...*
...SAYYYY... OVER LUNCH...?
GLADLY, GREEN LANTERN.
LET'S GET GOING--
WE'RE *LEAVING?!* YOU'RE *KIDDING*, RIGHT--?
--AND WHAT HAPPENS TO *THEM?*
YEAH, THERE'VE GOTTA BE SOME *BAD GUYS* MIXED IN WITH THE REFUGEES. BUT TO STOP *THEM--*
--THE GOVERNMENT TROOPS WILL SLAUGHTER THE *INNOCENT* AS WELL!
WHAT'S OUR *ALTERNATIVE--?*
--BUILD OUR NEW HEADQUARTERS *HERE...*POLICE THIS CONFLICT? AND OTHERS *LIKE* IT?
I'VE LEARNED...THROUGH *HARD* EXPERIENCE... THIS IS THE *REALITY* OF *WAR--*
--THIS IS *NOT* WAR.
WAR MEANS SOMEBODY FIGHTS *BACK.*
THIS IS JUST PEOPLE GETTING *SLAUGHTERED*--US LEAVING IT TO *HAPPEN.*
THIS BUSINESS IS *TRIBAL.* THOUSANDS OF YEARS OLD. WHAT--
--WE SHOULD GO TO *PALESTINE* NEXT?
YOU MEAN ISRAEL--
DO I? DON'T YOU GET IT, JESS? ONE TRIBE SAYS PALESTINE, THE OTHER SAYS ISRAEL.
WE CAN'T CHOOSE SIDES. WE CAN'T BE IN THIS.
I AGREE.
THIS IS BIGGER THAN US. *WAY* BIGGER.
WE PROVIDE *SAFE PASSAGE* FOR THE REFUGEES--
WHAT'S "SAFE"?

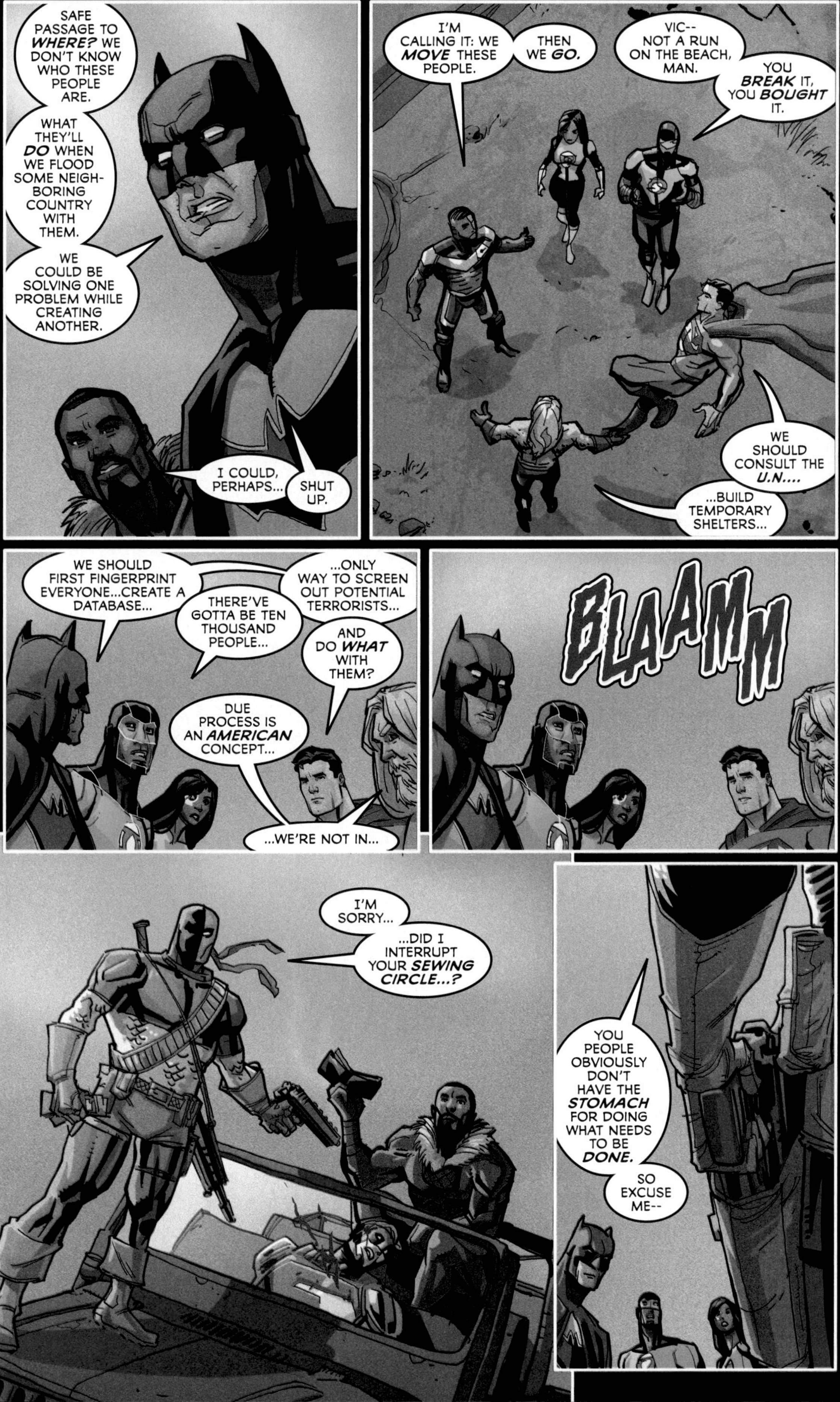

SAFE PASSAGE TO WHERE? WE DON'T KNOW WHO THESE PEOPLE ARE.
WHAT THEY'LL DO WHEN WE FLOOD SOME NEIGHBORING COUNTRY WITH THEM.
WE COULD BE SOLVING ONE PROBLEM WHILE CREATING ANOTHER.
I COULD, PERHAPS...
SHUT UP.
I'M CALLING IT: WE MOVE THESE PEOPLE.
THEN WE GO.
VIC-- NOT A RUN ON THE BEACH, MAN.
YOU BREAK IT, YOU BOUGHT IT.
WE SHOULD CONSULT THE U.N....
...BUILD TEMPORARY SHELTERS...
WE SHOULD FIRST FINGERPRINT EVERYONE...CREATE A DATABASE...
THERE'VE GOTTA BE TEN THOUSAND PEOPLE...
...ONLY WAY TO SCREEN OUT POTENTIAL TERRORISTS...
AND DO WHAT WITH THEM?
DUE PROCESS IS AN AMERICAN CONCEPT...
...WE'RE NOT IN...
BLAAMM
I'M SORRY...
...DID I INTERRUPT YOUR SEWING CIRCLE...?
YOU PEOPLE OBVIOUSLY DON'T HAVE THE STOMACH FOR DOING WHAT NEEDS TO BE DONE.
SO EXCUSE ME--

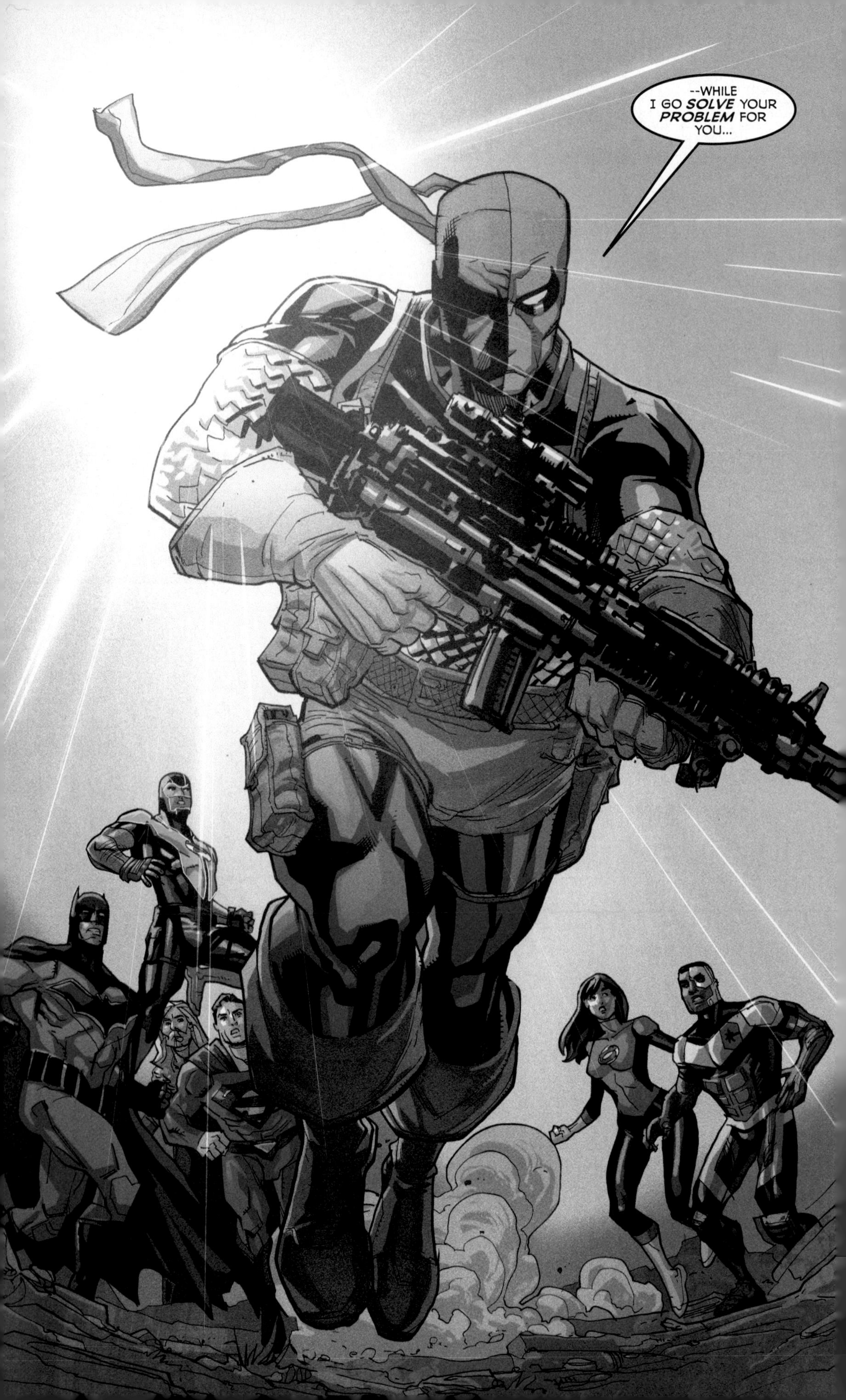
--WHILE I GO SOLVE YOUR PROBLEM FOR YOU...

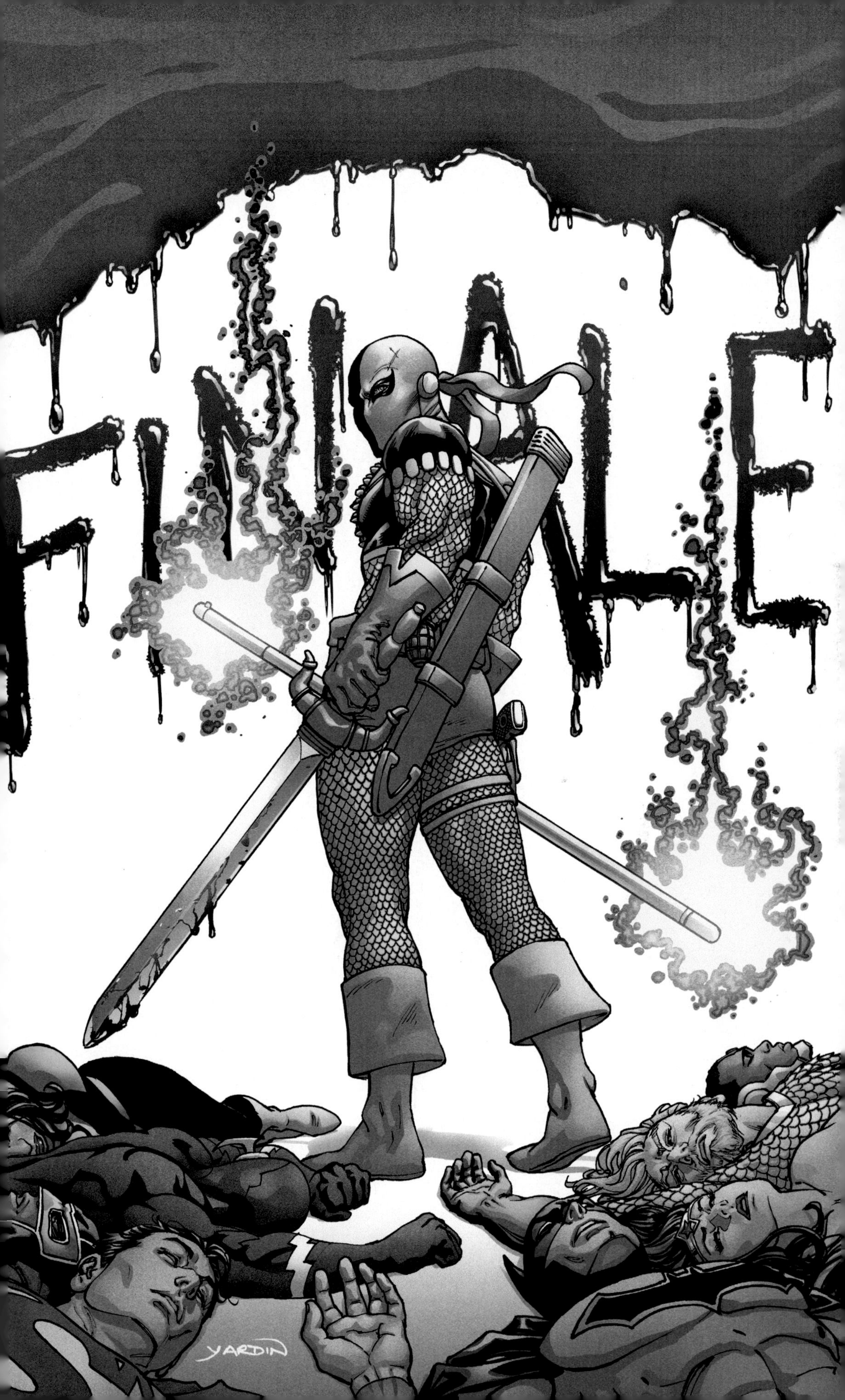
FINALE
YARDIN

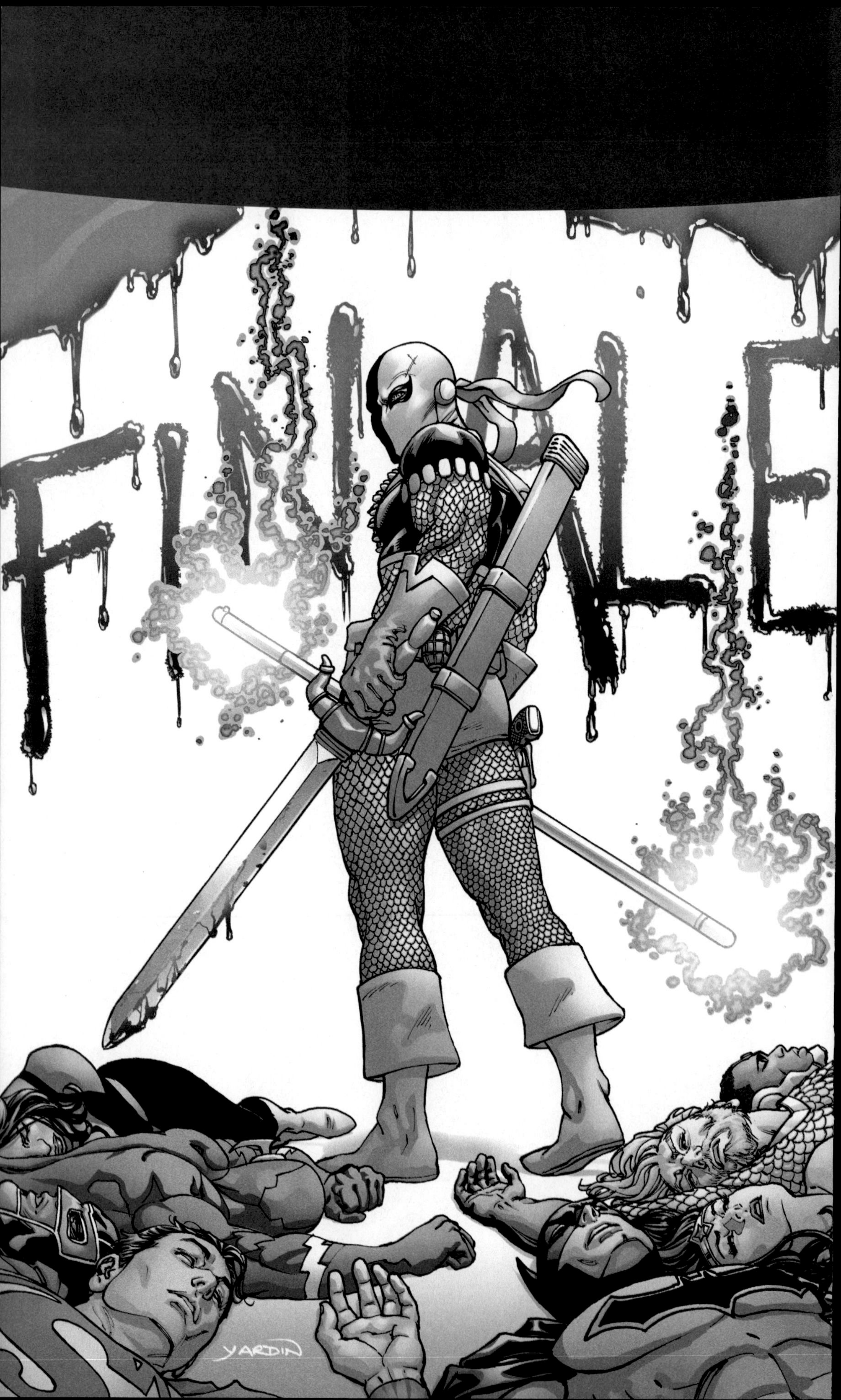
FINALE
YARDIN

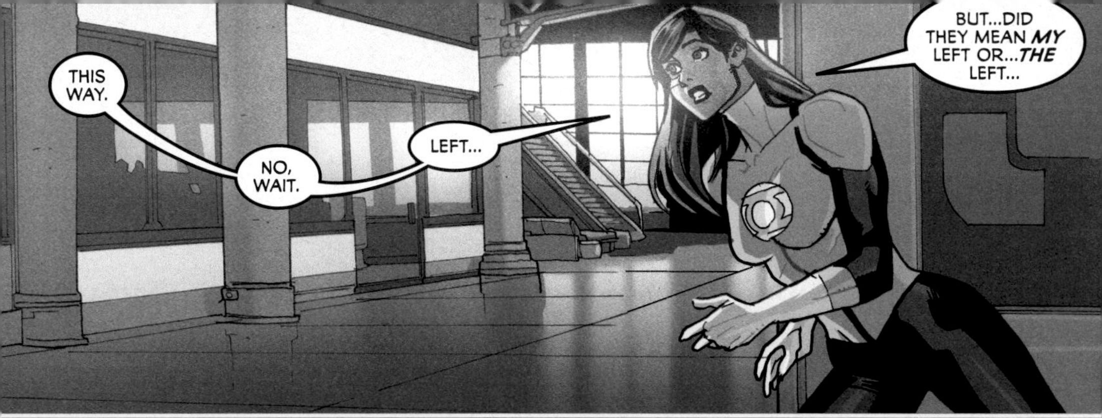
THIS WAY.
NO, WAIT.
LEFT...
BUT...DID THEY MEAN *MY* LEFT OR...*THE* LEFT...

"Leftist"

JLA RESEARCH CENTER, RHODE ISLAND

NOW

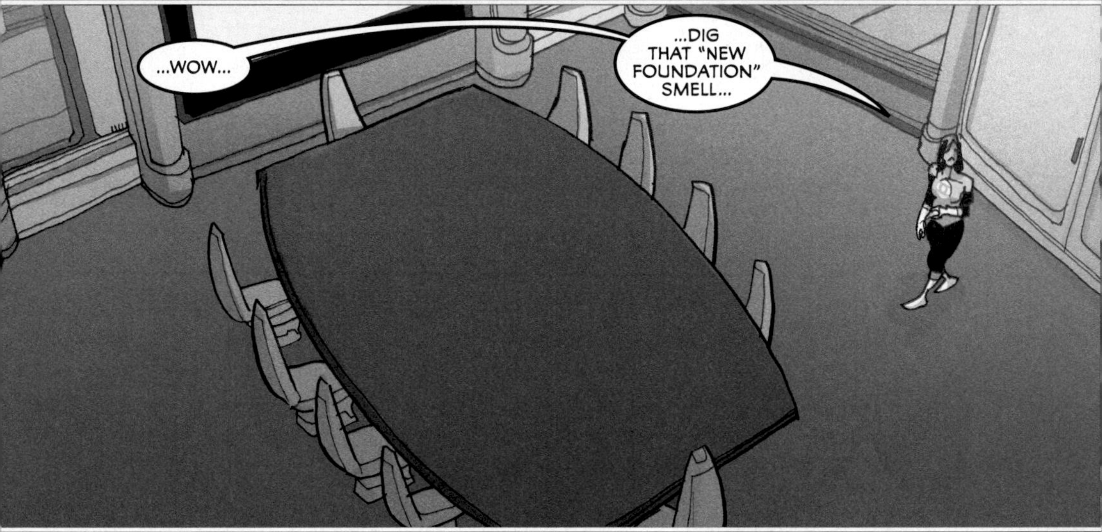
...WOW...
...DIG THAT "NEW FOUNDATION" SMELL...

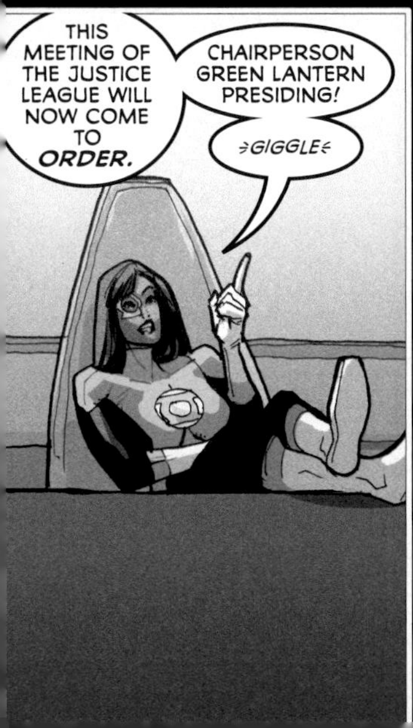
THIS MEETING OF THE JUSTICE LEAGUE WILL NOW COME TO *ORDER.*
CHAIRPERSON GREEN LANTERN PRESIDING!
GIGGLE

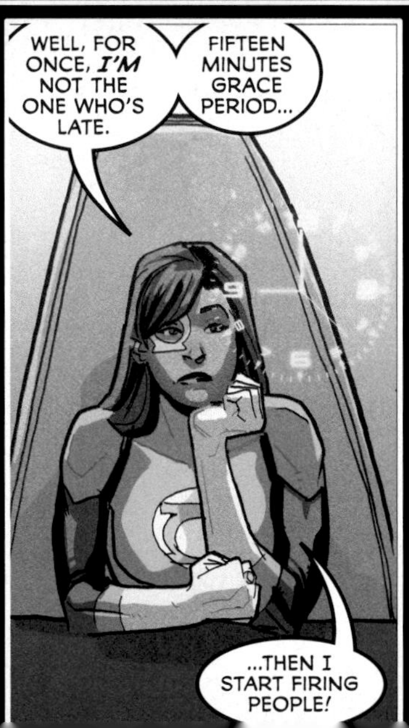
WELL, FOR ONCE, *I'M* NOT THE ONE WHO'S LATE.
FIFTEEN MINUTES GRACE PERIOD...
...THEN I START FIRING PEOPLE!

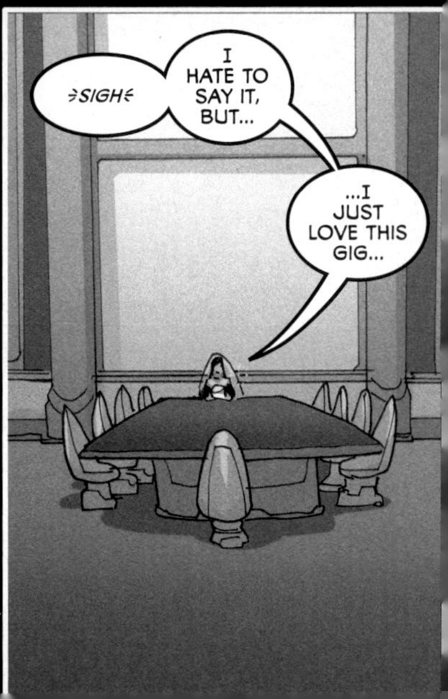
SIGH
I HATE TO SAY IT, BUT...
...I JUST LOVE THIS GIG...

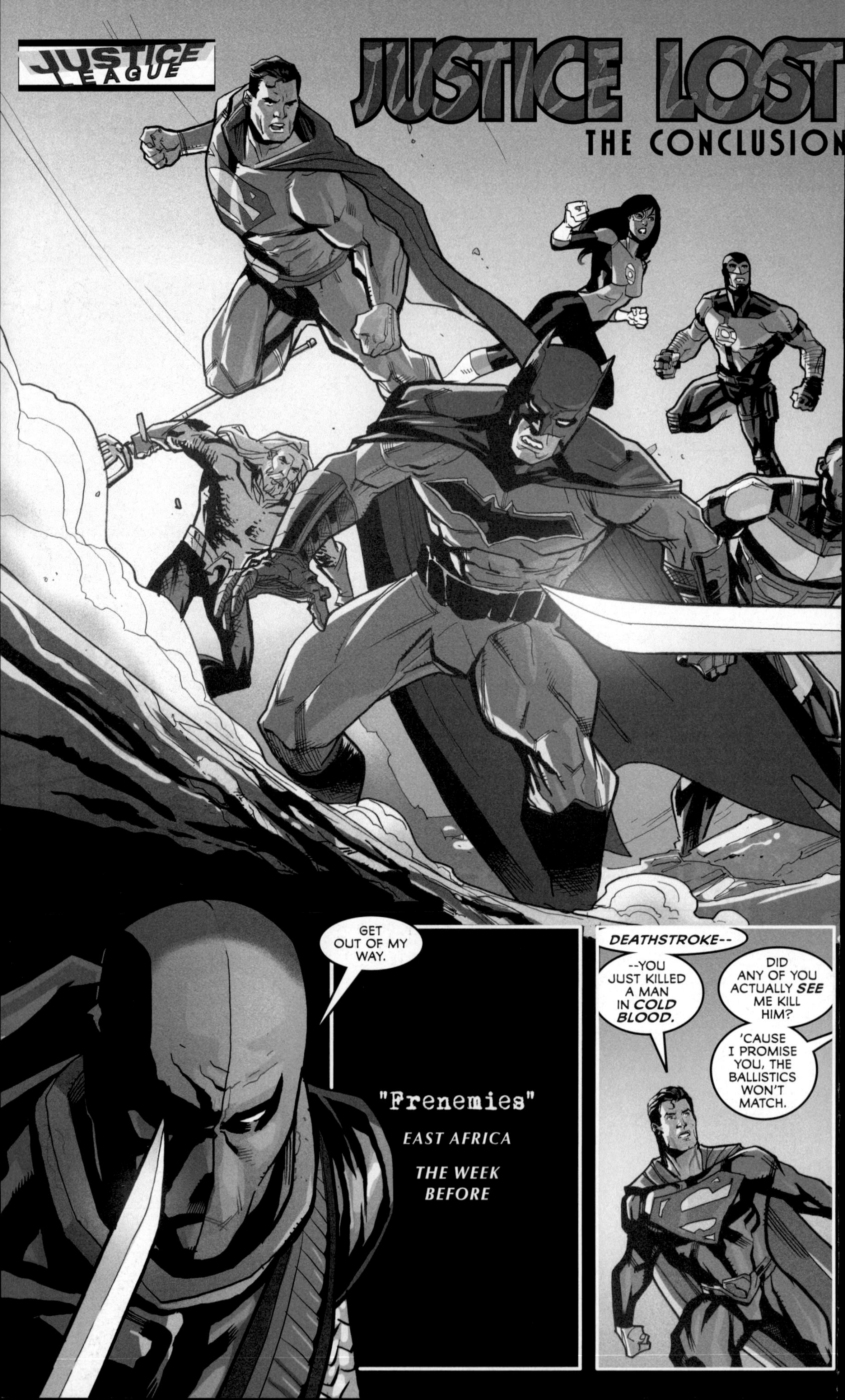

JUSTICE LEAGUE
JUSTICE LOST
THE CONCLUSION
GET OUT OF MY WAY.
"Frenemies"
EAST AFRICA
THE WEEK BEFORE
DEATHSTROKE--
--YOU JUST KILLED A MAN IN COLD BLOOD.
DID ANY OF YOU ACTUALLY SEE ME KILL HIM?
'CAUSE I PROMISE YOU, THE BALLISTICS WON'T MATCH.

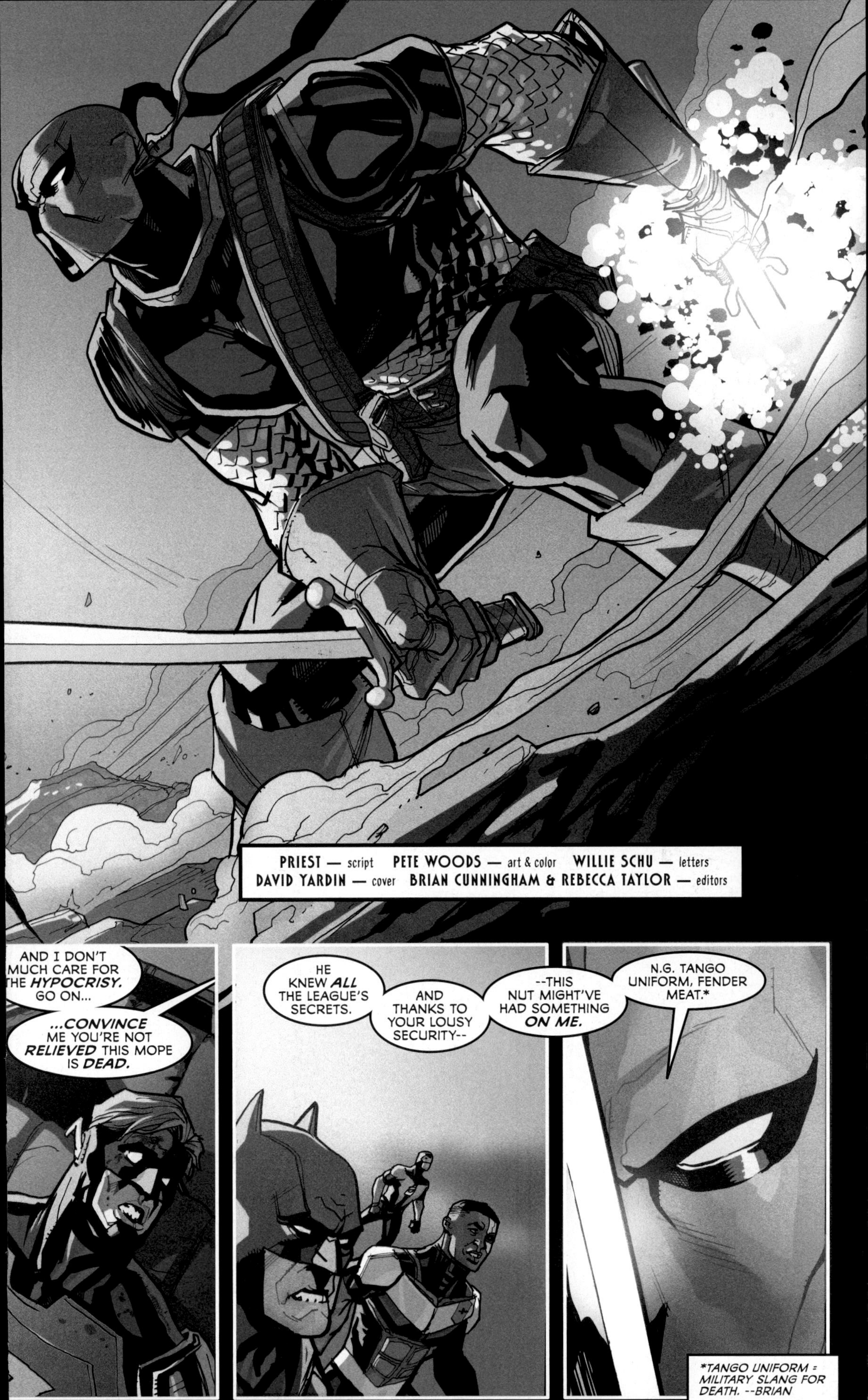

PRIEST — script PETE WOODS — art & color WILLIE SCHU — letters
DAVID YARDIN — cover BRIAN CUNNINGHAM & REBECCA TAYLOR — editors
AND I DON'T MUCH CARE FOR THE HYPOCRISY. GO ON...
...CONVINCE ME YOU'RE NOT RELIEVED THIS MOPE IS DEAD.
HE KNEW ALL THE LEAGUE'S SECRETS.
AND THANKS TO YOUR LOUSY SECURITY--
--THIS NUT MIGHT'VE HAD SOMETHING ON ME.
N.G. TANGO UNIFORM, FENDER MEAT.*
*TANGO UNIFORM = MILITARY SLANG FOR DEATH. --BRIAN

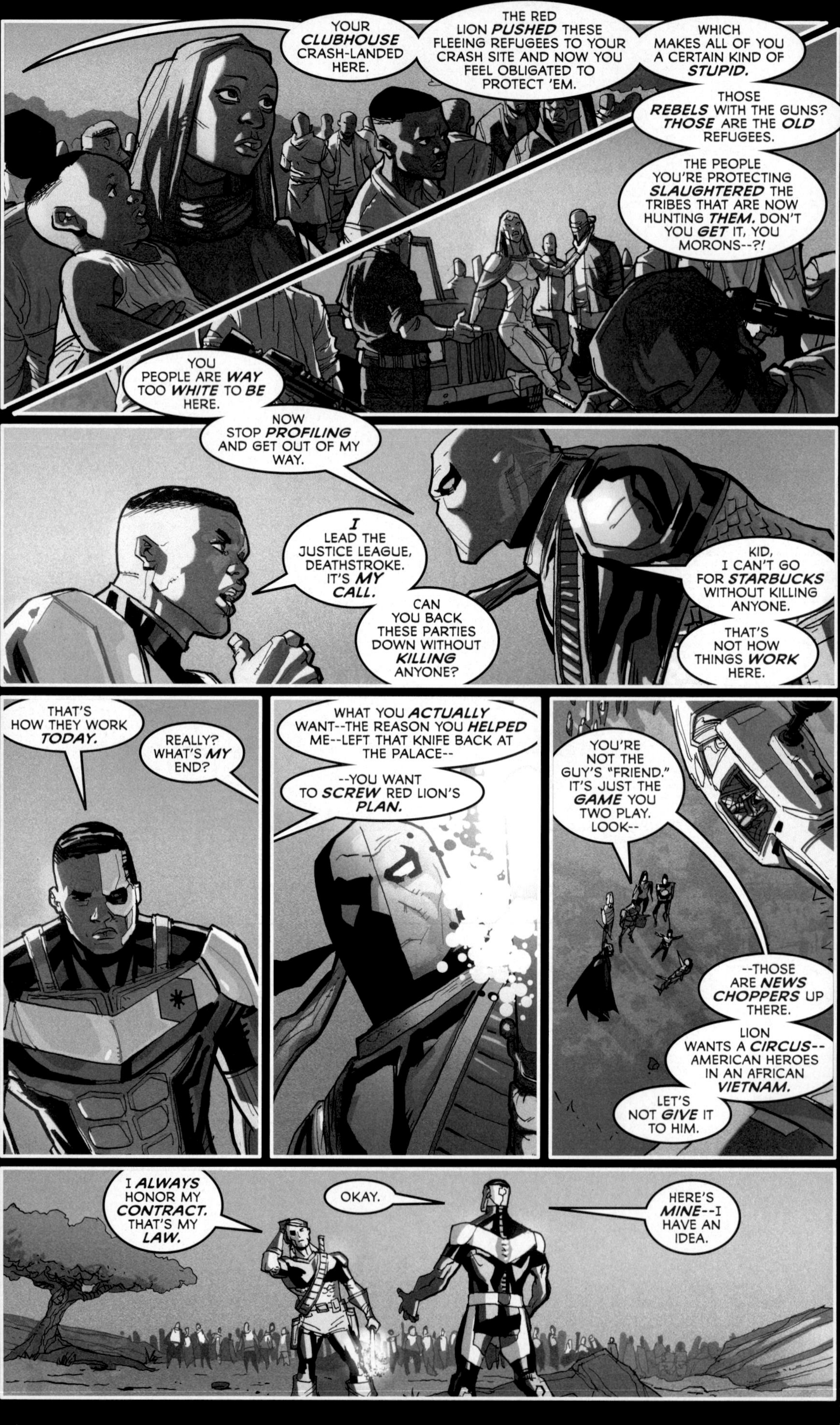
YOUR CLUBHOUSE CRASH-LANDED HERE.
THE RED LION PUSHED THESE FLEEING REFUGEES TO YOUR CRASH SITE AND NOW YOU FEEL OBLIGATED TO PROTECT 'EM.
WHICH MAKES ALL OF YOU A CERTAIN KIND OF STUPID.
THOSE REBELS WITH THE GUNS? THOSE ARE THE OLD REFUGEES.
THE PEOPLE YOU'RE PROTECTING SLAUGHTERED THE TRIBES THAT ARE NOW HUNTING THEM. DON'T YOU GET IT, YOU MORONS--?!
YOU PEOPLE ARE WAY TOO WHITE TO BE HERE.
NOW STOP PROFILING AND GET OUT OF MY WAY.
I LEAD THE JUSTICE LEAGUE, DEATHSTROKE. IT'S MY CALL.
CAN YOU BACK THESE PARTIES DOWN WITHOUT KILLING ANYONE?
KID, I CAN'T GO FOR STARBUCKS WITHOUT KILLING ANYONE.
THAT'S NOT HOW THINGS WORK HERE.
THAT'S HOW THEY WORK TODAY.
REALLY? WHAT'S MY END?
WHAT YOU ACTUALLY WANT--THE REASON YOU HELPED ME--LEFT THAT KNIFE BACK AT THE PALACE--
--YOU WANT TO SCREW RED LION'S PLAN.
YOU'RE NOT THE GUY'S "FRIEND." IT'S JUST THE GAME YOU TWO PLAY. LOOK--
--THOSE ARE NEWS CHOPPERS UP THERE.
LION WANTS A CIRCUS--AMERICAN HEROES IN AN AFRICAN VIETNAM.
LET'S NOT GIVE IT TO HIM.
I ALWAYS HONOR MY CONTRACT. THAT'S MY LAW.
OKAY.
HERE'S MINE--I HAVE AN IDEA.

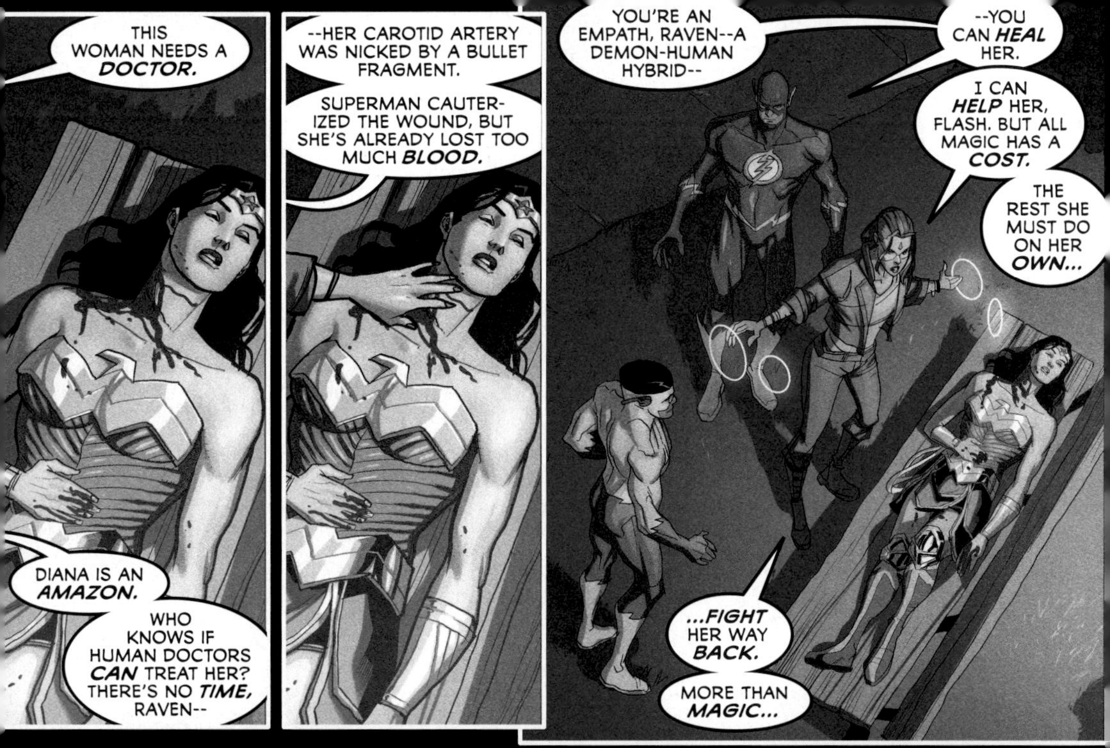
THIS WOMAN NEEDS A DOCTOR.
DIANA IS AN AMAZON.
WHO KNOWS IF HUMAN DOCTORS CAN TREAT HER? THERE'S NO TIME, RAVEN--
--HER CAROTID ARTERY WAS NICKED BY A BULLET FRAGMENT.
SUPERMAN CAUTERIZED THE WOUND, BUT SHE'S ALREADY LOST TOO MUCH BLOOD.
YOU'RE AN EMPATH, RAVEN--A DEMON-HUMAN HYBRID--
--YOU CAN HEAL HER.
I CAN HELP HER, FLASH. BUT ALL MAGIC HAS A COST.
THE REST SHE MUST DO ON HER OWN...
...FIGHT HER WAY BACK.
MORE THAN MAGIC...

"Empathy"

GOLDEN GATE PARK

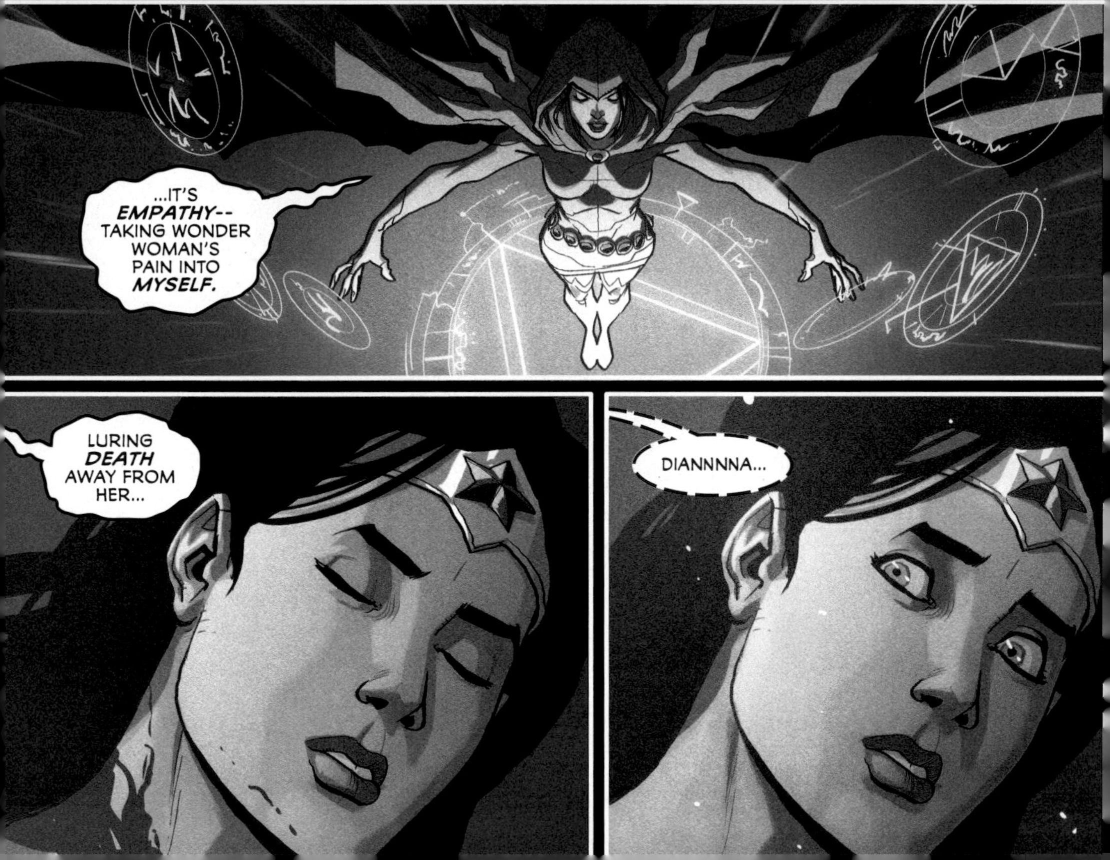
...IT'S EMPATHY--TAKING WONDER WOMAN'S PAIN INTO MYSELF.
LURING DEATH AWAY FROM HER...
DIANNNNA...

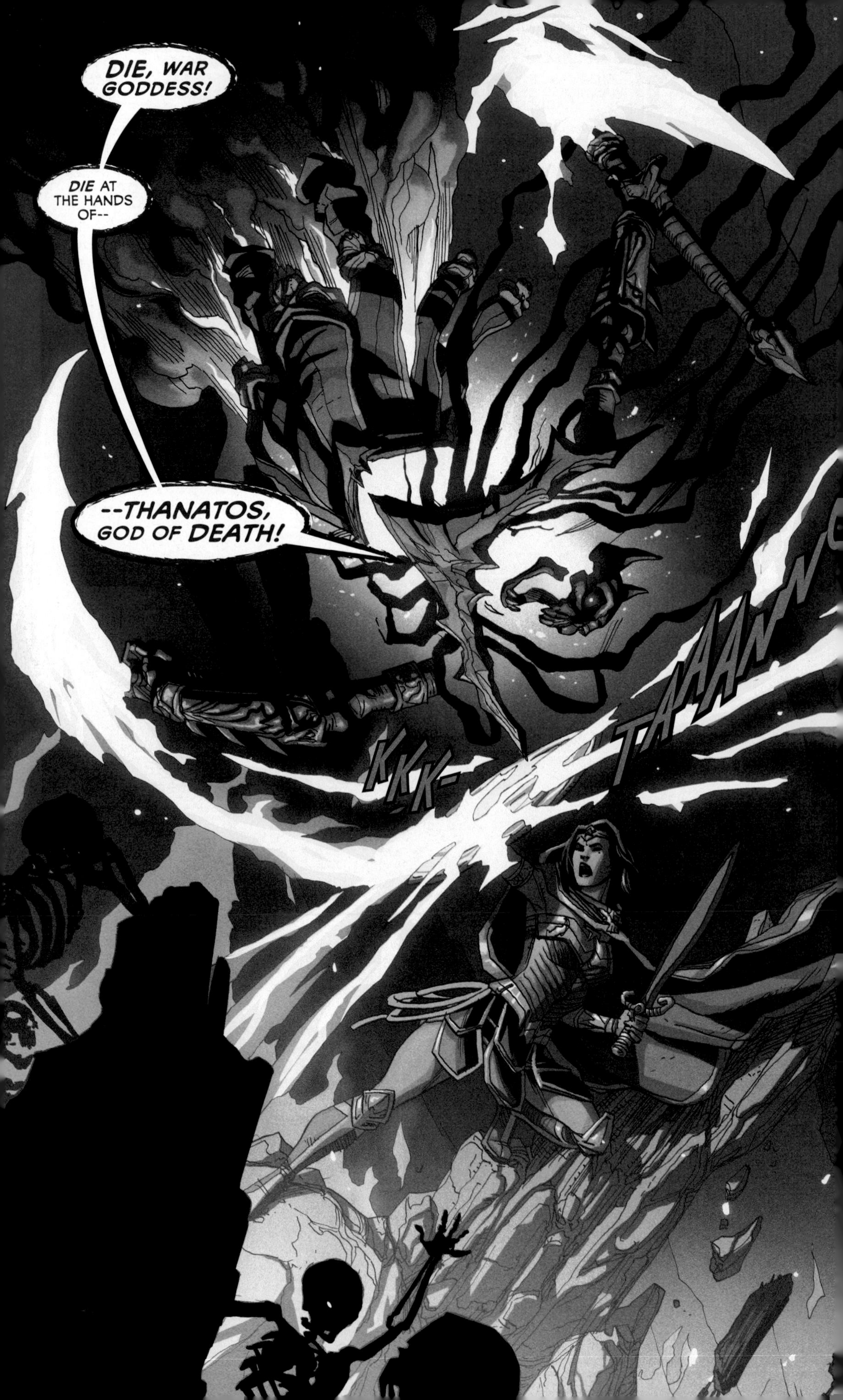

DIE, WAR GODDESS!
DIE AT THE HANDS OF--
--THANATOS, GOD OF DEATH!
KKK-
TAAANNG

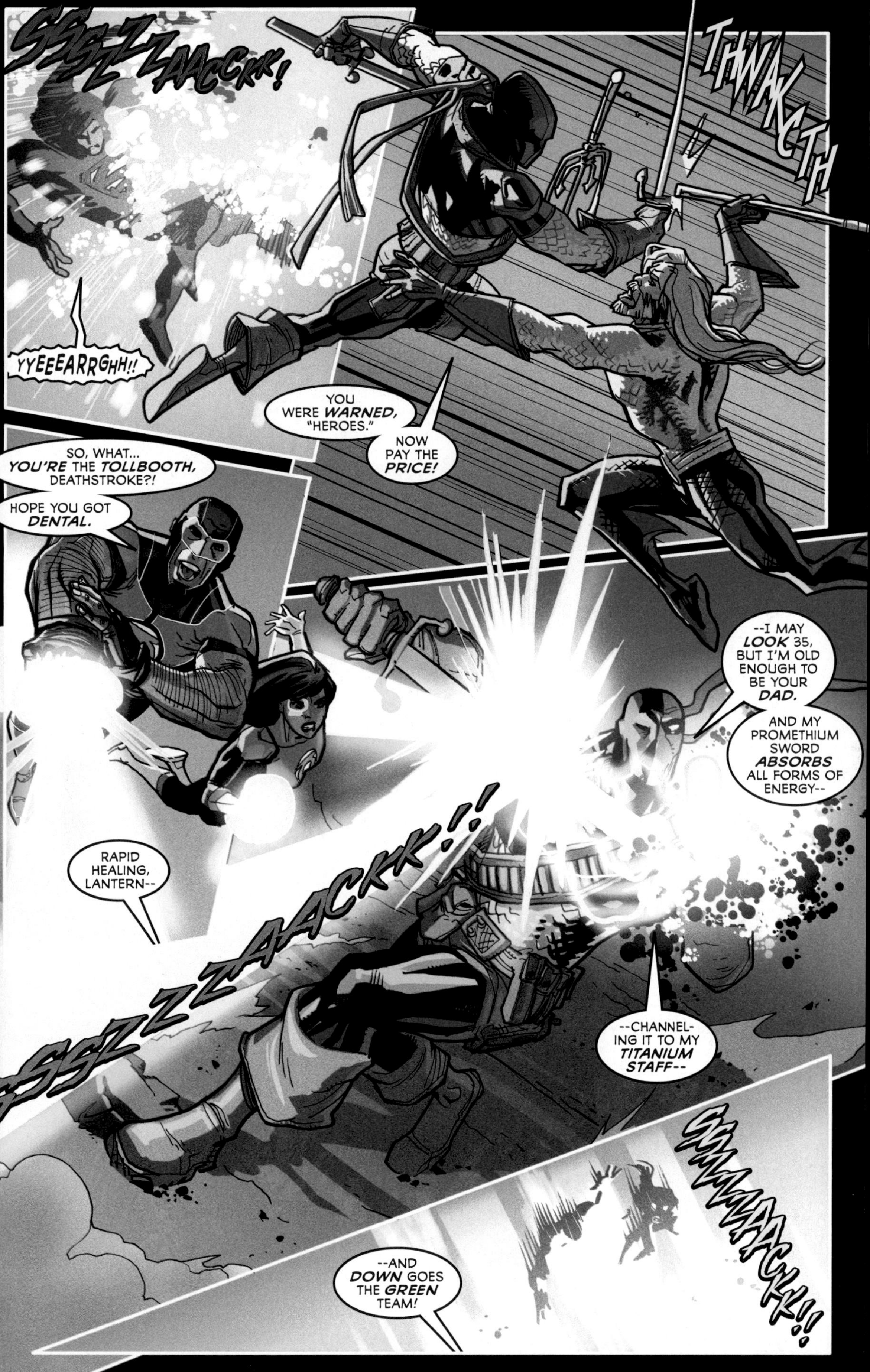

SSSZZZAACCKK!
THWAKCTH
YYEEEARRGHH!!
YOU WERE WARNED, "HEROES."
NOW PAY THE PRICE!
SO, WHAT... YOU'RE THE TOLLBOOTH, DEATHSTROKE?!
HOPE YOU GOT DENTAL.
RAPID HEALING, LANTERN--
--I MAY LOOK 35, BUT I'M OLD ENOUGH TO BE YOUR DAD.
AND MY PROMETHIUM SWORD ABSORBS ALL FORMS OF ENERGY--
SSSZZZZAACKK!!
--CHANNEL-ING IT TO MY TITANIUM STAFF--
SMMAACK!!
--AND DOWN GOES THE GREEN TEAM!

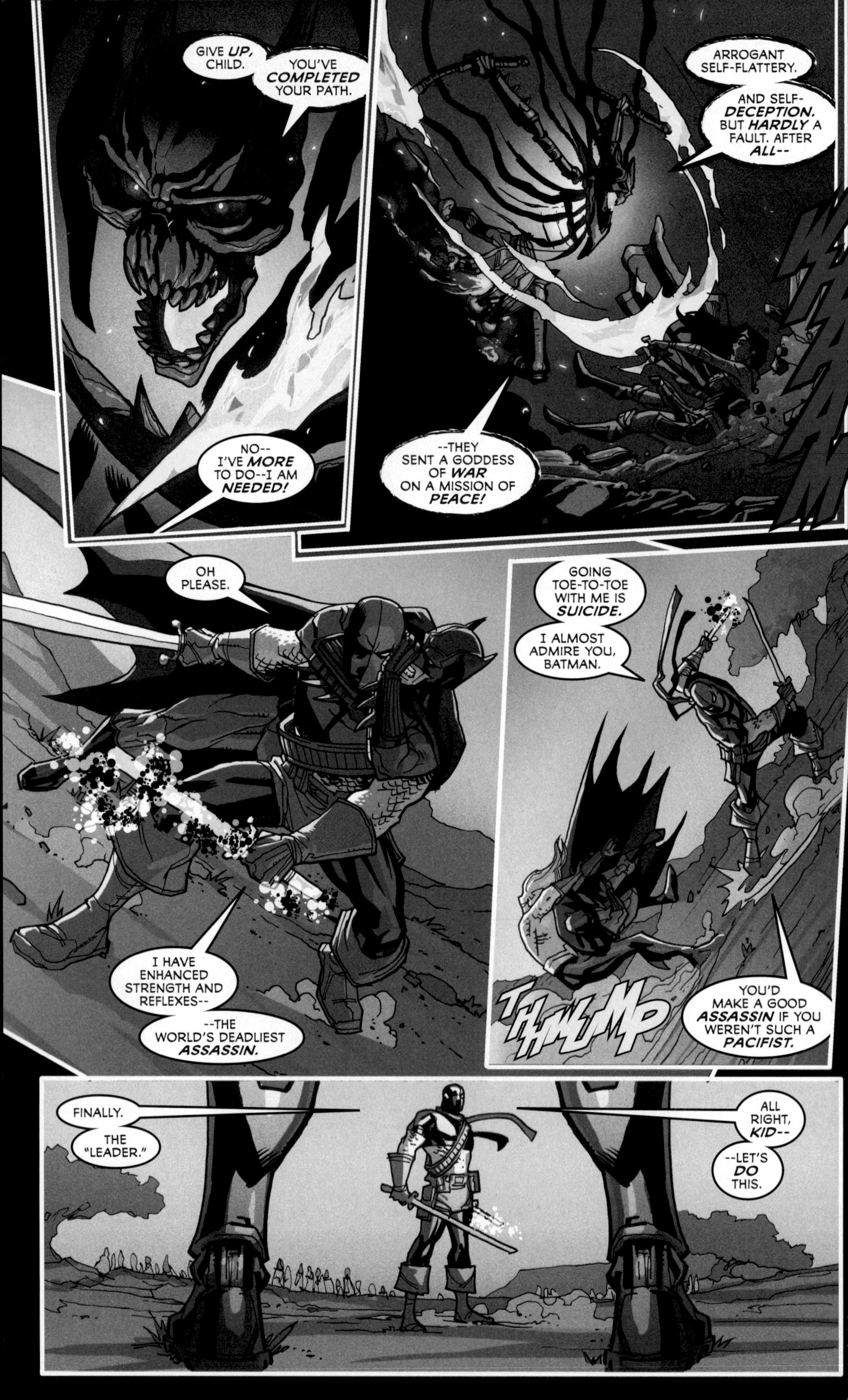
GIVE UP, CHILD.
YOU'VE COMPLETED YOUR PATH.
NO-- I'VE MORE TO DO--I AM NEEDED!
ARROGANT SELF-FLATTERY.
AND SELF-DECEPTION. BUT HARDLY A FAULT. AFTER ALL--
--THEY SENT A GODDESS OF WAR ON A MISSION OF PEACE!
OH PLEASE.
I HAVE ENHANCED STRENGTH AND REFLEXES--
--THE WORLD'S DEADLIEST ASSASSIN.
GOING TOE-TO-TOE WITH ME IS SUICIDE.
I ALMOST ADMIRE YOU, BATMAN.
THHWUMP
YOU'D MAKE A GOOD ASSASSIN IF YOU WEREN'T SUCH A PACIFIST.
FINALLY.
THE "LEADER."
ALL RIGHT, KID--
--LET'S DO THIS.

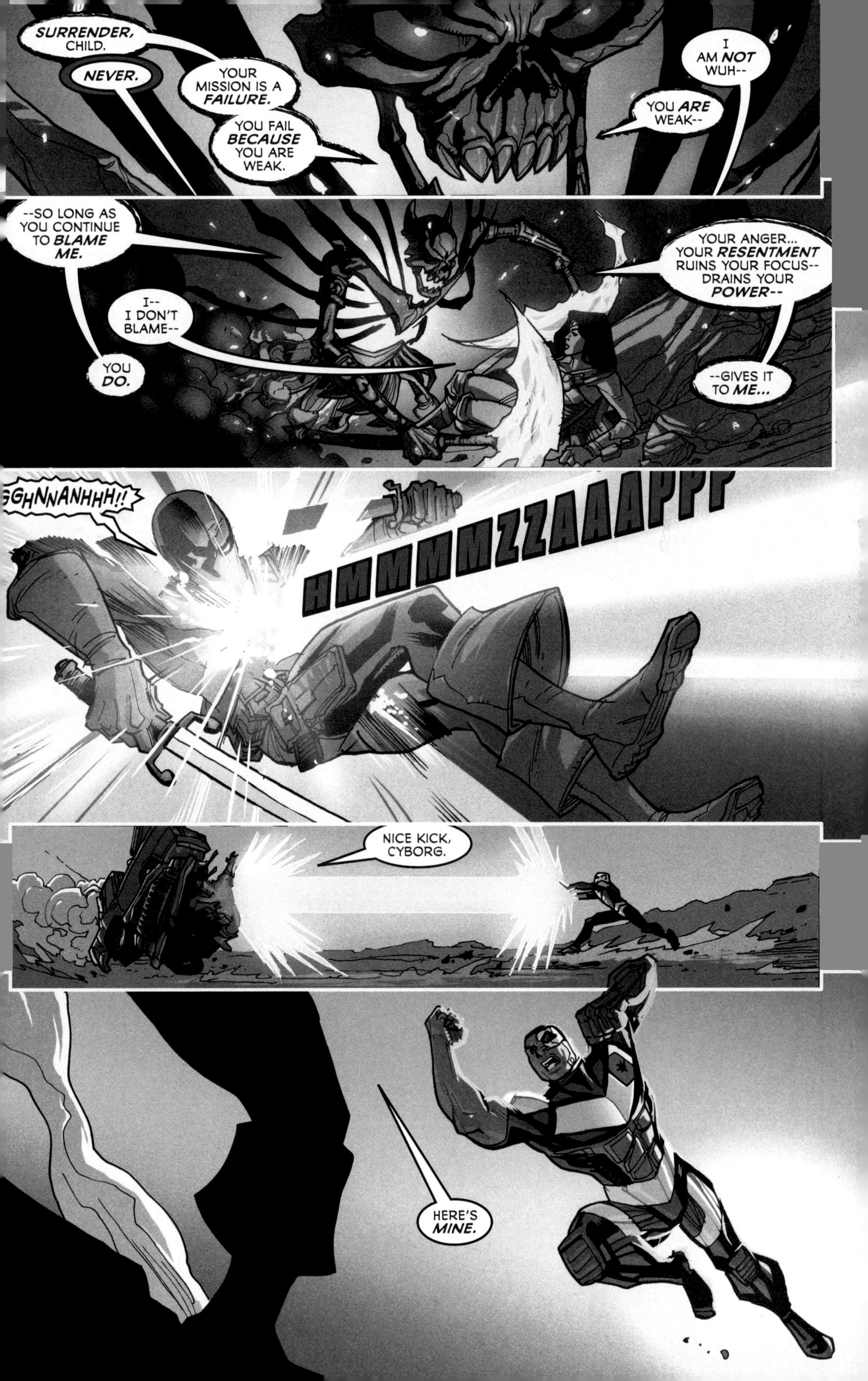
SURRENDER, CHILD.
NEVER.
YOUR MISSION IS A FAILURE.
YOU FAIL BECAUSE YOU ARE WEAK.
I AM NOT WUH--
YOU ARE WEAK--
--SO LONG AS YOU CONTINUE TO BLAME ME.
I-- I DON'T BLAME--
YOU DO.
YOUR ANGER... YOUR RESENTMENT RUINS YOUR FOCUS-- DRAINS YOUR POWER--
--GIVES IT TO ME...
GHNNANHHH!!
HMMMMZZAAAPPP
NICE KICK, CYBORG.
HERE'S MINE.

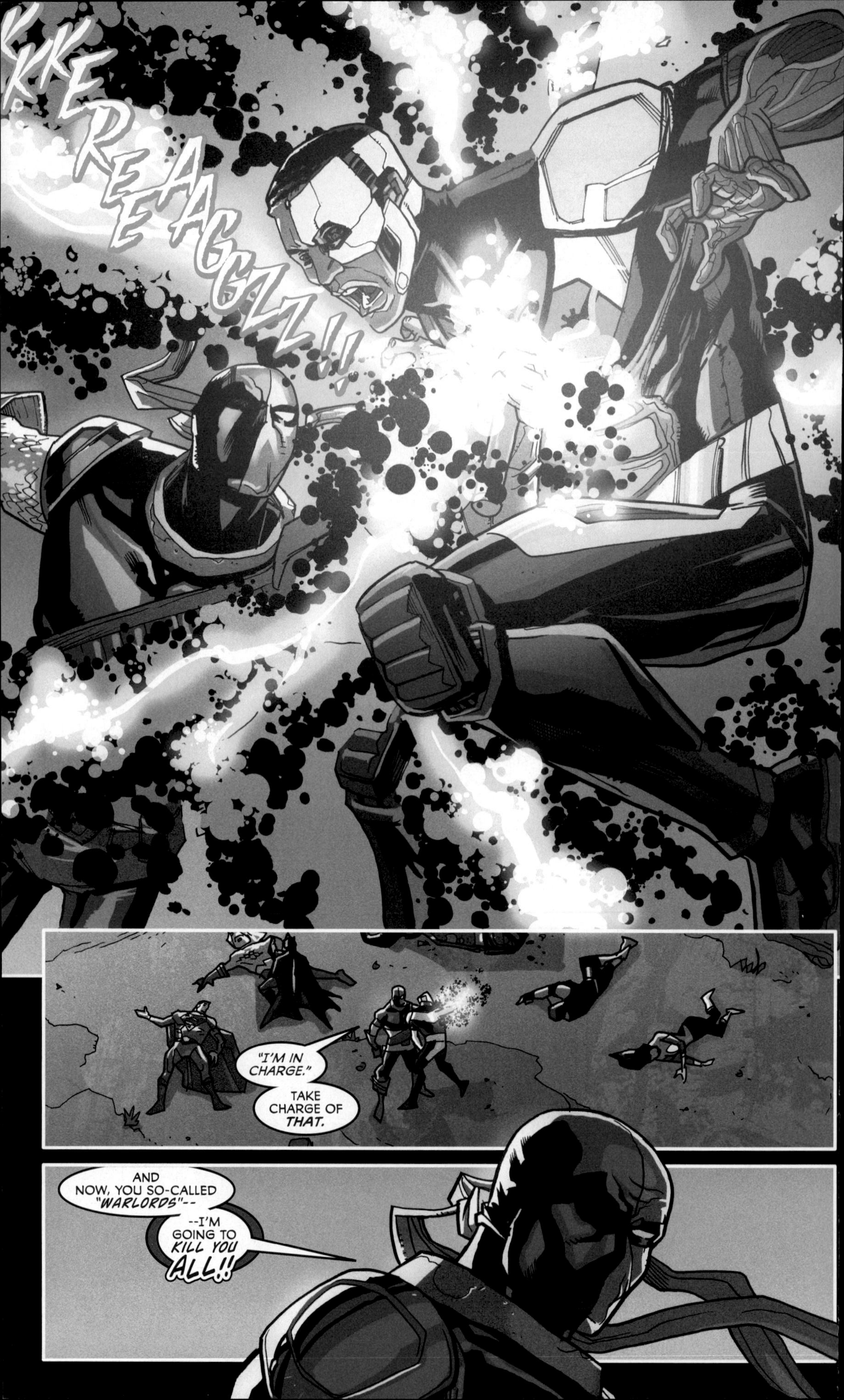
KKEREEAAGGZZ!!
"I'M IN CHARGE."
TAKE CHARGE OF *THAT.*
AND NOW, YOU SO-CALLED "*WARLORDS*"--
--I'M GOING TO *KILL YOU ALL!!*

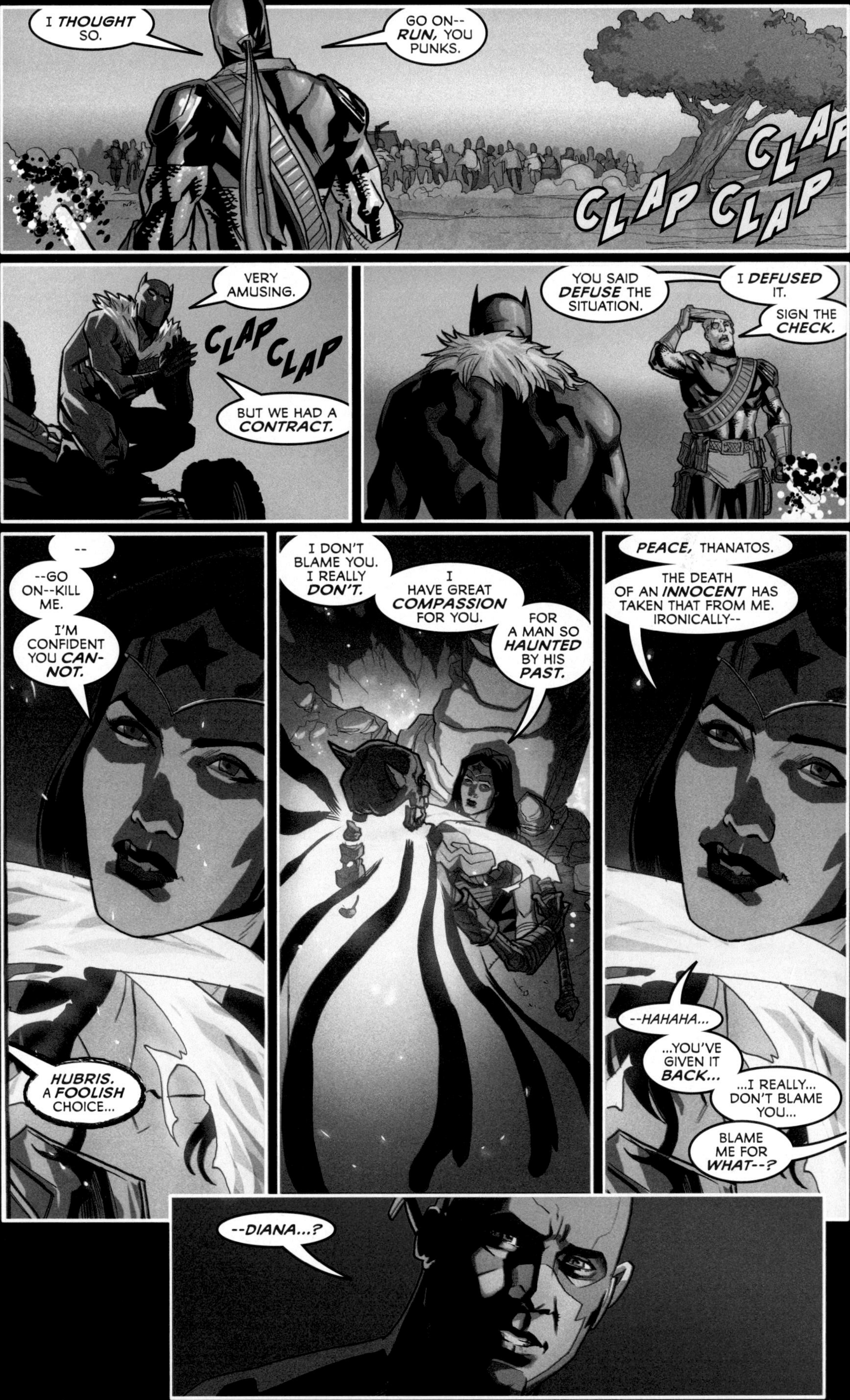
I THOUGHT SO.
GO ON-- RUN, YOU PUNKS.
CLAP CLAP CLAP CLAP
VERY AMUSING.
CLAP CLAP
BUT WE HAD A CONTRACT.
YOU SAID DEFUSE THE SITUATION.
I DEFUSED IT.
SIGN THE CHECK.
--
--GO ON--KILL ME.
I'M CONFIDENT YOU CAN-NOT.
HUBRIS. A FOOLISH CHOICE...
I DON'T BLAME YOU. I REALLY DON'T.
I HAVE GREAT COMPASSION FOR YOU.
FOR A MAN SO HAUNTED BY HIS PAST.
PEACE, THANATOS.
THE DEATH OF AN INNOCENT HAS TAKEN THAT FROM ME. IRONICALLY--
--HAHAHA...
...YOU'VE GIVEN IT BACK...
...I REALLY... DON'T BLAME YOU...
BLAME ME FOR WHAT--?
--DIANA...?

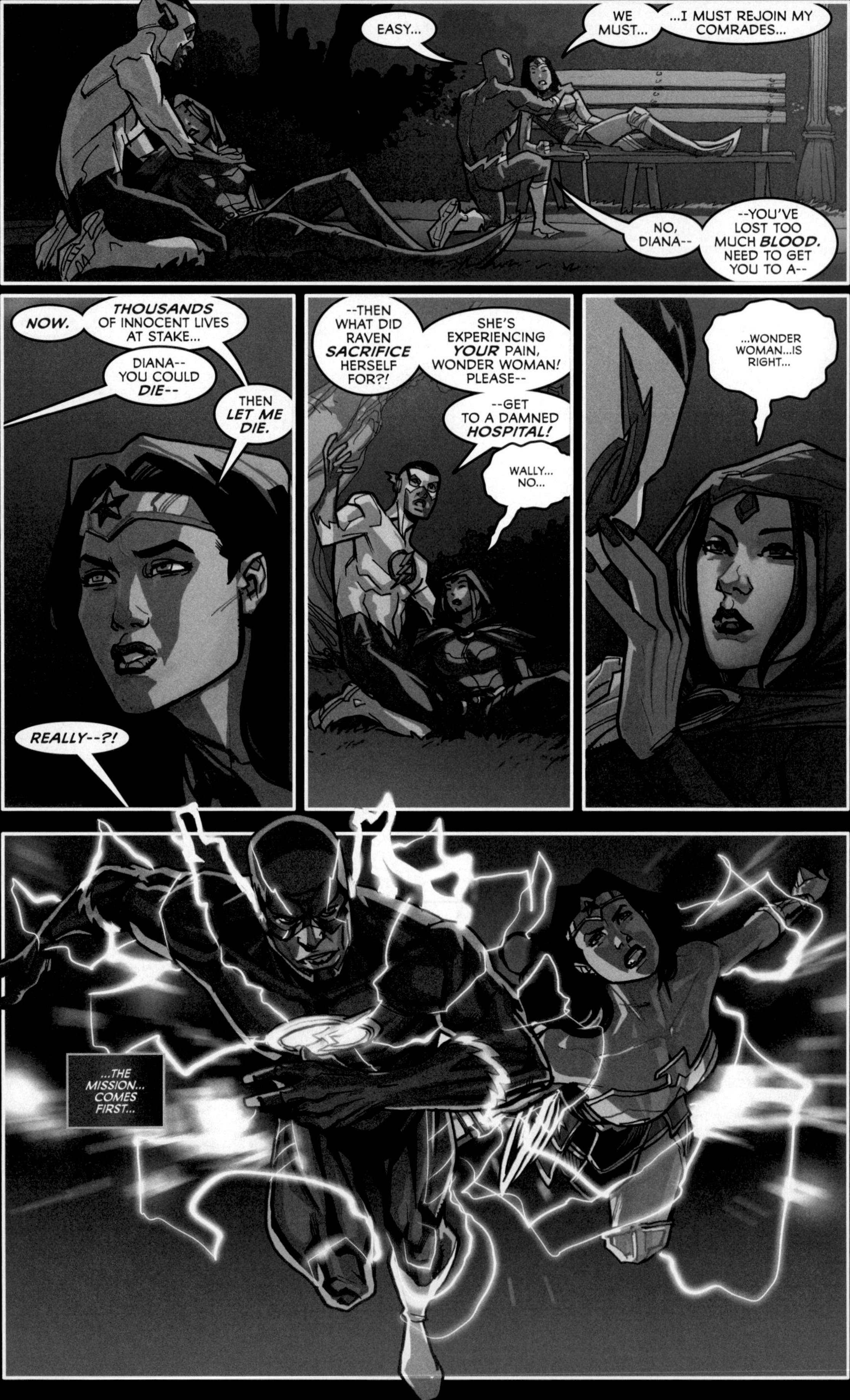

EASY...
WE MUST...
...I MUST REJOIN MY COMRADES...
NO, DIANA--
--YOU'VE LOST TOO MUCH BLOOD. NEED TO GET YOU TO A--
NOW.
THOUSANDS OF INNOCENT LIVES AT STAKE...
DIANA-- YOU COULD DIE--
THEN LET ME DIE.
REALLY--?!
--THEN WHAT DID RAVEN SACRIFICE HERSELF FOR?!
SHE'S EXPERIENCING YOUR PAIN, WONDER WOMAN! PLEASE--
--GET TO A DAMNED HOSPITAL!
WALLY... NO...
...WONDER WOMAN...IS RIGHT...
...THE MISSION... COMES FIRST...

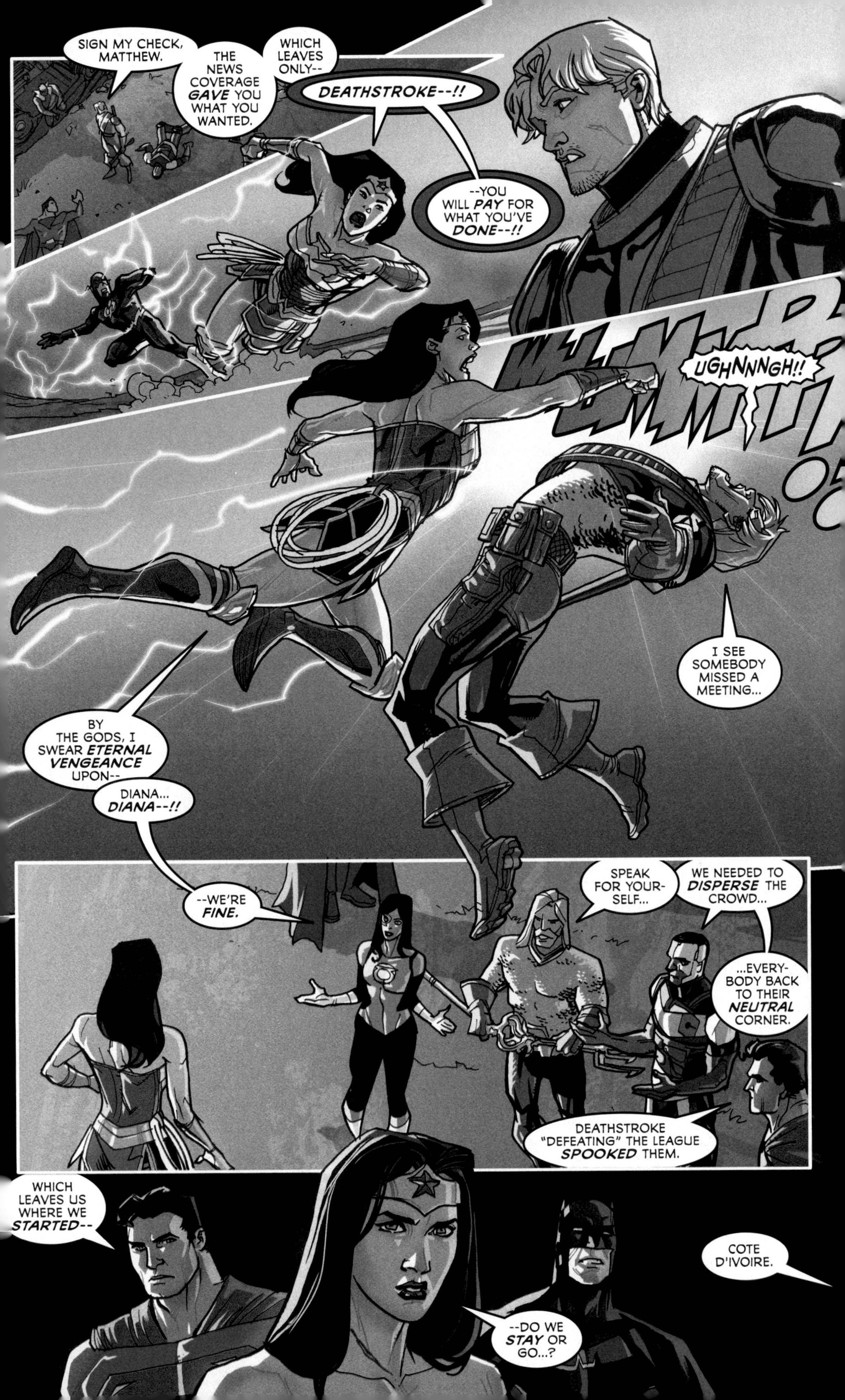
SIGN MY CHECK, MATTHEW.
THE NEWS COVERAGE GAVE YOU WHAT YOU WANTED.
WHICH LEAVES ONLY--
DEATHSTROKE--!!
--YOU WILL PAY FOR WHAT YOU'VE DONE--!!
UGHNNNGH!!
I SEE SOMEBODY MISSED A MEETING...
BY THE GODS, I SWEAR ETERNAL VENGEANCE UPON--
DIANA... DIANA--!!
--WE'RE FINE.
SPEAK FOR YOURSELF...
WE NEEDED TO DISPERSE THE CROWD...
...EVERYBODY BACK TO THEIR NEUTRAL CORNER.
DEATHSTROKE "DEFEATING" THE LEAGUE SPOOKED THEM.
WHICH LEAVES US WHERE WE STARTED--
--DO WE STAY OR GO...?
COTE D'IVOIRE.

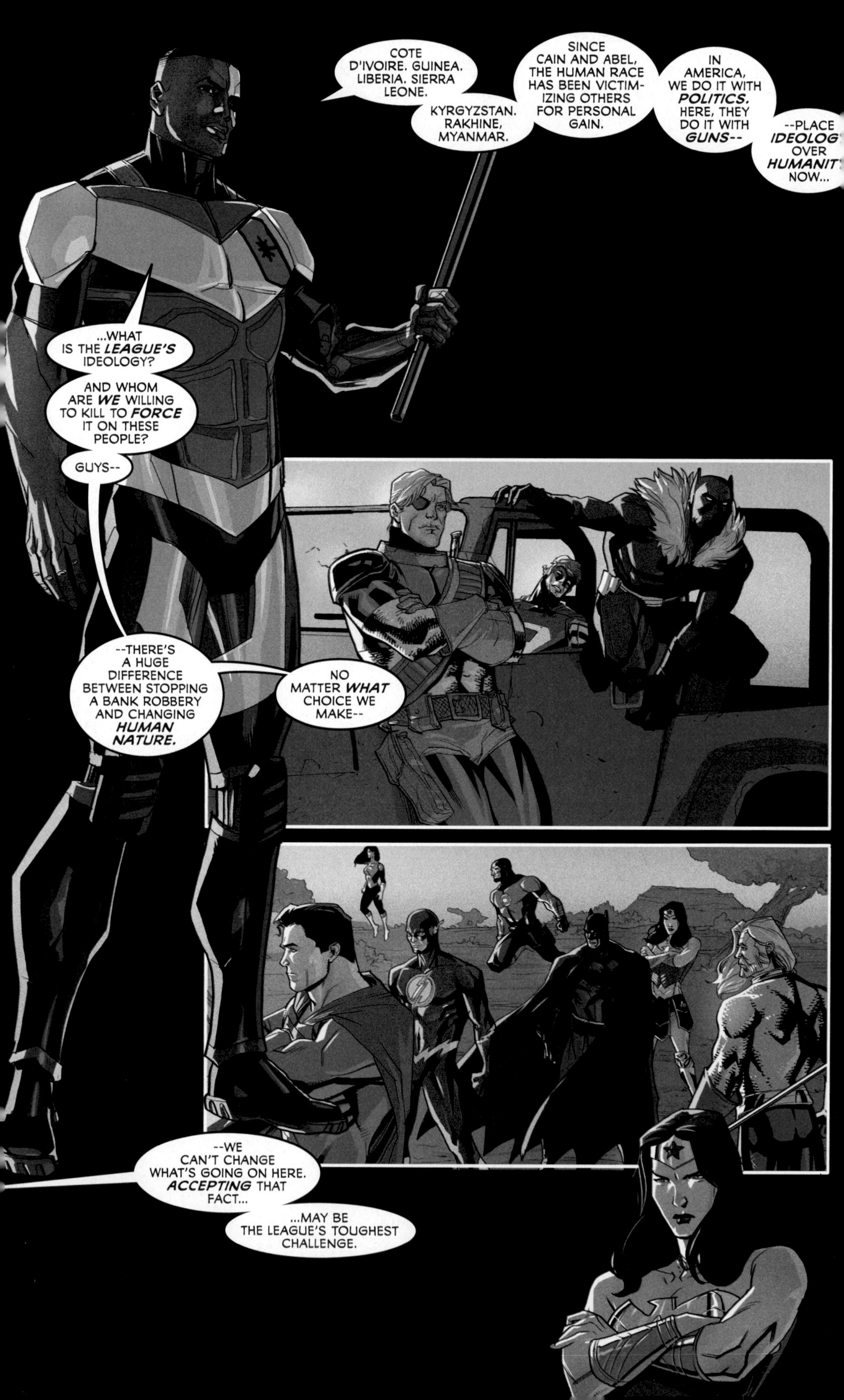
COTE D'IVOIRE. GUINEA. LIBERIA. SIERRA LEONE.
KYRGYZSTAN. RAKHINE, MYANMAR.
SINCE CAIN AND ABEL, THE HUMAN RACE HAS BEEN VICTIMIZING OTHERS FOR PERSONAL GAIN.
IN AMERICA, WE DO IT WITH POLITICS. HERE, THEY DO IT WITH GUNS--
--PLACE IDEOLOG OVER HUMANIT NOW...
...WHAT IS THE LEAGUE'S IDEOLOGY?
AND WHOM ARE WE WILLING TO KILL TO FORCE IT ON THESE PEOPLE?
GUYS--
--THERE'S A HUGE DIFFERENCE BETWEEN STOPPING A BANK ROBBERY AND CHANGING HUMAN NATURE.
NO MATTER WHAT CHOICE WE MAKE--
--WE CAN'T CHANGE WHAT'S GOING ON HERE. ACCEPTING THAT FACT...
...MAY BE THE LEAGUE'S TOUGHEST CHALLENGE.

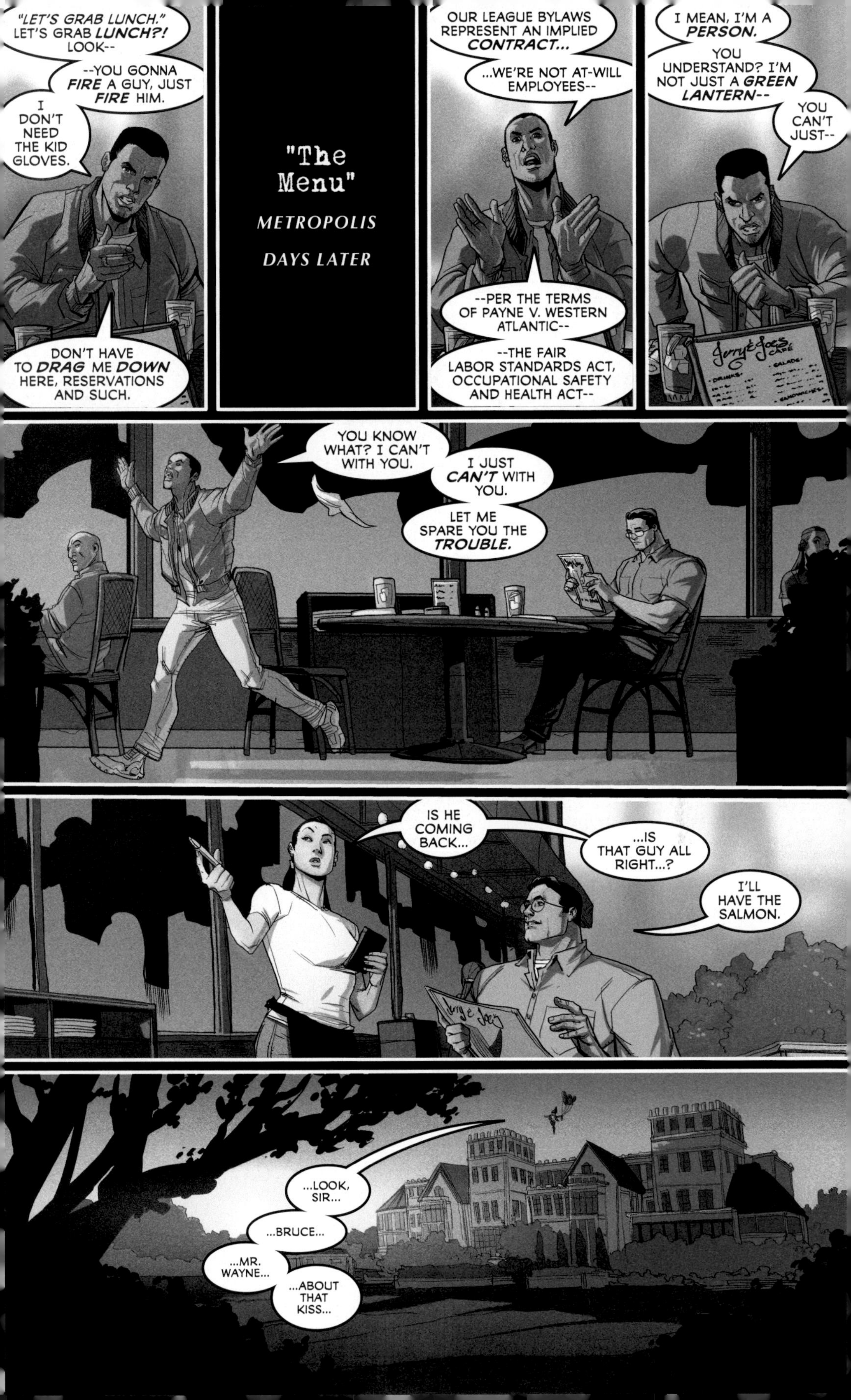
"LET'S GRAB LUNCH." LET'S GRAB LUNCH?! LOOK--
--YOU GONNA FIRE A GUY, JUST FIRE HIM.
I DON'T NEED THE KID GLOVES.
DON'T HAVE TO DRAG ME DOWN HERE, RESERVATIONS AND SUCH.
"The Menu"
METROPOLIS
DAYS LATER
OUR LEAGUE BYLAWS REPRESENT AN IMPLIED CONTRACT...
...WE'RE NOT AT-WILL EMPLOYEES--
--PER THE TERMS OF PAYNE V. WESTERN ATLANTIC--
--THE FAIR LABOR STANDARDS ACT, OCCUPATIONAL SAFETY AND HEALTH ACT--
I MEAN, I'M A PERSON.
YOU UNDERSTAND? I'M NOT JUST A GREEN LANTERN--
YOU CAN'T JUST--
YOU KNOW WHAT? I CAN'T WITH YOU.
I JUST CAN'T WITH YOU.
LET ME SPARE YOU THE TROUBLE.
IS HE COMING BACK...
...IS THAT GUY ALL RIGHT...?
I'LL HAVE THE SALMON.
...LOOK, SIR...
...BRUCE...
...MR. WAYNE...
...ABOUT THAT KISS...

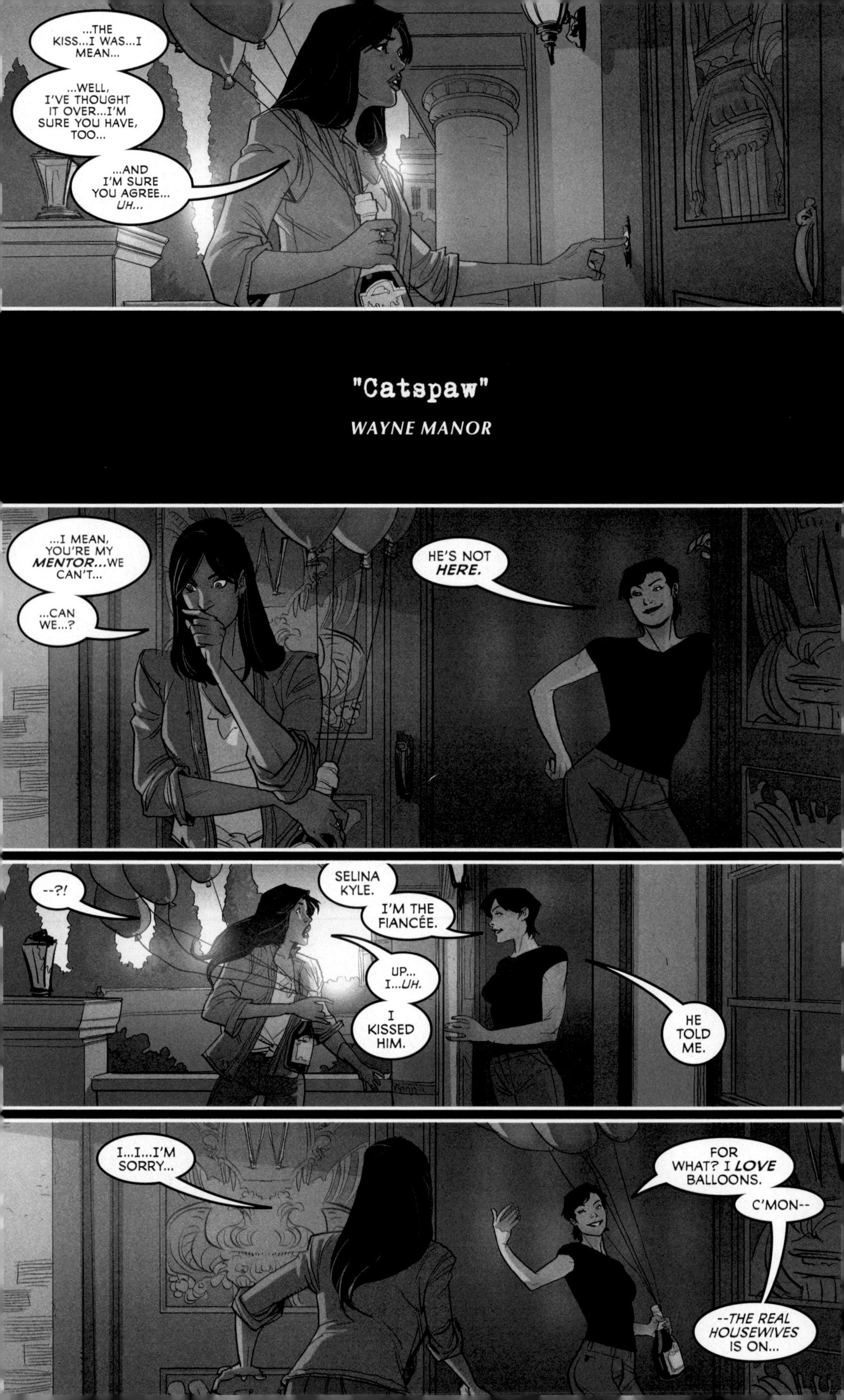
...THE KISS...I WAS...I MEAN...
...WELL, I'VE THOUGHT IT OVER...I'M SURE YOU HAVE, TOO...
...AND I'M SURE YOU AGREE... *UH...*
"Catspaw"
WAYNE MANOR
...I MEAN, YOU'RE MY ***MENTOR...*** WE CAN'T...
...CAN WE...?
HE'S NOT ***HERE.***
--?!
SELINA KYLE.
I'M THE FIANCÉE.
UP... I...*UH.*
I KISSED HIM.
HE TOLD ME.
I...I...I'M SORRY...
FOR WHAT? I ***LOVE*** BALLOONS.
C'MON--
--THE REAL HOUSEWIVES IS ON...

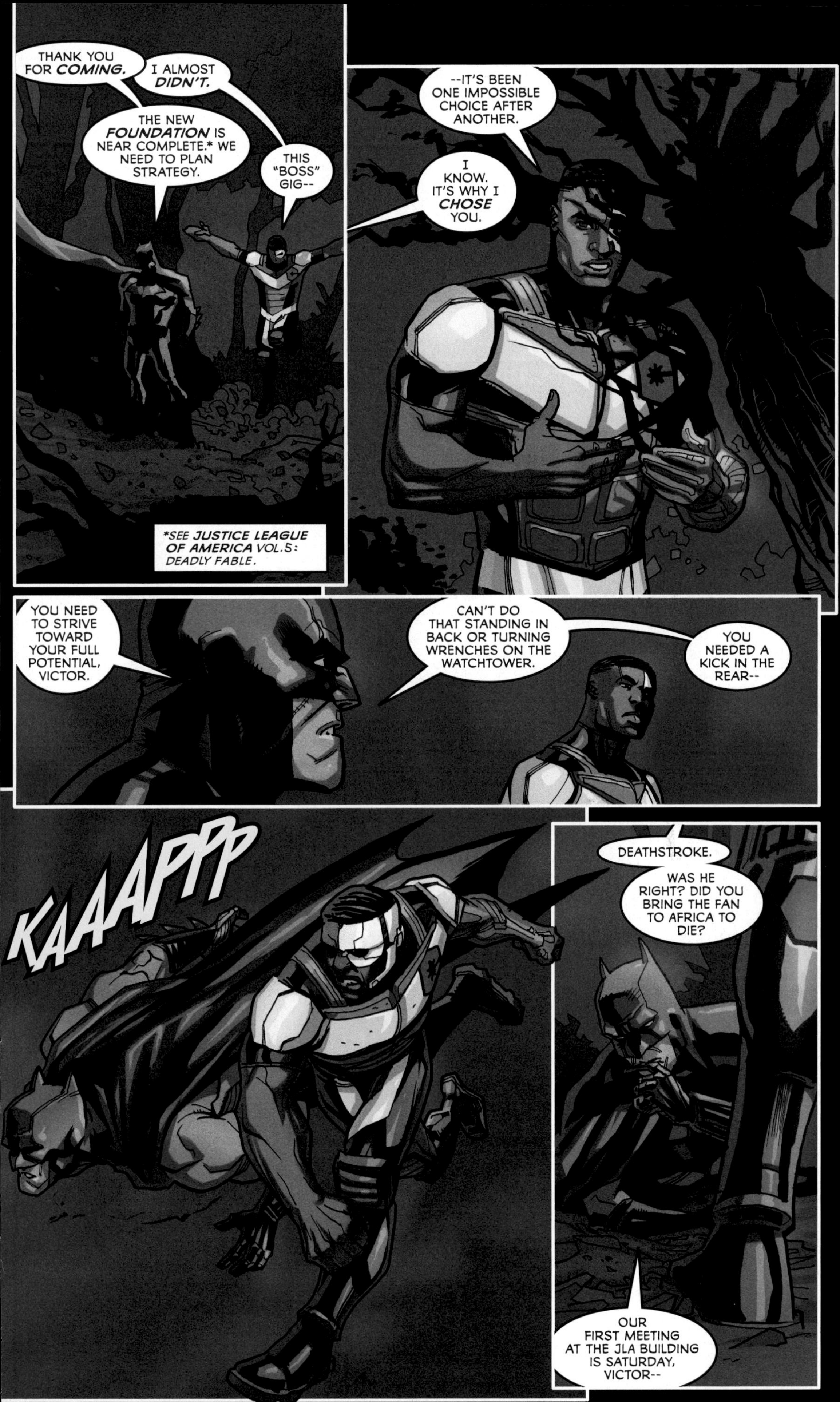
THANK YOU FOR COMING.
I ALMOST DIDN'T.
THE NEW FOUNDATION IS NEAR COMPLETE.* WE NEED TO PLAN STRATEGY.
THIS "BOSS" GIG--
*SEE JUSTICE LEAGUE OF AMERICA VOL.5: DEADLY FABLE.
--IT'S BEEN ONE IMPOSSIBLE CHOICE AFTER ANOTHER.
I KNOW. IT'S WHY I CHOSE YOU.
YOU NEED TO STRIVE TOWARD YOUR FULL POTENTIAL, VICTOR.
CAN'T DO THAT STANDING IN BACK OR TURNING WRENCHES ON THE WATCHTOWER.
YOU NEEDED A KICK IN THE REAR--
KAAAPPP
DEATHSTROKE.
WAS HE RIGHT? DID YOU BRING THE FAN TO AFRICA TO DIE?
OUR FIRST MEETING AT THE JLA BUILDING IS SATURDAY, VICTOR--

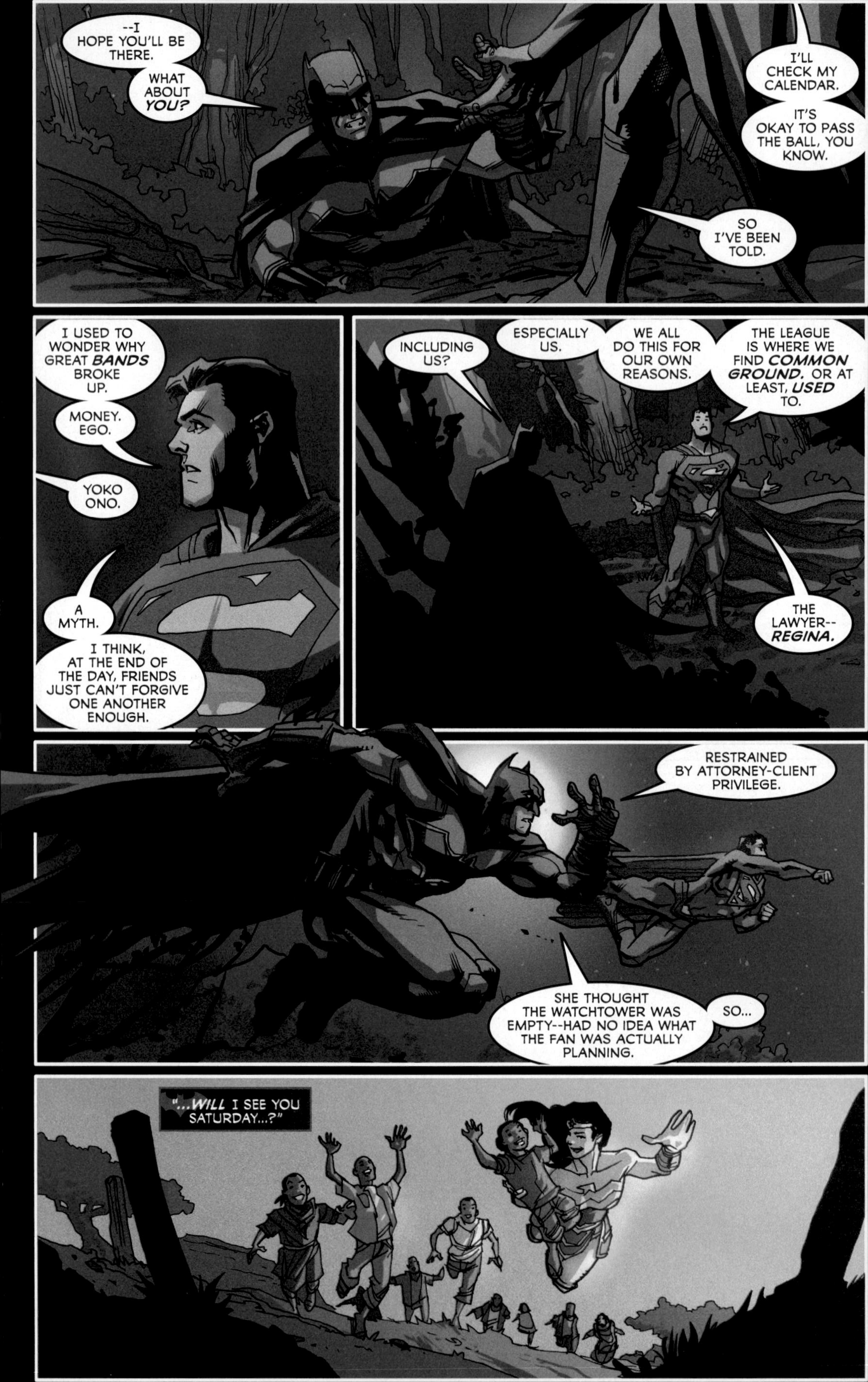
--I HOPE YOU'LL BE THERE.
WHAT ABOUT *YOU?*
I'LL CHECK MY CALENDAR.
IT'S OKAY TO PASS THE BALL, YOU KNOW.
SO I'VE BEEN TOLD.
I USED TO WONDER WHY GREAT *BANDS* BROKE UP.
MONEY. EGO.
YOKO ONO.
A MYTH.
I THINK, AT THE END OF THE DAY, FRIENDS JUST CAN'T FORGIVE ONE ANOTHER ENOUGH.
INCLUDING US?
ESPECIALLY US.
WE ALL DO THIS FOR OUR OWN REASONS.
THE LEAGUE IS WHERE WE FIND *COMMON GROUND.* OR AT LEAST, *USED* TO.
THE LAWYER-- *REGINA.*
RESTRAINED BY ATTORNEY-CLIENT PRIVILEGE.
SHE THOUGHT THE WATCHTOWER WAS EMPTY--HAD NO IDEA WHAT THE FAN WAS ACTUALLY PLANNING.
SO...
"...*WILL* I SEE YOU SATURDAY...?"

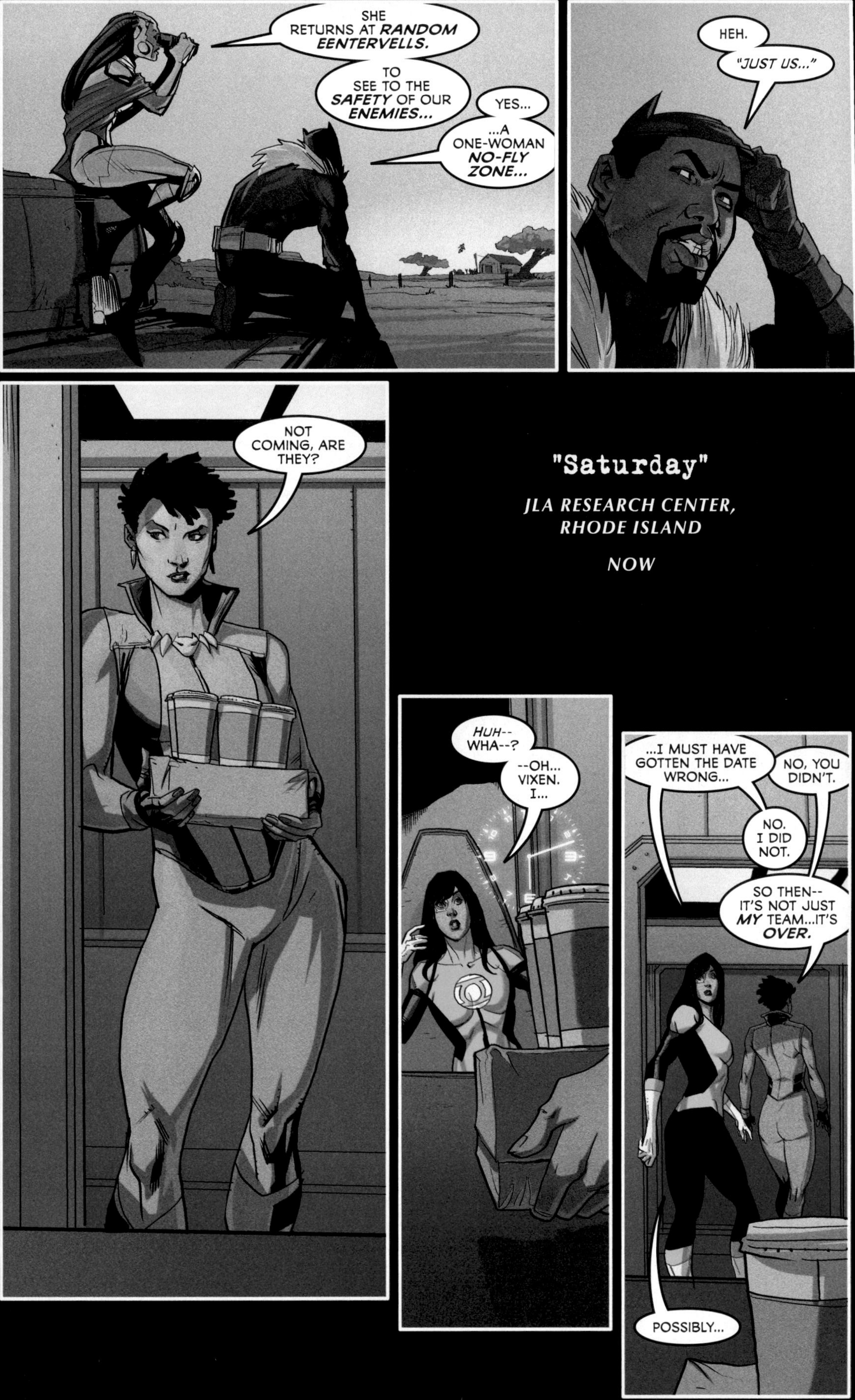
SHE RETURNS AT RANDOM EENTERVELLS.
TO SEE TO THE SAFETY OF OUR ENEMIES...
YES...
...A ONE-WOMAN NO-FLY ZONE...
HEH.
"JUST US..."
NOT COMING, ARE THEY?
"Saturday"
JLA RESEARCH CENTER, RHODE ISLAND
NOW
HUH-- WHA--?
--OH... VIXEN. I...
...I MUST HAVE GOTTEN THE DATE WRONG...
NO, YOU DIDN'T.
NO. I DID NOT.
SO THEN-- IT'S NOT JUST MY TEAM...IT'S OVER.
POSSIBLY...

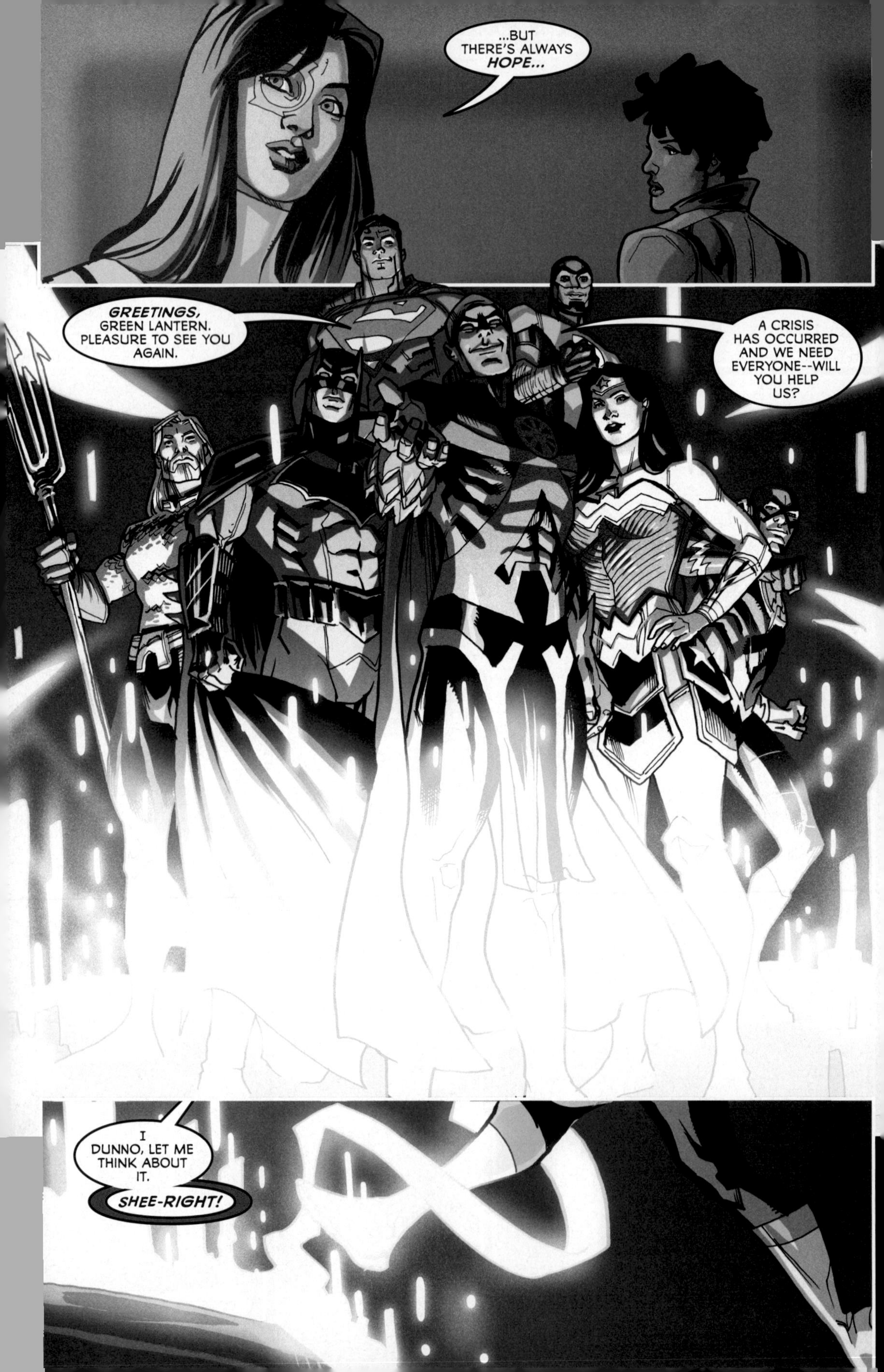
...BUT THERE'S ALWAYS HOPE...
GREETINGS, GREEN LANTERN. PLEASURE TO SEE YOU AGAIN.
A CRISIS HAS OCCURRED AND WE NEED EVERYONE--WILL YOU HELP US?
I DUNNO, LET ME THINK ABOUT IT.
SHEE-RIGHT!

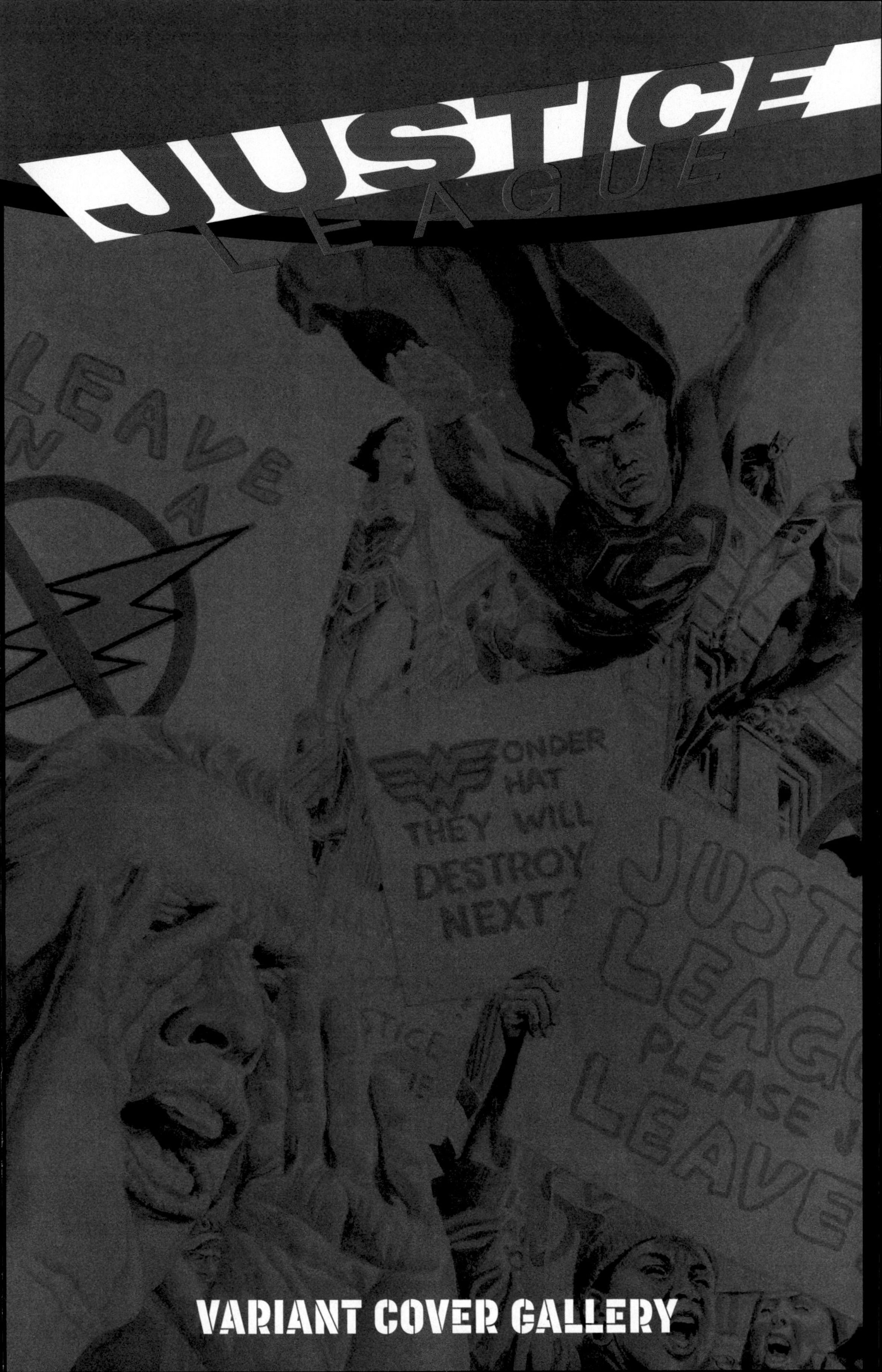
JUSTICE LEAGUE
LEAVE
ONDER HAT THEY WILL DESTROY NEXT?
PLEASE
LEAVE

VARIANT COVER GALLERY

JUSTICE LEAGUE #39 variant cover by J.G. JONES

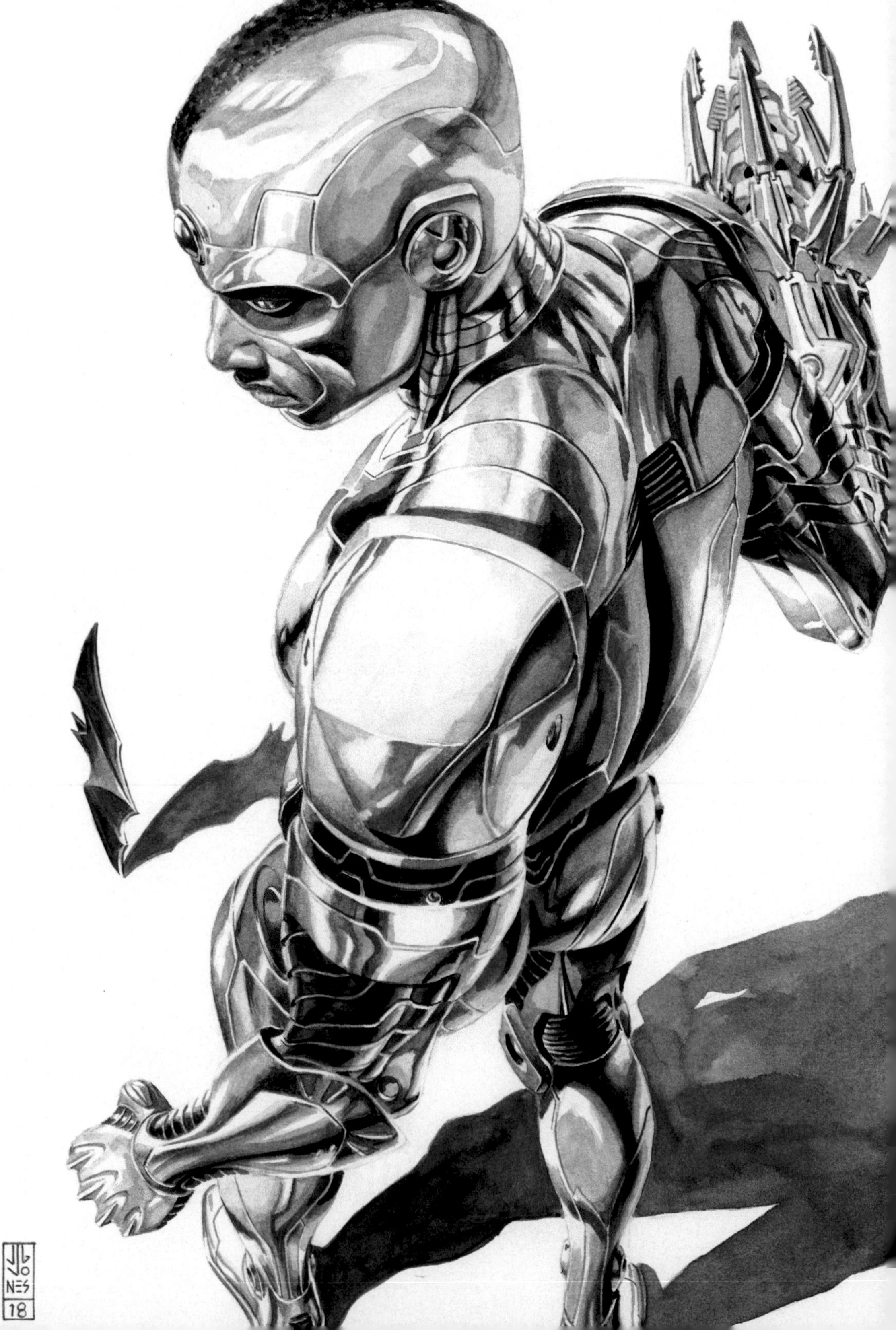
JG
JO
NES
18

JUSTICE LEAGUE #40 variant cover by J.G. JONES

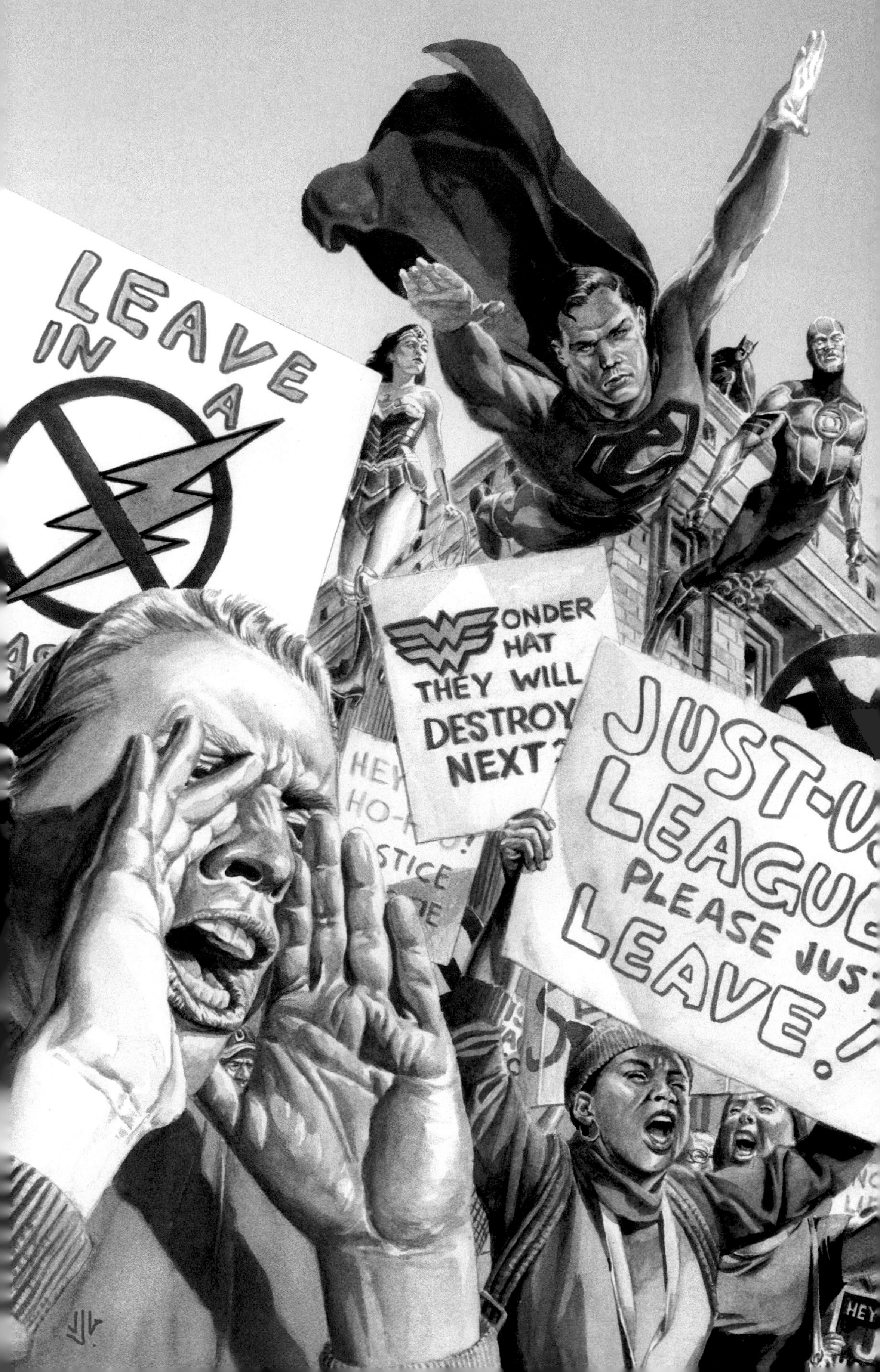
LEAVE
IN
A
ONDER
HAT
THEY WILL
DESTROY
NEXT
JUST-U
LEAGU
PLEASE JUS
LEAVE!
HEY
HO-
STICE

JUSTICE LEAGUE #41 variant cover by J.G. JONES

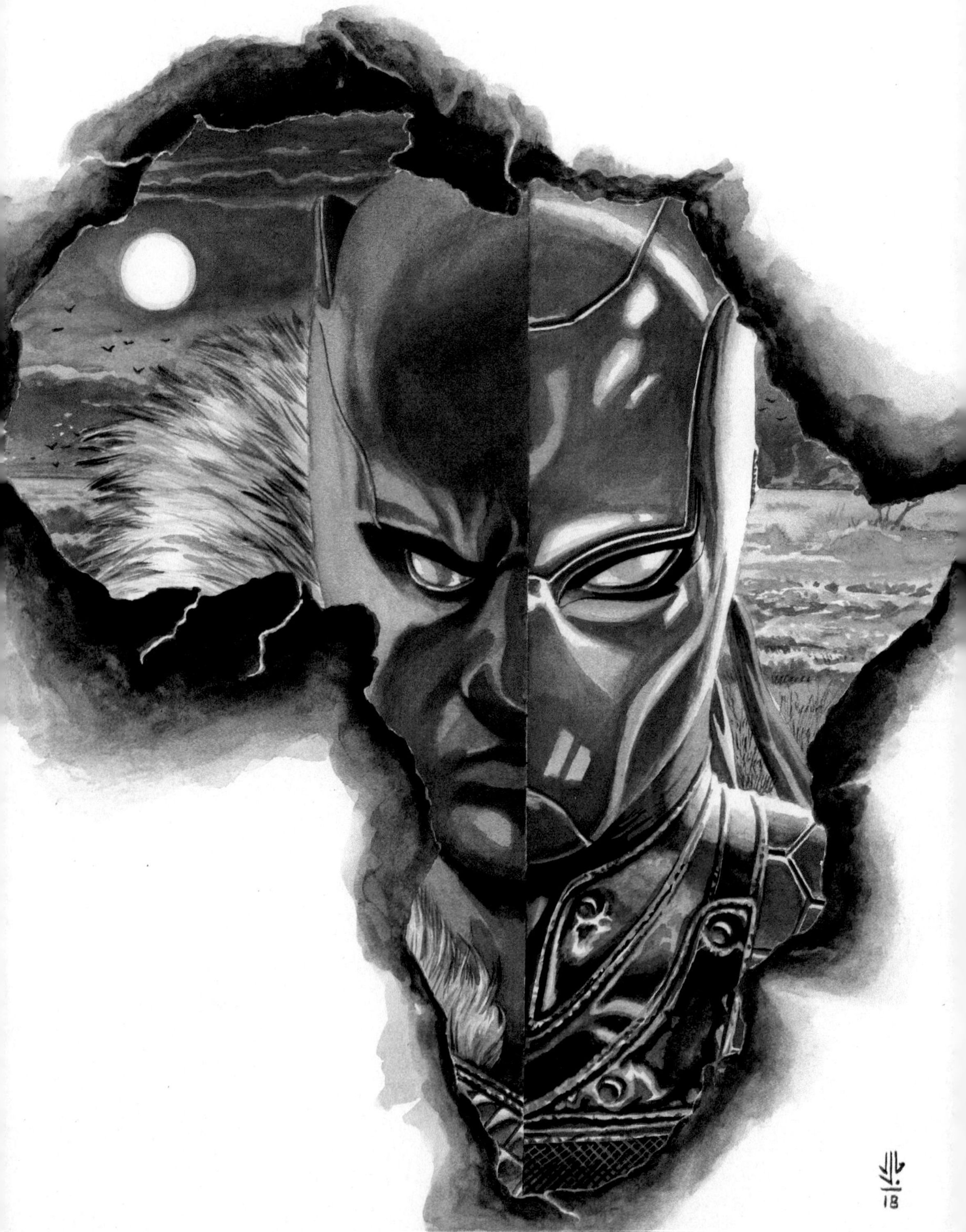

JUSTICE LEAGUE #42 variant cover by J.G. JONES

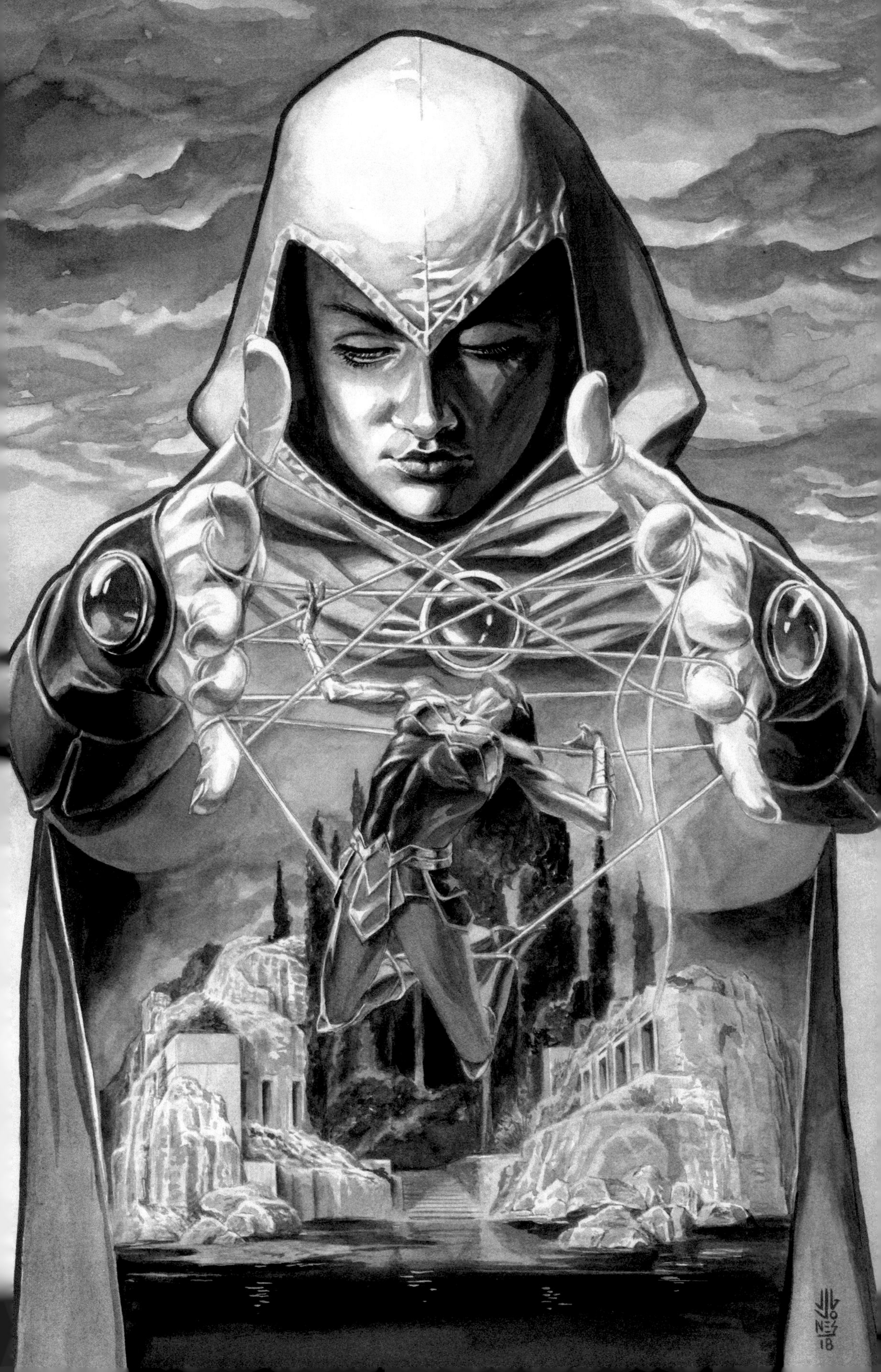

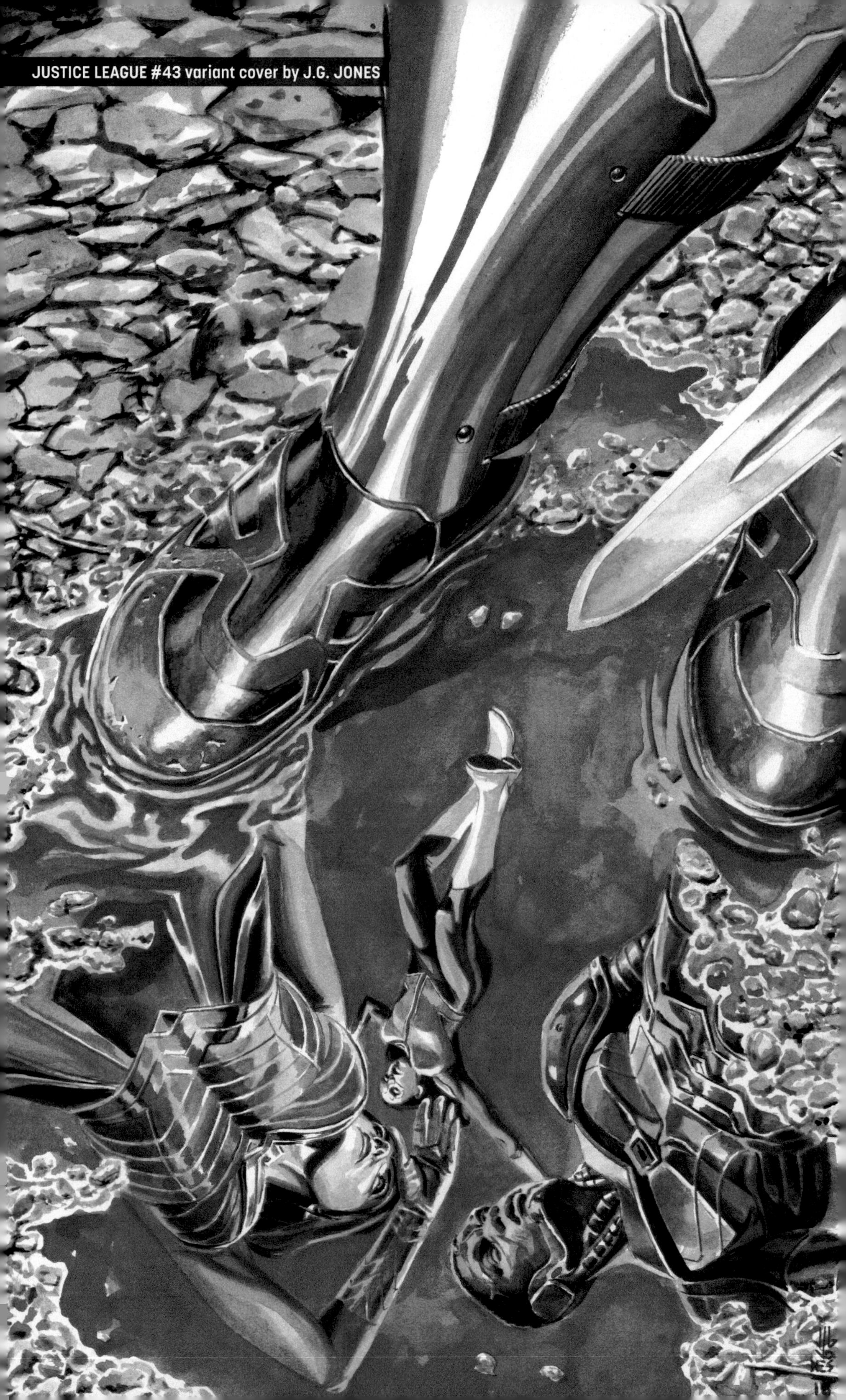

JUSTICE LEAGUE #43 variant cover by J.G. JONES

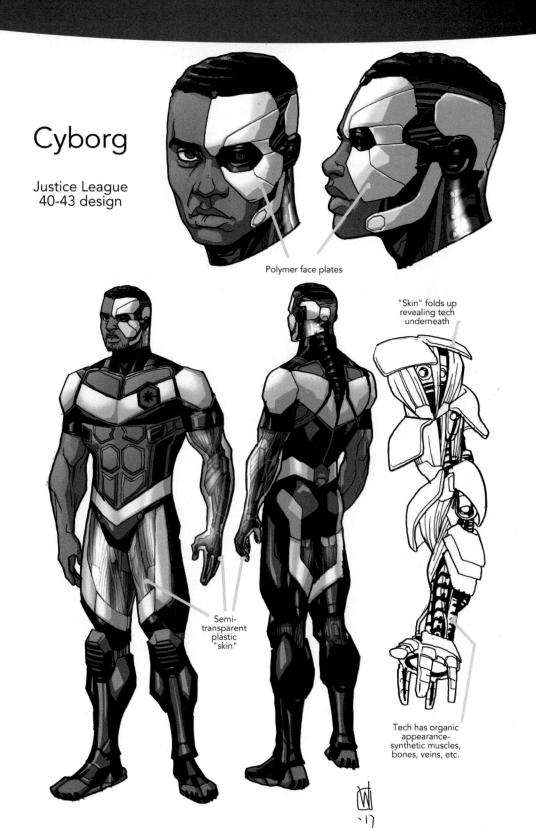

Cyborg

Justice League
40-43 design

Polymer face plates

"Skin" folds up revealing tech underneath

Semi-transparent plastic "skin"

Tech has organic appearance-synthetic muscles, bones, veins, etc.

Cyborg costume redesign by Pete Woods

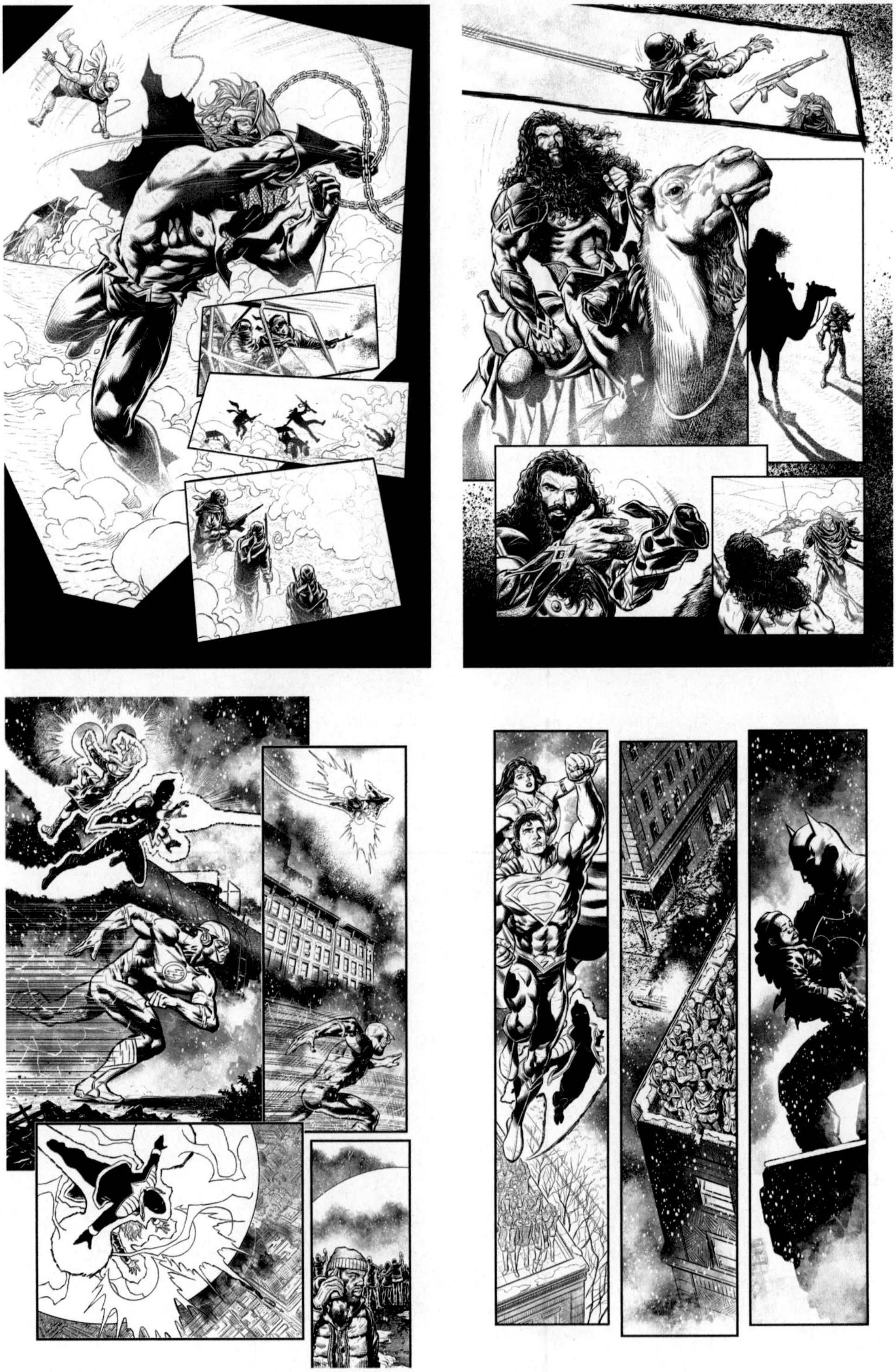

Inked art for JUSTICE LEAGUE #39 pages 3, 5, 17 and 19 by Ian Churchill

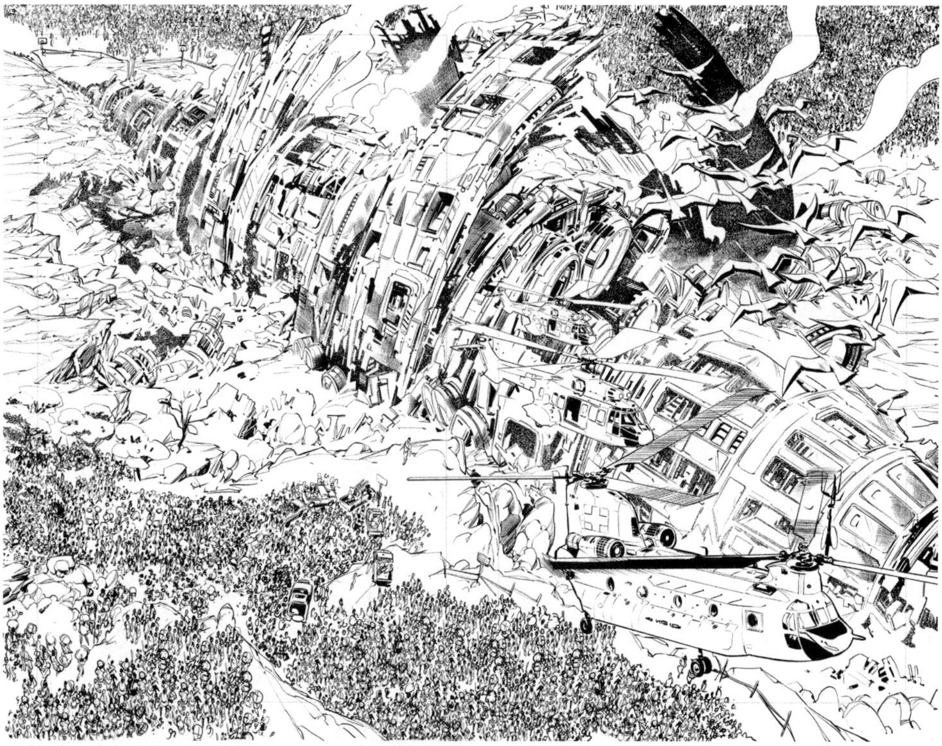

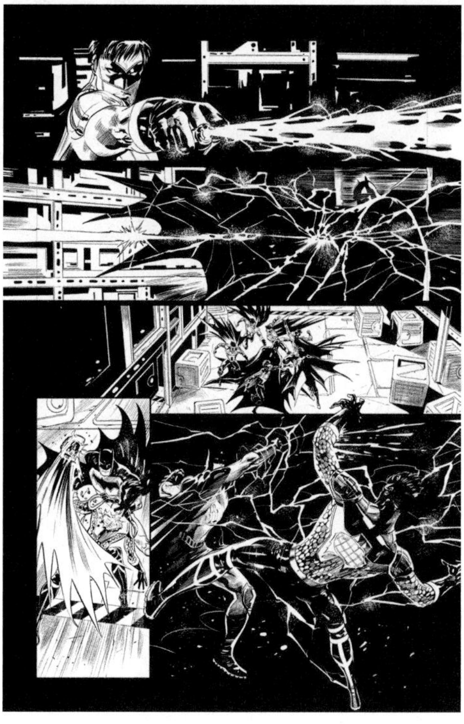

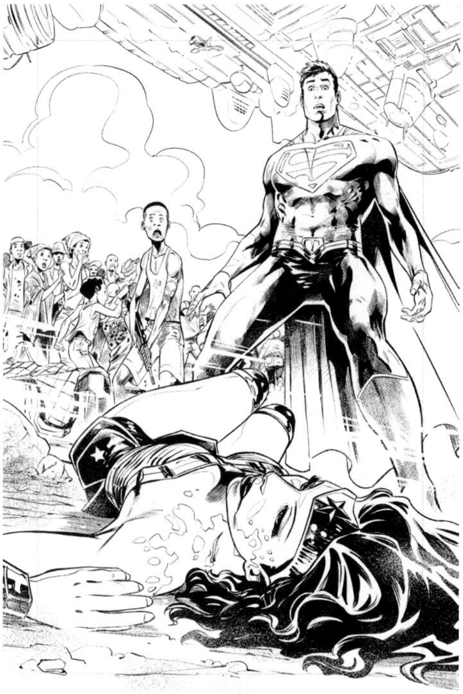

Inked art for JUSTICE LEAGUE #41 pages 4, 5, 15 and 18 by Philippe Briones

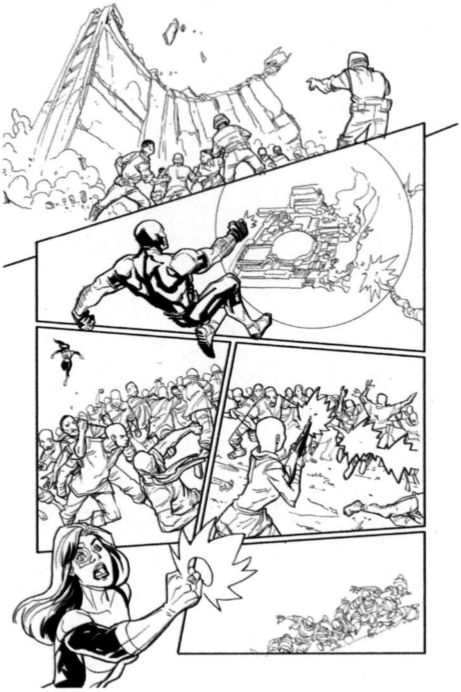

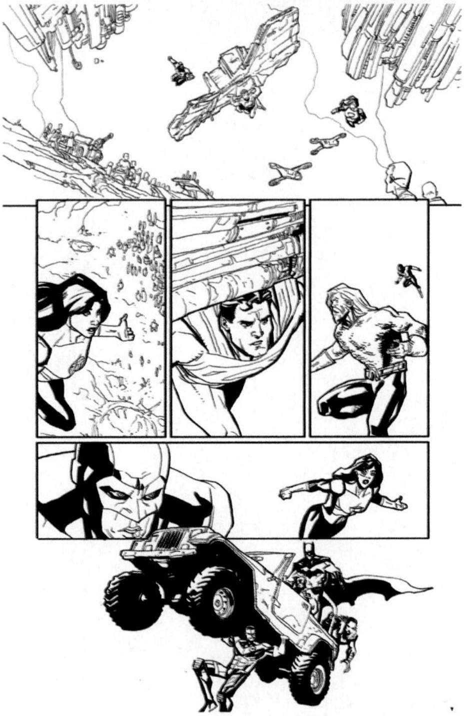

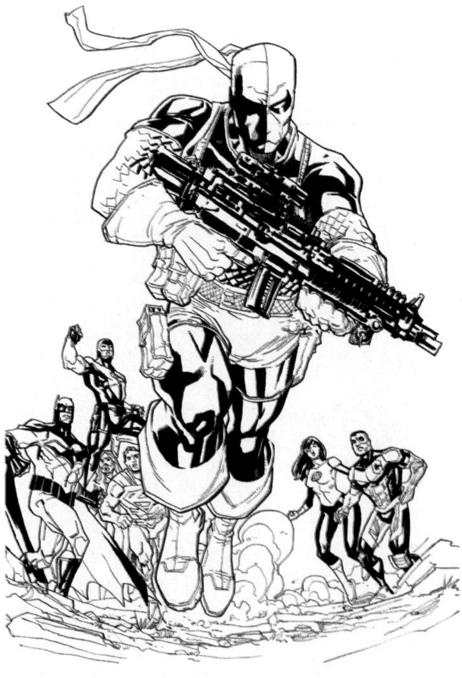

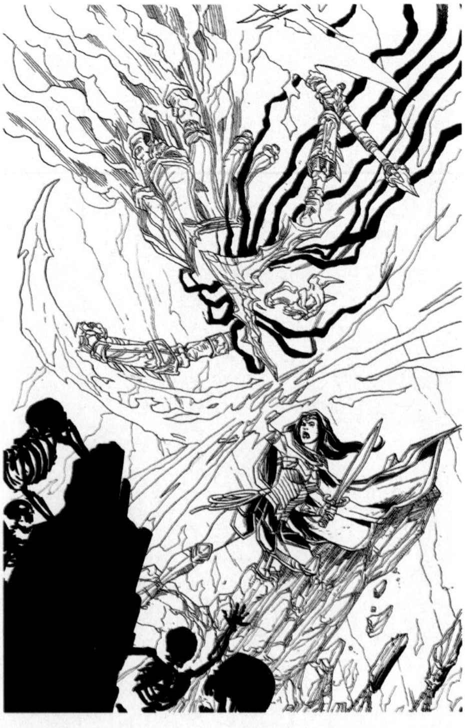

Inked art for JUSTICE LEAGUE #42 pages 13, 18 and 20 and JUSTICE LEAGUE #43 page 6 by Pete Woods

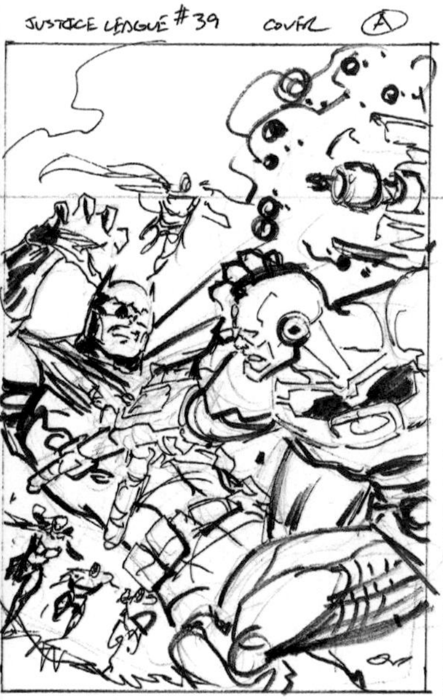
JUSTICE LEAGUE #39 COVER A
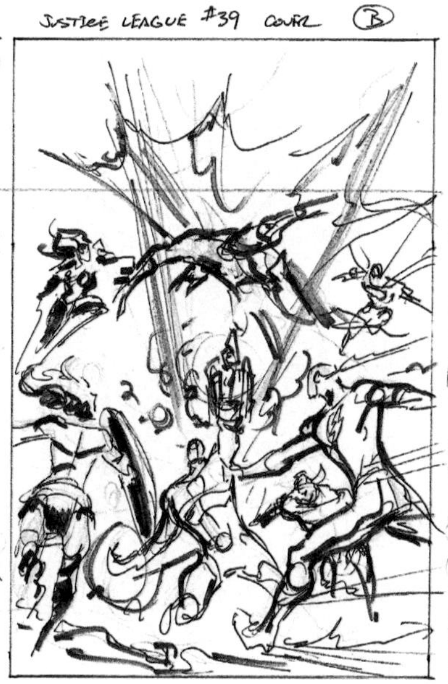
JUSTICE LEAGUE #39 COVER B
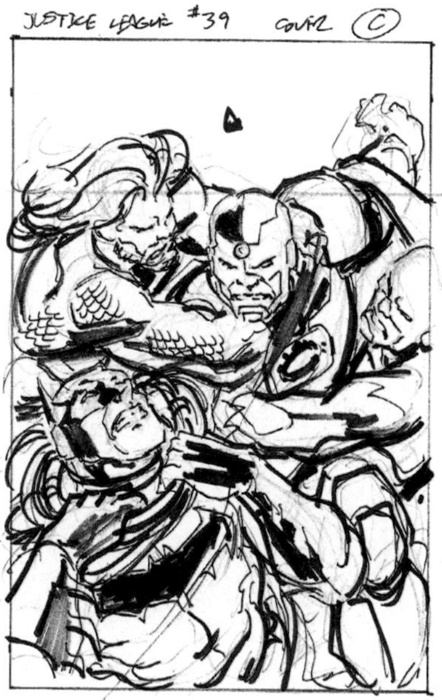
JUSTICE LEAGUE #39 COVER C
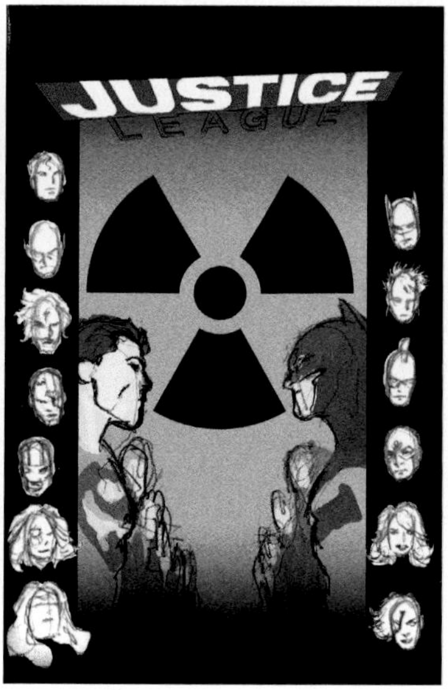
JUSTICE
LEAGUE
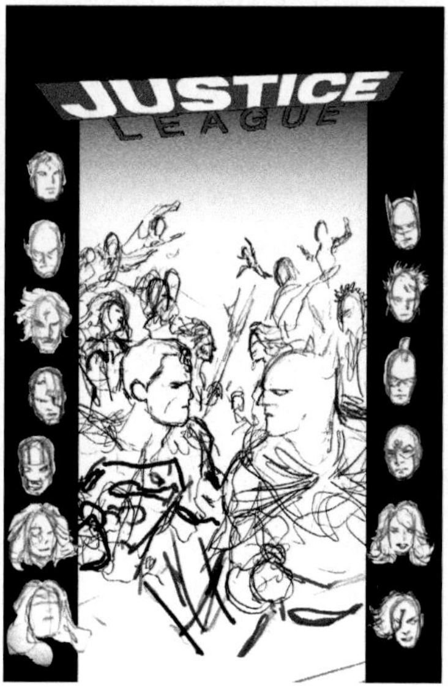
JUSTICE
LEAGUE
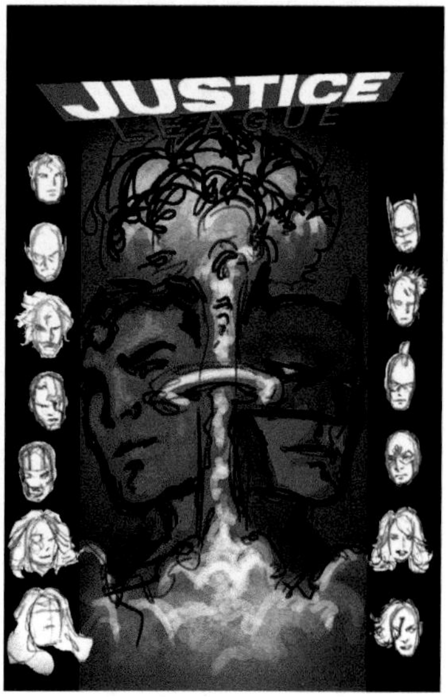
JUSTICE
LEAGUE

Cover sketches for JUSTICE LEAGUE #39 by Paul Pelletier and JUSTICE LEAGUE #40 by David Yardin

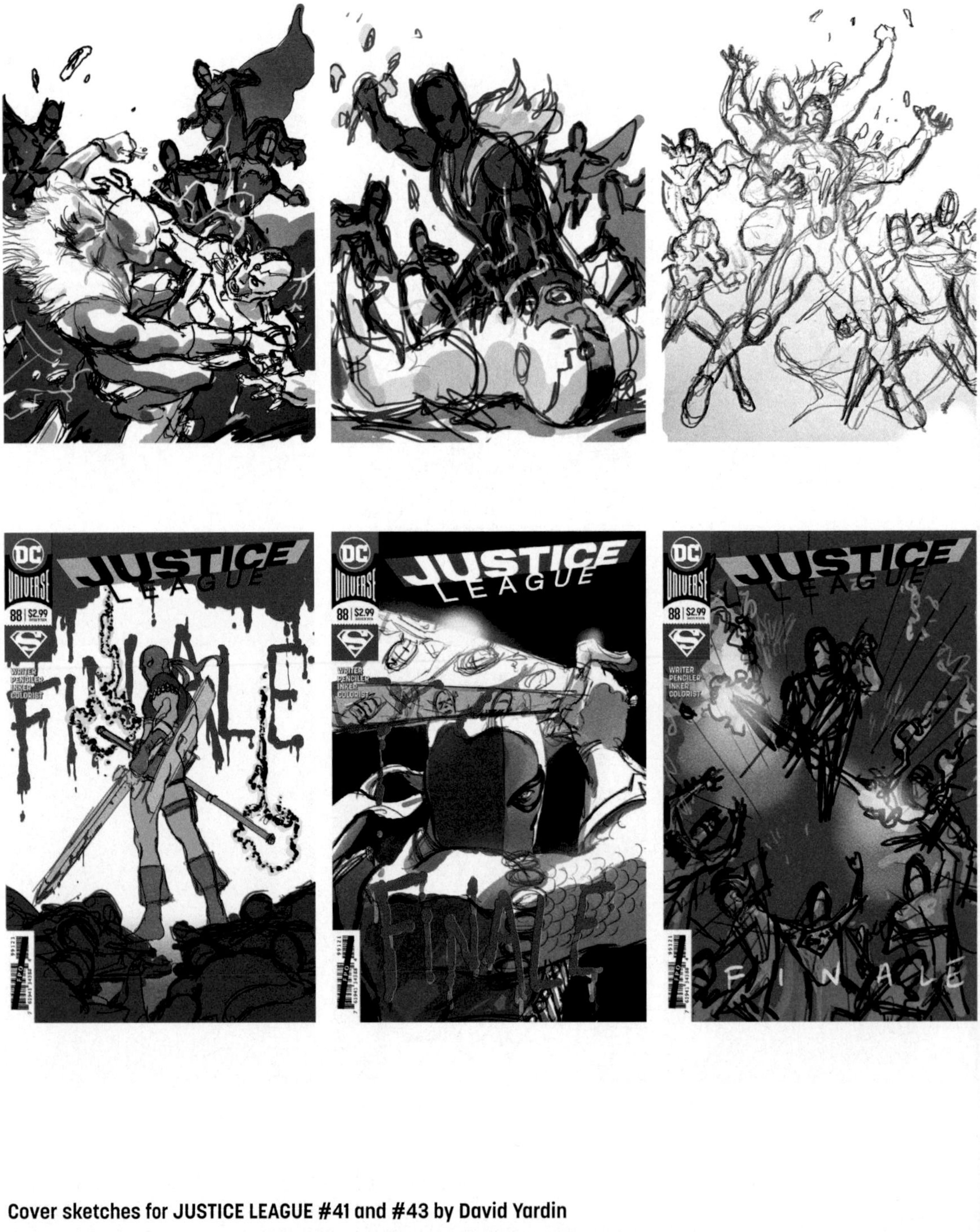
DC UNIVERSE
JUSTICE LEAGUE
88 $2.99
WRITER
PENCILER
INKER
COLORIST
FINALE
DC UNIVERSE
JUSTICE LEAGUE
88 $2.99
WRITER
PENCILER
INKER
COLORIST
FINALE
DC UNIVERSE
JUSTICE LEAGUE
88 $2.99
WRITER
PENCILER
INKER
COLORIST
FINALE

Cover sketches for JUSTICE LEAGUE #41 and #43 by David Yardin

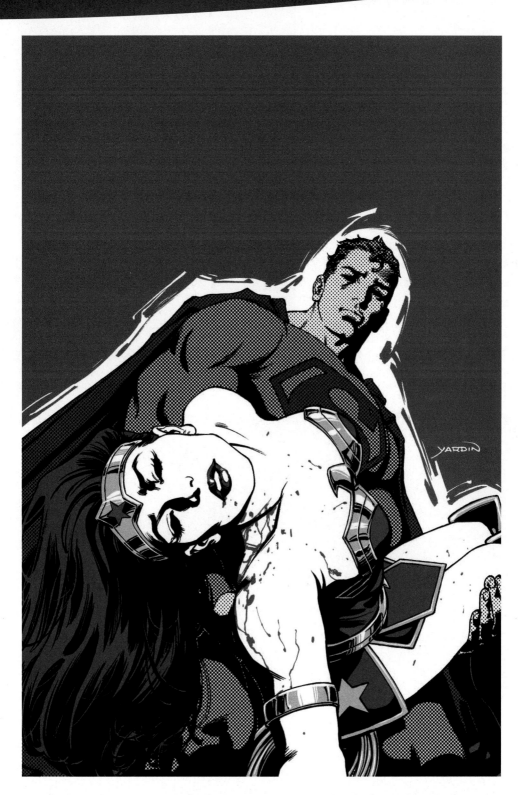

Alternate unused version of David Yardin's cover to JUSTICE LEAGUE #42

JUSTICE LEAGUE

VOL. 1: ORIGIN
GEOFF JOHNS and JIM LEE

GEOFF **JOHNS** JIM **LEE** SCOTT **WILLIAMS**

**JUSTICE LEAGUE
VOL. 2: THE VILLAIN'S JOURNEY**

**JUSTICE LEAGUE
VOL. 3: THRONE OF ATLANTIS**

Get more DC graphic novels wherever comics and books are sold!